W9-CEU-753

Advance Praise for *The Sustainability Advantage*

In *The Sustainability Advantage*, Bob Willard has performed a service of inestimable value: quantifying the business case for sustainability. By focusing at the level of the firm, Willard has bypassed the overriding but somewhat esoteric question, *"How long can the rape of Earth by the modern industrial system go on before ecological collapse?"* The answer to this big question lies in the cumulative effect of millions of firms, large and small, waking up to the untapped profit potential that's all around them. Bob Willard has shown how to capture that potential in real profits. Consequently, the answer to the big question is: *Let the rape stop now; there's a better way to make a bigger profit.* Read this book to learn how.

— Ray Anderson, CEO, Interface, Inc.

For managers in search of practical tools for quantifying the value of environmental and social initiatives in their businesses, Bob Willard's new book, *The Sustainability Advantage*, offers a treasure trove of resources. Willard has assembled an exhaustive, yet readable inventory of seven "bottom line" benefits of sustainability. But even more importantly, he has created a set of easy-to-use spreadsheets that enable managers to estimate these benefits for their own businesses. As a former IBM manager, Willard demonstrates convincingly that, even using the most conservative estimates, the potential for a "sustainability advantage" is huge.

— Professor Stuart Hart, Director, Center for Sustainable Enterprise, Kenan-Flagler Business School, University of North Carolina

I believe, and the 150 companies of the *World Business Council for Sustainable Development* all believe, that the pursuit of sustainability creates more competitive companies. Bob Willard makes this case. He has laid out a powerful but practical guide to the ways in which companies can use the sustainability concept to do things like improve productivity and decrease expenses while increasing revenue and shareholder value. He even offers a "sustainability spreadsheet" into which executives can plug their own companies' data. His book is a delightful combination of creativity and rigor.

— Stephan Schmidheiny, Honorary Chairman, World Business Council for Sustainable Development

My dozen years of involvement in the socially responsible investment industry have demonstrated to me that companies that integrate social and environmental parameters into their business decision making are better long-term financial performers than their industry counterparts that ignore the realities of the new marketplace. *The Sustainability Advantage* lays out, for the first time, a quantitative model that highlights why this is true. It provides the tools that senior executives, across all sectors and industries, can use to quantify the financial advantage of managing under a sustainability framework. Corporate executives will discover through *The Sustainability Advantage* that the "triple bottom line" not only means a more productive workforce and greater environmental efficiency, but greater competitive advantage, reduced costs, improved profits, and enhanced shareholder value.

— Michael Jantzi, President, Michael Jantzi Research Associates Inc.

The Sustainability Advantage makes the most compelling argument yet for how business can profit from a strategy that focuses on the health of people and the planet. Bob Willard shows us in rich detail — with case examples, financial spreadsheets, and practical applications — that sustainability is not only the ethical thing to do, it's the economic thing to do. And, after reading Willard's book, I think you'll be as convinced as I am that in the long term it's the only thing to do. By putting *The Sustainability Advantage* lessons into practice you'll save your company, you'll preserve the environment, and you'll earn new respect for yourself.

— Jim Kouzes, co-author,
***The Leadership Challenge* and *Encouraging the Heart*,**
Chairman Emeritus, tompeters!company

As companies worldwide move into a new era of corporate responsibility, Bob Willard has developed a comprehensive guide to frame the costs vs. benefits debate on the topic of sustainability. Well researched, it provides a good summary of value propositions to move the sustainability agenda forward. Recommended reading for those investing to build a business case for the corporation of tomorrow.

— Sunil A. Misser, America's Leader — Sustainability Advisory Services, PricewaterhouseCoopers

The Sustainability Advantage is a breakthrough. Hard numbers sell corporate executives and, on top of that, they are plausible. All told, they make a compelling case for operationalizing sustainable development. The book has other strengths as well. It is full of real-world examples. It is straightforwardly written, with no fluff. And it has plainly been written by a business professional for business professionals — one of its main strengths. *The Sustainability Advantage* represents a very positive contribution to the ongoing conversation about the bottom-line merits of sustainability. If it gets the readers it deserves — and if they are paying attention — it will make a real difference.

— Carl Frankel, author *In Earth's Company: Business, Environment, and the Challenge of Sustainability*

If we aspire to a future in which the power of innovation, organizational learning, and leadership in business is harnessed to create a truly sustainable future that we would all be proud to describe to our grandchildren, this book delivers a set of credible strategies to get there. Bob Willard has created a robust template for focusing energy to achieve business results, that fills in an important gap in the evolution of a new story for business in society. A much-needed job well done.

— Dr. Bryan Smith, President, Broad Reach Innovations Inc.

A social conscience delivers business value. This book shows how corporate social responsibility balances environmental and social imperatives with long-term business success and shareholder value. Bob Willard has provided us with the most complete and quantified description of the business benefits that we have seen to show that corporate social responsibility is a win/win/win proposition for business, the ecological health of the planet, and society. This book is a must-read for progressive business leaders.

— George Khoury, Director, Canadian Centre for Business in the Community, The Conference Board of Canada

Practitioners are plagued with the dilemma of how to make a strong business case for sustainability. What are the sacrifices? What are the payback timelines? What are the personnel implications? How do you justify the investments? How do you define the benefits of a robust sustainability program in traditional terms, ratios and business language? *The Sustainability Advantage* provides any practitioner, or any individual within a company, no matter the size or nature of the business, the means to make the case for sustainability and waste reduction using the examples and worksheets in this book. *The Sustainability Advantage* is a well-researched and organized collection of sustainability thought, applications, and real world trials — a must for your reference shelf.

— Catherine Greener, Principal, Team Leader, Commercial and Industrial Services, Research and Consulting, Rocky Mountain Institute

Drawing on a wealth of experience as a human resources professional, Bob Willard presents compelling arguments for the financial benefits of better practices in recruitment, retention, and employee productivity. He also deals with issues of eco-efficiency and liability reduction to make the case for enhanced attractiveness to investors and other stakeholders. In each case, Willard uses the novel device of accounting spreadsheets and the example of a fictional IT company to demonstrate real cash savings and advantages of pursuing a sustainability strategy. *The Sustainability Advantage* will be read avidly by commentators and students of sustainability in business, but perhaps it will be of greatest value to practitioners seeking to ground their own 'business case' in the organizations for which they work.

— Dr. David Wheeler, Erivan K. Haub Professor of Business and Sustainability, Schulich School of Business, York University

The Sustainability Advantage

The Sustainability Advantage

SEVEN BUSINESS CASE BENEFITS OF A TRIPLE BOTTOM LINE

BOB WILLARD

NEW SOCIETY PUBLISHERS

Cataloguing in Publication Data: A catalog record for this publication is available from the National Library of Canada.

Cover design: Diane McIntosh. Book design/layout: Greg Green/Jeremy Drought.

Printed in Canada by Friesens. Third printing January 2007.

New Society Publishers acknowledges the support of the Government of Canada through the Book Publishing Industry Development Program (BPIDP) for our publishing activities, and the assistance of the Province of British Columbia through the British Columbia Arts Council.

Hardcover ISBN 13: 978-0-86571-451-9

To order directly from the publishers, please call toll-free (North America) 1-800-567-6772, or order online at www.newsociety.com :

New Society Publishers
P.O. Box 189, Gabriola Island, British Columbia V0R 1X0, Canada

The Sustainability Advantage worksheets in digital form can be ordered from New Society Publishers' website: see below.

New Society Publishers' mission is to publish books that contribute in fundamental ways to building an ecologically sustainable and just society, and to do so with the least possible impact on the environment, in a manner that models this vision. We are committed to doing this not just through education, but through action. We are acting on our commitment to the world's remaining ancient forests by phasing out our paper supply from ancient forests worldwide. This book is one step towards ending global reforestation and climate change. It is printed on acid-free paper that is **100% old growth forest-free** (100% post-consumer recycled), processed chlorine free, and printed with vegetable based, low VOC inks. For further information, or to browse our full list of books and purchase securely, visit our website at www.newsociety.com

NEW SOCIETY PUBLISHERS www.newsociety.com

Dedication

To my family,
Sherrill, Neil, Graham, and Kendra,
for their inspiration and support
on my journey.

Contents

Acknowledgments

This could be very short or very long.

My thanks go to my editor, Audrey McClellan, for her invaluable suggestions and her eagle eye. She is a pleasure to work with and the book is better for her many thoughtful ideas. Thanks also to my family for their patience as I got this book out of my system.

I also acknowledge the hundreds of authors, speakers, lecturers, activists, colleagues, and friends who helped shape my thinking about sustainable development. Many of the experts are listed in the bibliography and endnotes, so I won't repeat them here. Consider the bibliography as a continuation of my acknowledgments to those whose research I researched. Standing on the shoulders of giants wonderfully improved my perspective.

Thanks to all of you.

Foreword

John Elkington and Oliver Dudok van Heel

SustainAbility Ltd.

Many CEOs and other business leaders will read this book — and those that don't should be given a brief on its key messages. Bob Willard has his finger on the pulse of the emerging business agenda. Indeed, it's a privilege to have been invited to contribute this foreword.

In helping major, brand-name corporations to understand the emerging agenda, identify strategic priorities and then move towards implementation within their operations, the biggest barriers we encounter invariably have been linked to the perceived absence of a business case for sustainability.

To paraphrase a common response: 'Sustainability is all very nice, but I'm trying to run a business here!'

The Sustainability Advantage provides convincing arguments that sustainability and 'running a business' are potentially (although not automatically) complimentary, not contradictory. Whatever industry you operate in, *The Sustainability Advantage* is designed to help you and your colleagues make an increasingly powerful case for the inclusion of the triple bottom line (TBL) of sustainable development within your business operations.

The Sustainability Advantage is an important book, providing what we believe to be the first systematic quantification of the business case for TBL performance. To date, many people outside — and growing numbers inside — business believed there was a convincing business case for corporate sustainability. But this was often an act of faith, with few companies making serious attempts to quantify the business case. Early corporate contenders in this area have included: Axel Springer Verlag, BAA, BASF, British Telecom, Baxter, Henkel Group, IBM, Kirin Brewing Company, Novo Nordisk, STMicroelectronics and Volkswagen Group [1].

Bob Willard shows that, even under the most conservative estimates, real financial bottom line benefits are there for the taking. Using the model provided here, smart executives will be impatient to discover how the numbers add up for their company.

Happily, the conclusions of *The Sustainability Advantage* very much mirror the conclusions of *Buried Treasure*, a report SustainAbility completed

[1] See pages 38-39, *The Global Reporters*, SustainAbility and UNEP, 2001.

in early 2001. Sound environmental performance — managed in the right way — drives costs down, revenues up and increases shareholder value. At the same time, in an overwhelming percentage of studies we reviewed, sustainable corporations are found to be highly productive ones. Corporate and personal values, the evidence shows, go hand in hand, empowering and powerfully motivating employees.

That said, a commitment to sustainability will only reap maximum benefits when it is fully incorporated in a company's core business models, strategies and processes. And, even today, the number of companies that have got this far remains precariously small.

Clearly, the work doesn't end with the publication of this book. Three key challenges lie ahead for the sustainability community.

First, the existence of a positive business case needs to be communicated beyond 'the usual suspects.' Company executives and the financial markets must be briefed on the sustainability advantage, so that they can start taking this advantage into account in their decision-making processes.

Second, the measurement of social and environmental performance needs to be refined through the development of appropriate key performance indicators. Only once we can comprehensively measure sustainability performance (good, bad, and ugly) can we fully quantify its financial benefits.

And, third, we must be sure that enthusiasm does not get the better of us. Where there is a positive business case, we should say so. Where there isn't, we should also say so. The uncomfortable fact is that the business case is still weak in many areas, because markets have not yet worked out how to value human, social, and natural forms of capital appropriately. Where such market weaknesses become clear, business will need to work with governments and other stakeholders to change markets, whether through regulation or — increasingly — taxes and fiscal instruments.

Read on. And a final message to Bob Willard. Don't rest easy. If the business case community moves as fast as we hope it will, we are all going to need a new edition of *The Sustainability Advantage* in a year or two.

John Elkington and Oliver Dudok van Heel
SustainAbility Ltd., London, U.K.

Introduction

Managers should look at environmental problems as business issues. They should make environmental investments for the same reasons they make other investments: because they expect them to deliver positive returns or reduce risks.

Forest Reinhardt[1]

PICTURE THIS. It's three years from today. You've just been interviewed by a writer from *Harvard Business Review*, who is doing an article on your company's remarkable success in an economy that has wiped out some of your toughest competitors and ruthlessly downsized others. You are the senior executive who is reputed to have led the three-year turnaround of your company, SD Inc., and the writer has come to you for the straight goods on this magic "sustainable development" thing—is it really the silver bullet that other articles in the business press are claiming it to be?

The interview was fun—once you got the writer past the usual business press desire to find the one secret to SD Inc.'s success and the one leader-hero who made it happen. It's never that simple. At first it sounded like a cliché when you explained it had been a team effort involving everyone in the company and that many little things were instrumental in SD Inc.'s profit growth. When the writer asked for details and examples, though, the story came alive.

- You described how three years earlier you and the CEO had invited all employees to help revitalize the company's vision so that it compelled and inspired everyone to pursue sustainable business goals energetically, creatively, relentlessly.

- You explained the company's commitment to a five-year investment in company-wide education on what sustainability means to the planet, society, the business community, and especially to SD Inc. In the first sessions, senior executives led discussions on what the company was already doing on the "triple bottom line" (an expression that you needed to explain to the writer), what it planned to improve next, and how the company needed everyone's creative ideas to make it all happen. The status reports by executives in the last two annual education sessions had reinforced that this was not just another management fad. These training sessions were also turning out to be wonderful opportunities to celebrate progress on the sustainability journey.

- You admitted that you thought some employees would be energized by the move to sustainability, but you had been amazed by how the individual and team efforts of passionate folks had raised the overall productivity of the company. Employees were voluntarily working harder and smarter to ensure the company did well and continued to address environmental and social issues that they cared about. The chance to contribute to "saving the world" had unleashed their potential beyond anything you had heard about in the business literature.

When the writer probed further, asking what this had to do with SD Inc.'s success, it had been satisfying to pull numbers from the latest annual report, which now included the environmental, health and safety, and corporate community relations reports that used to be produced separately each year. You showed how, over the past three years:

- profits had improved by 25%, as revenues increased by 5% and expenses were reduced by 20% in a variety of creative ways throughout the business;
- productivity had risen by 5 to 10% across the company and was still improving;
- customer satisfaction had reached new highs;
- markets once viewed as unprofitable were now returning margins that were better than traditional markets;
- the service and consulting arms of the business were generating over half the revenue, and the volume of products that were leased had surpassed the volume of outright sales; and
- new products designed to appeal to "green customers" were helping to change SD Inc.'s image in the market and were, surprisingly, more profitable than most products in its traditional product line.

There was so much more to tell and so little time to tell it. After the writer leaves, congratulating you on your recent appointment to senior vice-president of SD Inc.'s Sustainable Development Profit Center, you realize that you forgot to mention how helpful it had been to have a business case template that you initially used to demonstrate to the CEO and your executive colleagues how compelling the business benefits of sustainable development could be for SD Inc. Oh, well. You'll make sure to start the interview with that story when you meet with the *Wall Street Journal* reporter who is coming tomorrow.

Back to the present.

This story does not need to be fiction. Today's companies are squandering bottom-line benefits that could easily be achieved by adapting sustainable development strategies. The business benefits are quantifiable and real—the return on investment from aggressively improving company-wide sustainable development knowledge and initiatives can make other traditional investment opportunities seem trivial. Whichever company captures these benefits soonest will have a significant competitive edge. Sustainable development gives companies a sustainable advantage. It's a race to the top.

Businesspeople do not have to be transformed into tree-hugging environmental activists to reap these benefits. They can remain just what their shareholders expect them to be—hard-nosed executives who evaluate proposals on their bottom-line merits. Saving the world and making a profit is not an either/or proposition; it is a both/and proposition. Good environmental and social programs make good business sense. Benefits from more aggressive and creative attention to environmental and social projects throughout a company create a win/win approach for both the corporate bottom-line and the restoration of the health of the planet. As George Molenkamp, chairman of KPMG Environmental Consulting, reported after a 1999 KPMG study of the Fortune 250 companies and the top 100 firms in 11 countries:

> More big multinational firms are seeing the benefits of improving their environmental performances.... Firms are saving money and boosting share performance by taking a close look at how their operations impact the environment.... Companies see that they can make money as well [as improve the environment].[2]

Addressing environmental and sustainability issues in a systematic way provides new opportunities to focus on core business objectives such as reducing hiring and retention costs, improving productivity, reducing expenses at manufacturing and commercial sites, increasing revenue and market share, reducing risk, increasing shareholder value, and increasing profit.

External Pressures

More and more, business leaders influence world decisions. Without their support, environmental restoration will take longer—and time is running out. It is vital that companies become leaders in corporate social and environmental responsibility. Companies experience a variety of external pressures to improve their sustainable development performance: lobbying by non-governmental organizations;[3] government environmental policies and regulations;[4] insurance company encouragement to reduce the risk of environmental liability;[5] pressure from large investors like pension funds, insurance companies, and banks that are seeking ethical investments;[6] trade association image-building efforts;[7] labor groups' and consumers' health and safety concerns;[8] and local community concerns about the impact of company operations on long-term air, water, and land quality.[9] The World Business Council for Sustainable Development sums up the pressures on the environmental attributes of a business (italics in original).

> The environment is not going to disappear as an issue for business. Companies are, and will continue to remain, under pressure from *customers, investors, employees, legislators* and increasingly, from *banks* and *insurance companies* to be eco-efficient.[10]

Most firms would prefer to pursue their environmental strategies voluntarily, rather than be legislated or externally pressured into doing so.[11] Frequently, external pressures are seen as being at odds with the internal desire of the firm to generate strong bottom-line results for another group of external constituents—shareholders. However, if a compelling internal business case could be made for quantum leaps in environmental and social performance that result in improvements in the bottom line, companies would voluntarily want to capitalize on this business opportunity.

Do companies already care about corporate social responsibility? Most would claim that they do. How they interpret the phrase, why they care, and the degree to which they display an active interest in environmental and social issues will differ. Some get it, some don't. Some are voluntary leaders, some are unwilling followers driven by regulations. Unfortunately, some also attempt to co-opt and dilute the terminology, so it is helpful to clarify commonly used labels.

Clarifying the Terminology

Are "sustainable development," "corporate social responsibility," and "eco-efficiency" all the same? Not quite.

"Sustainable development" was the theme of *Our Common Future*, the 1987 report prepared by the World Commission on Environment and Development, led by then Norwegian prime minister Gro Harlem Brundtland. Commonly known as the Brundtland report, it described sustainable development as "meeting the needs of the present without compromising the ability of future generations to meet their own needs."[12] In economic language, it means we should live off the Earth's interest, not its capital. For a business, it means sustaining nature's resources as well as sustaining the company. Sustainable development is like a three-legged stool. Its legs are economic prosperity, environmental stewardship, and social responsibility.[13] If one of the legs is missing, the stool is not going to work, so we need to be sure all three legs are in good shape (see Figure 1.1).

The *economic prosperity* element is easily understood and accepted by companies—it is about the long-term economic health of global, local, and corporate economies. It's not just about individual corporations being profitable over the short term. It's also about multilevel, interdependent economies being healthy and sustainable for the long term.

The *environmental stewardship* dimension of sustainable development not only requires companies to "do no harm" to the environment with their operations and products, but also stretches them to help restore the environment from harm already done. This requires reducing the amount of energy, water, and material consumed in the manufacture of products, reducing waste, and remediating contaminated sites.

"Eco-efficiency" marries these first two economic and environmental elements of sustainable development. The term is a contraction of *eco*logical and *eco*nomic *efficiency*—doing more with less over the full life cycle of a product. Stephan Schmidheiny, with 50 business leaders in the Business Council for Sustainable Development, elaborated in *Changing Course* on what eco-efficient companies would look like.

> Corporations that achieve ever more efficiency while preventing pollution through good housekeeping, materials substitution, cleaner technologies, and cleaner products and that strive for more efficient use and recovery of resources can be called "eco-efficient."[14]

"Eco-efficiency" is a more palatable term to business leaders than "sustainable development," which may seem abstract and unwieldy at first. The seven guidelines of eco-efficiency proposed by Livio DeSimone and Frank Popoff in *Eco-efficiency: The Business Link to Sustainable Development* are refreshingly explicit.[15]

Sustainable Development

a.k.a. Corporate Social Responsibility, Good Corporate Citizenship, Conscientious Commerce, Sustainable Capitalism

The Triple Bottom Line... 3 Es, 3 Ps

Economy/Profit *Sustainable Business*

- Profits
- Taxes/Expenditures
- Jobs, R&D
- Compensation/Benefits
- Training/Productivity
- Fair trade
- Ethical Behaviour
- Core values

Environment/Planet *Eco-Efficient Business*

- Manufacturing eco-efficiency
- Supplier eco-inspections
- Operations eco-efficiency
- Product eco-characteristics
- Cradle-to-cradle product responsibility/take-back
- Beyond compliance
- Restorative to nature

Equity/People *Ethical Business*

INTERNAL EMPLOYEES

- Respect for diversisty
- Respect for human rights
- Health & safety protection
- Empowerment & caring

REST OF THE WORLD

- Charitable contributions
- Corporate relations
- Closing the gap between rich and poor

Figure 1.1 Sustainable Development

- Reduce the material intensity of goods and services
- Reduce the energy intensity of goods and services
- Reduce toxic dispersion
- Enhance material recyclability
- Maximize sustainable use of renewable resources
- Extend product durability
- Increase the service intensity of products

Eco-efficiency is a significant element of sustainable development, but it is not synonymous, as it excludes the third element, social responsibility. *Social responsibility* calls for a global view of society and seeks to ensure that resources and wealth are more equitably shared among citizens of the world. For a corporation, social responsibility includes observing human rights, improving working conditions and labor relations, adhering to business ethics, making charitable contributions, reducing aesthetic impacts of factory and commercial sites on the local community, helping employees develop transferable job skills, supporting public health, and fostering community relations. Although some observers debate whether all these are a legitimate responsibility of corporations,[16] social responsibility is a powerful attractor for some employees who are deeply committed to sustainable development, and there are clear indications that social responsibility is gaining importance in the civil society movement.[17]

The Natural Step, an international educational organization working to accelerate the movement toward a sustainable society, espouses four systems conditions that echo the components of sustainable development.[18]

1. Nature's functions and diversity must not be subject to increasing concentrations of substances extracted from the earth's crust.
2. Nature's functions and diversity must not be subject to increasing concentrations of substances produced by society.
3. Nature's functions and diversity must not be impoverished by overharvesting or other forms of ecosystem manipulation.
4. Resources are used fairly and efficiently in order to meet basic human needs worldwide.

Eco-efficiency addresses the efficiency aspect of this fourth condition, but not the fairness aspect of meeting basic human needs worldwide.

There is concern that if companies fail to address corporate social responsibility and its underlying issue of trust, social unrest will boil over and undermine progress in the environmental and economic areas. As the authors of *Mapping the Journey* contend, to overlook the social aspect is to overlook an important "sleeper discontinuity" of sustainable development.

> There is mounting evidence that our "old-world" "trade-off" paradigm, pitting economic success against environmental and social goals, is seriously flawed. Both research studies and practical experience have demonstrated that improved environmental and social responsibility increase value to shareholders, customers, employees, and society (rather than adding costs). Improving environmental and social performance in fact leads to enhanced profitability and value: cost reductions from eco-efficiencies, waste reductions and process improvements; price premiums, especially for those first to market; enhanced brand equity and customer loyalty; lowered cost of capital due to reduced liability and risk; increased revenue from new products, markets, and even new businesses; and enhanced asset management.... Superior environmental and social performance has also been found to lead to intangible benefits: higher employee job satisfaction and commitment, increased innovation and creativity, and motivation from a higher sense of purpose.[19]

We will explore all these benefits as we examine how integrating the three elements of sustainable development is smarter than trading them off against each other. They are all part of the same whole, not separate from each other. When people talk about "trading off" or "balancing" economic progress against environmental and social impacts versus "integrating" these three dimensions, it betrays a lack of understanding of sustainable development.[20]

Several mnemonic devices have been developed to make it easier to remember the triple bottom line of sustainable development. For example, there is the acronym SEE. The letters stand for society, environment, and economics.[21] A second memory trigger for sustainable development is the 3 Es: economics, environment, and equity. A more targeted version of the 3 Es was coined by a group of telecom CEOs in 1999: e-business (as a component of economics), environment, and education (as a component of equity).[22] Some people prefer to think of the 3 Ps: profits, planet, and people. The nuances of meaning are different for each of these terminology triplets, but the basic ingredients are the same.

More recently, corporate social responsibility has been embraced by the business community as another synonym for sustainable development. It has even been given the acronym CSR, [23] increasing its aura of legitimacy. The elements of CSR do align nicely with the three elements of sustainable development: financial sustainability in CSR aligns with economics/profits of sustainable development; environmental responsibility in CSR aligns with environment/planet in sustainable development; and community investment, employee relations, and human rights in CSR align with the society/equity/people element of sustainable development.[24] The only drawback is that the environmental dimension is not explicit in the term "corporate social responsibility," which may require coining the longer phrase "corporate social and environmental responsibility" for those who do not realize CSR includes environmental dimensions. In this book, corporate social responsibility and sustainable development will be used synonymously, and I will focus on the economic and environmental aspects much more than the social.

To wrap up our terminology discussion, and to suggest a state of sustainable development to which companies might aspire, here are nine principles of corporate social responsibility that have been defined by the Social Venture Network.[25]

- **Ethics**. The company deals with all stakeholders ethically.
- **Accountability**. Stakeholder "need to know" takes precedence over inconvenience and cost to the company.
- **Governance**. The company balances conscientious management of resources with the interests of all stakeholders.
- **Financial Returns**. Profits sustain long-term growth and shareholder value.
- **Employment Practices**. The company fosters employee development, diversity, empowerment, fair labor practices, competitive wages and benefits, and a safe, harassment-free, family-friendly work environment.
- **Business Relationships**. The company is fair and honest with all business partners and monitors the CSR of business partners.
- **Products and Services**. The company offers the highest level of service and quality.
- **Community Involvement**. The company has an open, honest, transparent, proactive relationship with the community.

- **Environmental Protection**. The company protects and restores the environment by minimizing use of resources and energy, decreasing waste and harmful emissions, and embedding these considerations into day-to-day management decisions.

Happily, the idea of sustainable development is not new to CEOs. The consulting firm Arthur D. Little recently surveyed a group of North American and European business leaders and found that 95% of them viewed sustainable development as genuinely important, while 83% of them believed they could derive business value from sustainable development initiatives.

> Companies are finding that the benefits of pursuing a sustainable development approach range from opening new avenues to innovation in products, processes, and stakeholder relationships to accelerating learning organization skills throughout the company.[26]

Chances are, when you hear the term "socially responsible business" a handful of companies (and their founders) leap to mind: Ben & Jerry's Homemade Ice Cream (Ben Cohen and Jerry Greenfield); the Body Shop International (Anita and Gordon Roddick); Smith & Hawken (Paul Hawken); Patagonia (Yvon Chouinard). They set up shop, espousing "principles before profits" and a commitment to making the world—from the New York City subways to the Pentagon to the Amazon rain forest—a better place, back in the late 1970s or the 1980s, and most of them grew fast and furiously to become the paragons of companies that care about more than just making profits.

CEOs of larger corporations already know about sustainable development and agree that a commitment to sustainable development is good for business. As Trevor Eyton, senior chairman of Canada's Edper Brascan conglomerate of businesses in the natural resources, commercial properties, energy, and financial services industries, says:

> Our corporate group—including the directors and senior officers of Noranda [mining company]—have concluded that sustainable development is an inevitability. We have no choice but to develop a sustainable economy, and the ecological imperative can no longer be ignored. The sooner a corporation reaches that conclusion and begins to work toward true sustainable development, the greater its advantage in the future.[27]

It is worth noting that Eyton is referring to sustainable companies within a sustainable economy. A sustainable economy is a larger topic than the corporate sustainable development addressed in this book, although it is touched on later when we discuss the need for more supportive public policies.

The Need For a Business Case

Business people pursue sustainable development for three reasons: morality, compliance, or opportunity.[28] The morality motivation is based on the assumption that business owes it to society to improve people's lives and the environment in exchange for the privilege to operate. It is usually an outgrowth of the personal values of key senior executives. The compliance motivation is driven by the threat of current or anticipated environmental and social regulations that could affect the company's right to operate. The opportunity motivation is the result of companies seeing a chance for increased revenues and profits. Smart businesses respond better to opportunities than to threats. We will focus on the opportunity side of sustainable development more than on the morality and compliance sides. Companies that voluntarily show social and environmental leadership enhance their reputations, build trust and meaningful connections with their communities, and prosper.

Though some companies have recognized the opportunity and adopted some eco-efficiency initiatives, these are seldom fully exploited to drive innovation, new market development, new services, and new technologies. One of the reasons that businesses have been slow in getting off the ground with sustainable development is that there is no appropriate business case to quantify the opportunities. A study by The Alliance for Environmental Innovation reinforces the need for a sound business case that would encourage the business community to effectively address sustainability issues. The Alliance was founded as a joint project of the Environmental Defense Fund (EDF) and the Pew Charitable Trusts in 1994. It works cooperatively with companies to create aggressive environmental initiatives that yield substantial, direct, and measurable business benefits such as increased revenues or reduced costs.[29] In February 1999 the Alliance released a report, *Catalyzing Environmental Results: Lessons in Advocacy Organization-Business Partnerships*, which distills the lessons of almost a decade of work with individual companies, starting with the EDF-McDonald's Waste Reduction Task Force established in 1991, and continuing through the Alliance's current portfolio of projects with such companies as SC Johnson, Starbucks, United Parcel Service, and Dell. They found that, in most cases, environmental initiatives will only sustain themselves and grow within a company when they deliver specific, measurable business benefits, particularly with regard to a company's core business functions.[30] No business benefits, no momentum.

Business leaders need proof of quantifiable financial benefits from an increased focus on environmental and social factors. Saving the world is a daunting agenda for any business—it is challenging enough to find business initiatives that reduce costs, improve profit, and increase shareholder value. Corporations are scrambling for market share in an increasingly competitive business environment. Going out of business to save the world would be a tough strategy to propose in a boardroom. Sometimes senior corporate managers recognize the value their company can give to environmental and social issues, but their suggestions are rebuffed by colleagues who are focused solely on the next quarter's bottom-line results.

What the socially responsible managers have been overlooking is the beauty of the "If you can't fix it, feature it" strategy. They shouldn't fight the profit orientation of their colleagues; they should appeal to it. They can show their colleagues new ways to make money for their shareholders by adopting sustainable development business practices. To be effective when lobbying their hard-nosed colleagues, enlightened managers must use business language so that it is obvious how the cause relates to day-to-day business priorities. If it doesn't help the business, it's not on business leaders' radar screens. The trick is to focus on the "selfish" bottom-line benefits, not the seemingly altruistic societal and environmental results. Environmental benefits can be a happy by-product, not necessarily the initial motivating rationale.

Money is the language of business. Most environmentalists know less about accounting than accountants know about the environment.[31] Wall Street demands quarterly results, a stringent return on investment, and a short payback period. Mandatory pollution prevention projects can save the companies big money in fines, so their costs are readily justified. However, the business case for more proactive environmental initiatives, such as energy efficiencies and use of renewable energy, may be less evident. Executives need to be shown that environmental projects outside the pollution prevention realm will lead to quick, positive business results as well as longer term benefits. That is, the business benefits of sustainability initiatives not only need to be identified; they also need to be quantified and expressed in business language as bottom-line benefits relevant to the short- and long-term priorities of senior executives.

This book will show how big those benefits can be. It will present quantifiable evidence that investing in sustainable development pays off with real bottom-line benefits. Sustainable development is a profit driver, and at the same time it adds value to local economies, society, and the environment. We will explore simple, manageable, and economical measures to reap these bottom-line, social, and environmental benefits.

The Intent of This Book

There are many books about how humanity, led by transnational corporations, cannot continue destroying our own habitat at an ever-accelerating rate in the name of progress.[32] They make a powerful case for change. Other books despair of corporations ever practicing conscientious commerce sincerely. In fact, some authors claim that corporations are deliberately or ignorantly colluding against sustainability.[33] More hopefully, a body of literature identifies the benefits of corporate sustainability—especially environmental initiatives—and cites encouraging case studies.[34] The authors generalize about approaches that work and cite specific cases that help quantify the savings, increased revenue, or increased productivity from eco-efficiency efforts, though none provide comprehensive formulae for calculating the benefits.

This book fits in the last, more optimistic category. It will assess seven areas of business benefit associated with corporate environmental and social initiatives, including three often overlooked human resource benefit areas. The intent is to quantify the benefits of sustainability leadership and to offer a persuasive argument for companies to be genuinely responsible corporate citizens. Using frameworks and success stories, it breaks sustainable development down into ideas small enough to grasp and powerful enough to lead to new, important business opportunities. The real power of the book is in the Appendix, which contains generic Sustainability Advantage worksheets. Executives can insert their own data and assumptions into these worksheets so they can see for themselves whether the business case for aggressively supporting sustainable development is a compelling one for their company.

Finally, a word about the book's intended audience. The primary audience is senior executives and shareholders. It is also useful for consultants working with these executives and for environmental affairs department directors or corporate community relations department directors who are struggling with the business case for more pervasive corporate social responsibility initiatives—that is, initiatives which touch all employees and permeate all aspects of the company's operations. It is for human resources directors and staff looking for ways to attract and retain top talent, and looking for ways to increase the productivity of all employees. It is for talented prospective employees choosing which company they want to work for, and for employees who want to engage their companies in proactive social and environmental initiatives. It is for academics in business and environmental faculties at universities. It is for government agencies, non-governmental organizations, and environmental lobby groups seeking a credible rationale for their proposed environmental recommendations. It is for shareholders who seek less "emotional" reasons for the companies that they invest in to be more socially responsible. In fact, it is for all citizens who wish to be better informed about criteria by which they can assess the social responsibility of companies when considering purchasing their goods or services. I hope this audience includes you.

The Proposal

When viewed within the context of sustainable development, environmental concerns become not just a cost of doing business, but a potent source of competitive advantage. Enterprises that embrace the concept can effectively realize the advantages: more efficient processes, improvements in productivity, lower costs of compliance, and new strategic market opportunities. Such businesses may expect to reap advantages over their competitors who lack vision. Companies that fail to change can expect to become obsolete.

Stephan Schmidheiny[1]

MOST COMPANIES ALREADY HAVE environmental management systems, they have pollution prevention processes in place, they are working on saving energy, and they have company policies on environmental protection. So what's the problem?

The Problem

The problem is that the low-hanging fruit has been picked—the easy energy and waste savings have already been harvested and applied to the company bottom line. Many companies already have annual targets for further waste and electricity reduction and for the further elimination of toxic substances used in manufacturing, but they are becoming increasingly difficult to meet. When all the incandescent light bulbs have been replaced with more energy-efficient fluorescent or halide bulbs, and after over 80% of waste has been eliminated, then what? The law of diminishing returns inhibits further savings from eco-efficiency programs. A new phase must be entered.

To continue to reap the bottom-line benefits from environmental initiatives, companies must bring their environmental strategies out of the closet and reframe them in the broader context of sustainable development. Companies are treating the environmental aspects of their operations in the same way they too often treated quality in the 1980s—as a specialized staff concern, which ensures that the right environmental things are done while the rest of the organization gets on with the real business of creating shareholder value. ISO 14001 environmental systems management certification may be to the environment what ISO 9000 certification was to quality management. Often the environmental affairs department is associated with other compliance-oriented areas, like health and safety. Company environmental staff do good work, but they are marginalized—their work is mostly invisible and deliberately unpublicized, even internally. They are treated as problem-avoiders rather than as business entrepreneurs. When creative, whole-systems, ecologically based thinking is married with intelligent engineering and ecological design throughout the business, big savings can actually cost less up front than small or no savings.

Companies are missing a business opportunity. Their myopic view, which sees a place for environmental strategies only in their design and manufacturing functions, is overlooking potential benefits throughout the entire company, and that's not smart business. If company shareholders woke up to what was being left on the table by company executives, they would not be pleased.

The Proposal

What would happen if companies unleashed the untapped creative energies of all their people and encouraged them to help fulfill the vision of sustainable development? Suppose the corporate purpose, vision, values, and business processes were overtly aligned with sustainable development objectives. Suppose companies educated all employees and empowered them to suggest and implement environmentally oriented expense-saving and revenue opportunities. Suppose the company invigorated its fledgling sustainable development infrastructure by connecting the dots between the environmental affairs department, the health and safety department, the philanthropic corporate community relations department, and the communications department. Once its own house was in order, suppose the company used advertising to inform the public about the sustainable development benefits of its products and operations, building the growing wave of environmentally and socially concerned customers and potential employees. Suppose it publicized its corporate sustainable development values and the benefits of its products and services to the ecological carrying capacity of the planet. Suppose the company stopped treating the environmental affairs department as a cost center and started treating it as a Sustainable Development Profit Center.

In short, imagine the environmental strategies of companies were more pervasive—spreading far beyond the design, development, and manufacturing functions. The marketing and sales organizations would be engaged; all staff organizations would be engaged; all executives, managers, and employees would be engaged—everyone would be engaged. Energy conservation strategies could evolve from using energy more efficiently to making all company facilities energy self-sufficient, and then to providing a new revenue stream by selling excess company-produced energy back to the utility-owned power grid. Products could be so energy efficient they would operate on renewable solar energy, the way a pocket calculator does. All products would be leased and completely recycled after being returned by customers. The company would not only be doing no environmental harm, but would also be helping to restore the economic, ecological, and social health of the planet.

Would it be expensive to follow this road map to the future? Not really. Companies only undertake projects that meet strict payback and rate-of-return criteria, and this approach should continue. There is ample evidence that environmental projects can increase revenues and save expenses. What is needed is a concerted, company-wide effort to identify and implement these projects, supported by a sound communications and education strategy. Companies already have budgets for communication, recruiting ads, and product advertising. Adjusting the content of internal and external communications to include environmental themes could be done without additional cost.

SD Inc.: A Hypothetical Company

What corporation should be used as a test case for the proposed business case methodology? Choosing any one particular company would bias the generic benefits calculations. However, a credible illustration needs to have some basis in the real world, so a hypothetical company in a particular industry would be helpful. A typical company from any industry could serve as an example, but I will use a hypothetical company from the computer industry to test assumptions throughout this book. Why? The sphere of influence of global high-tech companies is huge, they manufacture goods and also offer services, they deal with the typical issues faced in most industries, and they have significant potential for being a positive force for global change.

According to the *Fortune 500* listing of the top ten computer and office equipment companies for 1999, the top five computer companies (IBM, HP, Compaq, Dell, and Xerox) generated 85% of the revenue and 83% of the profit for the top ten (IBM, HP, Compaq, Dell, Xerox, Sun, Gateway 2000, NCR, Apple, and Pitney Bowes).[2] The top five also employed 83% of the employees. Therefore, I will use a composite of the top five high-tech companies, "Sustainable Development Inc." or "SD Inc.," as a representative

Derivation of "SD Inc." Assumptions

Source: FORTUNE 500 web site at http://www.fortune.com/fortune/fortune500/ind8.html for 1999

		1999 Revenue		1999 Profit		1999 Employees		1998	1998	1998
	FORTUNE 500 Revenues Ranking	US$ Millions	% Change from 1998	US$ Millions	% Change from 1998	Number	% Change from 1998	Revenue	Profit	Employees
Computers, Office Equipment										
Intl. Business Machines (IB	6	87,548	7%	7,712	22%	307,401	6%	81,821	6,321	290,001
Hewlett-Packard (HP)	13	48,253	3%	3,491	19%	84,400	32%	46,848	2,934	124,118
Compaq Computer	20	38,525	24%	569	0%	76,100	5%	31,069	569	80,105
Dell Computer	56	25,265	38%	1,666	14%	36,500	50%	18,308	1,461	24,333
Xerox	87	19,228	4%	1,424	261%	94,600	2%	20,029	394	92,745
Total		218,819	10%	14,862	27%	599,001	2%	198,074	11,680	611,302
Average of top 5 companies.		**43,764**	10%	**2,972**	27%	**119,800**	2%	39,615	2,336	122,260

The above data is used as the basis for the assumptions for the hypothetical "SD Inc." company used in sample calculations in the worksheets.
The following data about the rest of the top 10 companies "Computer & Office Equipment" companies is for information purposes only.

	FORTUNE 500 Revenues Ranking	1999 Revenue US$ Millions	% Change from 1998	1999 Profit US$ Millions	% Change from 1998	1999 Employees Number	% Change from 1998	1998 Revenue	1998 Profit	1998 Employees
Sun Microsystems	150	11,726	20%	1,031	35%	29,700	13%	11,703	1,027	29,661
Gateway 2000	203	8,646	16%	428	24%	20,726	9%	8,632	427	20,707
NCR	283	6,196	-5%	37	176%	32,800	-1%	6,199	331	32,803
Apple Computer	285	6,134	3%	601	94%	8,348	2%	6,132	595	8,346
Pitney Bowes	354	4,548	5%	636	10%	30,628	-2%	4,546	635	30,634
Total of Top 10		256,069	9%	17,895	22%	721,203	-2%	235,286	14,696	733,455
Average of Top 10		**25,607**	9%	**1,790**	22%	**72,120**	-2%	23,529	1,470	73,345
SD Inc. as a % of Top 10		**85%**		**83%**		**83%**		84%	79%	83%

Figure 2.1 Derivation of "SD Inc." Assumptions

sample of global high-tech companies. Our fictitious SD Inc. will be assumed to have 1999 revenues of $44 billion, profits of $3 billion, and 120,000 employees (see "Assumptions About the 'SD Inc.' Hypothetical Company" in the Appendix). Figure 2.1 elaborates on how these values were derived by averaging the financial results of the top five computer companies.

If the SD Inc. hypothetical company is much larger than your particular company of interest, just divide the assumed size by 10, 100, 1,000, or some other suitable factor. The logic used in the business case methodology is scalable. Further, if 1999 figures seem "old," remember that they are just examples. Current figures for any specific company could be substituted, and should be.

It is reassuring that a study done by Innovest Strategic Value Advisors in 1999 found a strong correlation between superior environmental performance and superior financial performance among computer companies.[3] Innovest studied computer companies' recycling programs for outdated products, and whether the products could be returned for disposal; the energy efficiency of the actual computers; and the pollution caused by manufacturing plants. The top five "eco-performers" were Dell, IBM, Compaq, Quantum, and Apple Computer. The worst eco-performers included Data General, Western Digital, Silicon Graphics, and Gateway. Innovest found that the environmentally friendly firms outperformed those ranked last by about 25%. Even if executives are skeptical about the causal connection between sound ecological practices and strong financial performance, they should be comfortable knowing that bottom-line results need not suffer because of increased attention to environmentally oriented strategies.

There have been similar results for other industries researched by Innovest. In fact, the arguments and quantifications outlined in this book are generic. The computer industry is simply used to illustrate the business case and to test the assumptions.

Do computer companies already care about the environment? Absolutely. Visit the websites for the Fortune 500 top ten largest computer and office equipment companies.[4] All except Gateway 2000 and NCR have "Environment, Health and Safety" reports publicly available on-line that reinforce corporate policies and actions geared toward environmental, health, and safety protection.

Do computer companies' environmental efforts already go beyond compliance? Sure. In its description of the Power Macintosh 7200, Apple Computer states:

> With the increasing importance of environmental attributes in consumer products, Apple Computer has made a transition from viewing environmental performance as a compliance issue to viewing it as a customer requirements issue. Environmental factors must now be considered as an integral part of business decision-making at both the strategic planning level and the day-to-day operating level.[5]

Most computer companies have at least partly instituted Design for the Environment (DfE) approaches to minimize toxic materials, energy consumption, chemical emissions, and waste. Most have also instituted Design for Disassembly (DfD) for some of their products, perhaps in anticipation of product take-back regulations, to minimize landfill disposal of rapidly obsolete computing products. Significant cost savings have already resulted from reducing, reusing, and recycling materials and energy in pursuit of eco-efficiency. It is on this base that the business case is built.

Major computer companies, like all major companies, also pride themselves on their donations to charities and to cultural, social, and community causes. They do good work. They care about the social aspect of sustainable development, although they are understandably selective about what causes to help. Companies can't possibly respond positively to the hundreds of donation requests they receive each year from deserving causes, so each company usually declares what its prime social focus is. For example, IBM focuses its corporate community relations efforts on education in schools through its Reinventing Education program. Throughout this book I will suggest how expanded efforts in the social area can lead to further business benefits.

I will assume that some money is invested in sustainable development up front, yet I will also demonstrate that the payoff is still positive. I will project future cash flows and include any incremental costs to implement the projects. Generally speaking, the most effective way in which to analyze projects is to use a discounted cash flow analysis. This methodology allows for consistent comparison of costs and benefits over time.[6] I will use this technique in our benefits calculations over a five-year period.

The Education Investment

Before outlining the potential areas of benefit, I should first outline the investment that I assume will be made in order to reap those benefits. Most companies will need to invest additional money in the area of employee education in sustainable development. Environmental education is already taking place in design and manufacturing departments at most companies, at least to ensure health and safety training. To responsibly empower every manager and employee to contribute to sustainability benefits requires more education in overall environmental and sustainability principles, current global ecological and social issues, life-cycle analysis and costing, design for the environment, the company's environmental and social track record, and the company's business, environmental, and social plans. This education could be done in classroom sessions, integrated with other business education, provided through self-study CD-ROMs, and/or delivered by on-line intranet training modules.

The "Education Investment Required to Achieve Benefits" worksheet in the Appendix shows how you would calculate the cost of providing the equivalent of two days of education for every employee in the first year, and one day of education in each of the next four years. To be conservative, factor the cost of the lost productivity of employees while they take this education into the calculation, although it is usually not included in companies' traditional training cost equations. Based on these assumptions, the five-year investment for increased environmental education for 120,000 employees and managers in our SD Inc. sample company would be about $372 million. For SD Inc., the net present value of this five-year environmental education investment is about $320 million.

The Seven Bottom-Line Benefits

When a company like SD Inc. makes the internal communications and educational investment in sustainable development, the foundation is laid for significant savings, revenue, and employee productivity opportunities in seven areas of potential benefit:

1. Easier hiring of the best talent
2. Higher retention of top talent
3. Increased employee productivity
4. Reduced expenses for manufacturing
5. Reduced expenses at commercial sites
6. Increased revenue/market share
7. Reduced risk, easier financing

The first three areas (hiring, retention, productivity) are about people benefits. The next two (reduced expenses at manufacturing and commercial sites) are about environmental benefits for the planet. Combined with the last two benefit areas (increased revenue and lower risk), all contribute to profits. People, planet, and profits—an integrated win/win/win case.

Why these seven—why not a different five, or ten, or fourteen benefit categories? In fact, various consulting companies have compiled lists of different lengths. Depending on their emphasis, they may explode one of my seven benefit areas into three or four component parts and treat them equally, or embed one or more of my seven within a single umbrella factor, or ignore one of my seven entirely. There are many ways to slice and dice the benefits categories. My experience is that a list of seven things is about as much as people can remember. I hope it works for you and that you can relate my seven benefit areas to other lists of sustainable development benefits with which you may be familiar.

The methodology will quantify these seven benefits, which are achieved when a powerful corporate sustainable development vision is transformed into reality. The business case is strong, even when the cost of the educational investment is deducted from the benefits. If the initiatives are framed and staged properly, they can yield enormous benefits to enlightened companies, with little or no downside risk.

In summary, the premise of this book is that companies are already doing good things on environmental and social issues. The base has been built. The proposed methodology acknowledges that good work and identifies additional savings which companies can capture. Some benefits may appear more qualitative than quantitative at first. However, by making explicit assumptions about the "so what?" of these benefits, the bottom-line impact can be verified. Using the worksheets in the Appendix, you can play out what-if scenarios using your own assumptions. By tuning the assumed values according to your own experience and good judgment, you can assess the business case for your own company. The business case is compelling for the sample company—it may be for yours, too.

Benefit 1: Easier Hiring of the Best Talent

In 15 years, there will be 15% fewer Americans in the 35 to 45-year-old range than there are now. At the same time, the U.S. economy is likely to grow at a rate of 3% to 4% per year. So over that period, the demand for bright, talented 35 to 45-year-olds will increase by, say, 25%, and the supply will be going down by 15%. That sets the stage for a talent war.

Charles Fishman[1]

The War For Talent

According to a 1999 Mercer/Angus Reid poll of 307 Canadian CEOs on business issues occupying their attention, executives were worried about attracting and retaining high-calibre employees. They said that this was harder to do than it was five years earlier, and 23% of the CEOs ranked this concern as their most important priority. In fact, this talent issue received the second highest number of votes, right behind improving profitability, which had the highest priority for 30% of the executives. As might be expected, most linked their profitability concern with their concern about attracting and retaining key employees.[2]

The Canadian situation is not unique. A 1999 Solomon Smith Barney report identified 350,000 information technology industry jobs open in the U.S. and 400,000 in Europe.[3] An August 1999 *Trend Alert* by Roger Herman and Joyce Gioia quantified the situation in high-tech industries in the United States.

> The high-tech arena is desperate for workers. The Bureau of Labor Statistics projects a 108 percent increase in the need for systems analysts, engineers and computer scientists from now until 2006. Today there are an estimated 933,000 jobs in these fields, and by 2006, the bureau estimates, that will rise to 1.9 million. Yet the nation's computer science programs each year are graduating only 25,000 students with bachelor's degrees.[4]

Given the scarce supply, the best companies are fiercely competing to attract and retain the best people. In 1997, the McKinsey consulting company did a landmark study of 77 companies and almost 6,000 managers and executives to assess the importance of this issue. Researchers found that the most important corporate resource over the next 20 years will be talent: smart, sophisticated business people who are technologically literate, globally astute, and operationally agile. In 2000 they updated the study and found, despite the economic slowdown and the end of the dot.com boom, the war for talent was intensifying dramatically. They found that 89% of those surveyed thought it was more difficult to attract talented people in 2000 than it had been three years earlier, and 90% thought it was now more difficult to retain them. McKinsey found that attracting and retaining talent was not just a valid desire—it was a business imperative.[5]

Attracting Top Talent

When the McKinsey researchers asked top people what they were looking for when they decided where to work, they got this answer: "a great company and a great job." More specifically, they found there are four kinds of messages that the best people respond to.

- **Go With a Winner.** This message attracts people who want to work for a high-performing company, a company where they're going to get lots of advancement opportunities.
- **Big Risk, Big Reward.** This message attracts people looking for an environment where they're challenged either to do exceptionally well or to leave — where there's considerable risk but good compensation, and where they can advance their career rapidly.
- **Lifestyles.** People who want flexibility and great lifestyle benefits, like a good location, are attracted to this message.
- **Save the World.** This message appeals to people seeking a company with an inspiring mission and an exciting challenge.

Interestingly, the survey found that high-tech companies are associated with the Save the World message. Coincidentally, IBM Canada's 1998 campus recruiting slogan was "Change the World."[7] The recruiting brochure referred to how e-business and e-learning are making educational opportunities available to people in remote areas, like the Inuit in Canada's North. IBM's more recent Why Work? global recruiting campaign encourages high-tech job seekers to ask eight questions of prospective employees (my italics).[8]

- Does the company have global reach?
- Does the technology count?
- Do the people matter?
- What about work/life balance?
- *Is the company's mission important?*
- *Does the company give back?*
- *Will the impact of my work endure?*
- *Will I make a difference?*

IBM's website expands on the fifth question, about the importance of the company's mission, by asking "What is worth doing? Is the place where you're working engaged in things that will change the world—in a good way?"[9] A business agenda in which sustainable practices were imbedded would provide a positive answer. The theme of worthwhile work relates to the Save the World attractor identified in the McKinsey study and suggests there is recruiting value in showing how a computer company is contributing to environmental sustainability and to society. The real question is: What is the bottom-line benefit of making this connection? The savings in recruiting costs are rather modest, as I will show next, so the hiring area may seem a weak benefit with which to launch this discussion of quantified benefits from sustainable development. However, it shapes the context for the other two human resource benefits in the hiring-retention-productivity trio, so I need to discuss it first.

The Cost of Recruiting

The opening calculations for SD Inc. in the "Attracting and Hiring the Best Talent" worksheet in the Appendix show it costs about $7,000 to recruit a new employee when the following factors are accounted for:

- **The cost of internal job posting or external advertisements**. External ads can range from $200 for a classified ad to $5,000 or more for a display advertisement. Agency costs are assumed to be 20 to 30% of annual compensation, although these are more likely to be incurred for executive-level recruiting. Employee referral costs range from $500 to $2,000 or more. An Internet posting costs $300 to $500 per listing. There is also the cost of the internal recruiter's or manager's time to understand the position requirements, develop and implement a sourcing strategy, and write the ad or job posting. Using a blend of these considerations, a very modest number of $5,000 is used for this line item.

- **Cost of initial candidate screening**. This cost includes the basic review of resumes and the administrative cost of handling, processing, and responding to applications for the opening. Included also are the costs of drug screening and educational and criminal background checks, especially if these tasks are outsourced. In addition, there is the cost of the pre-employment tests used to assess a candidate's skills, abilities, aptitude, attitude, values, and behaviors. The $500 cost further includes the time for the hiring department to do its own sourcing of candidates from networks, contacts, and other referrals.
- **Cost of doing interviews**. This reflects the time taken by recruiters and managers to review candidates' backgrounds, develop candidate interview schedules and make any travel arrangements for out-of-town candidates, prepare for interviews, conduct interviews, and prepare candidate assessments. The 30 hours of time assumed for the SD Inc. calculation also allows for lost productive time when internal candidates are away from their jobs while being interviewed.
- **Cost of making offers and hiring**. This is the cost to conduct reference checks on final candidates, to make the employment offer, and to notify unsuccessful candidates. The assumed expense of $500 includes the cost of orientation materials sent after the offer has been accepted.

The Potential Hiring Benefit of a Sustainable Development Image

Would this $7,000 expense be any lower if someone really wanted to join the company because he or she was attracted by the company's sustainable development agenda? Possibly. The savings would be minimal, however, since most of the costs are incurred before the job offer is made. Therefore, only a 5% savings of recruiting costs is used, assuming the need for recruiting will be slightly less because retention will be higher, as explained in the next chapter, and that word-of-mouth and a higher acceptance rate may also reduce hiring costs.

Furthermore, this 5% reduction would not apply to all recruits. It would apply only to those who are attracted and retained by SD Inc.'s superior corporate social responsibility image and reputation, aligned with the Save the World factor mentioned in the McKinsey study, so I'll now generate an assumption about the size of this group of recruits.

The *Millennium Poll on Corporate Social Responsibility* helps estimate the size of this group.[10] The survey, done in May 1999, polled approximately 1,000 citizens in 23 countries on six continents—a total of 25,000 surveys. It found that, worldwide, half the population is paying attention to the social behavior of companies. These people feel companies should not only focus on profitability, but should also protect employee health and safety, treat employees equally, protect the environment, not participate in bribery or corruption, and not use child labor. Note that these concerns all relate to the environmental and social aspects of sustainable development.

The *Millennium Poll* found that a corporation's overall image is most affected by perceptions of how it is fulfilling its social responsibilities (49% chose this as the most important factor), ahead of brand quality/reputation (40%) and business fundamentals (32%).[11] More importantly, based on how they perceive a company's social performance, 20% of respondents said they had either rewarded or punished companies in the previous year, and almost as many again had considered doing so. The survey defined punishing a company as avoiding its products and speaking out against it. Related to our discussion of how top talent might behave, those identified as opinion leaders were significantly more likely to have punished a socially irresponsible company in the past year—39% said they did. Assuming punishment would include not accepting a job offer, and assuming opinion leaders are top talent, 20 to 39% of talented potential recruits would care enough about the environmental image and reputation of a company to let it influence their decision to accept that company's job offer. To be conservative, I have used the lower estimate of 20%.

Therefore, if SD Inc. had a well-communicated and exceptional sustainable development reputation, the recruiting cost would be 5% lower for about 20% of those it is competing to hire. Assuming SD Inc. hires 10% of its employee base each year to offset attrition and to support growth, it recruits about 12,000 employees annually. The recruiting savings from the company's exceptional corporate social responsibility image would be about $840,000 (5% x 20% x 12,000 x $7,000). These calculations are shown in the "Attracting and Hiring the Best Talent" worksheet in the Appendix.

Admittedly, this is not a big saving. Consider it a placeholder that could be tuned higher, depending on company senior management's comfort level with the assumptions. The real benefit of attracting the best talent—people who value sustainable development—is not the saving of recruiting costs. The real benefit is the increased retention and productivity of these talented employees after they are hired, which is calculated next.

Benefit 2: Higher Retention of Top Talent

Employees who are highly committed to the organization work hard, are absent less often and are less likely to leave for a new job. Earning employees' commitment, therefore, is an important organizational goal.

Building a World-Class Workforce[1]

HIRING TOP TALENT is one challenge. Keeping it is another. The issue of worker retention in high-tech industries is a serious problem that is getting worse. At its annual Human Resources Conference and Exposition, the American Management Association (AMA) and Ernst & Young surveyed 350 senior human resource managers on employee turnover. As reported in the June 10, 1999, issue of *Trend Letter*, here are some of the findings:

- 46% said that skilled-worker retention was a "very serious" issue; another 28% believe it to be "serious."
- 51% said that turnover was particularly high among workers under 30 years of age.
- 37% reported problems retaining information technology workers, the highest percentage for any group of workers.[2]

The Cost of Turnover

What does it really cost when a good employee leaves and has to be replaced? A lot. The consulting company KPMG, together with the Canadian Advanced Technology Alliance (CATA), estimated that the cost of replacing a departed worker is at least $25,000,[3] which is certainly more than the $7,000 I estimated for hiring a new person. The cost of losing a typical employee is $50,000, according to a *BusinessWeek* article.[4] And in high-tech industries where knowledge is a hot commodity, the loss of intellectual property that accompanies each departed worker can be enormous.

The difficulty with these estimates is that they are not specific about what they include or do not include. Why are these two estimates so different from the $7,000 "cost of hiring" that we just calculated? Does the "cost of losing" equate to the "cost of replacing," or are the costs additive? What factors are allowed for and what assumptions are behind these claims? We need additional detail for the estimated costs to be understood and credible.

Bliss & Associates provide advisory services to entrepreneurial companies. Their "Cost of Turnover" article includes a comprehensive list of cost factors to consider when calculating the cost of turnover and is the basis for the "Retaining the Best Talent" worksheet in the Appendix.[5] The worksheet quantifies the costs from the time a typical experienced employee considers leaving until the replacement is hired, trained, and fully productive. The ten-month chronology includes:

- "Decide Time" while the valued employee privately decides to leave—One month
- "Save Attempt Time" during which the employer tries to convince the employee to stay—Half a month
- "Vacant Time" in the position before the employee's replacement arrives—Two months
- "New Hire Training Time" for basic orientation training by the company—Half a month
- "Department Training Time" for training on department- and job-specific operations—Six months

During the ten-month period, three phases of costs are incurred:

1. The costs associated with losing a good person
2. The costs of recruiting a new person
3. The costs of training a new person to be as productive as the person who left

The "Retaining the Best Talent" worksheet in the Appendix itemizes and quantifies the factors within each of these cost areas. The detail behind the assumed values for each factor is described below.

1. **Costs of losing a good person**. This cost is about $120,400 when the following factors are added up.

- **Cost of the person's lost productivity during "Decide Time."** This cost allows for the distraction while the employee considers the pros and cons of leaving, discusses the decision with confidants, secretly looks for a new job, quietly disengages from current activities in anticipation of possible departure, and shows a general lack of commitment to current activities. The assumed cost of $2,500 reflects the loss of half a month's productivity from the leaving employee, which may actually be stretched over several months or compressed into a shorter time frame.

- **Cost of the "Save Attempt Time."** The person's manager chews up productive time trying to save the person, to explain to others (especially the manager's own management) why the valued person is leaving, to make counterproposals, and to finally conduct an exit interview. The manager personally loses 25% productivity for two weeks, amounting to about $730. The person leaving is assumed to have a productivity loss during the "Save Attempt Time" of 50%. These productivity losses contribute another $1,250.

- **Cost of payroll and benefits administration**. When an employee resigns, payroll must be stopped and benefit deductions must be terminated. This often involves outside vendors of health coverage or insurance. There may also be costs for unemployment insurance premiums, for the time spent to prepare for an unemployment hearing, or for payment to a third party to handle the unemployment claim process. Specialized human resources staff need to complete various manual or on-line forms. This overall factor is minimal and is assumed to be the equivalent of only two days of a professional's time, or about $450.

- **Cost of separation allowance**. This $13,750 estimate assumes the person is leaving by mutual agreement and receives 11 weeks' pay as a separation allowance for five years of service. No additional payment in lieu of notice is assumed.

- **Cost of lost knowledge, experience, and contacts**. The company loses the value of the employee's personal network of associates built over the years, which expedited getting things done in the company's unique culture. The department loses productivity when the valued person is no longer available to guide, direct, and support the remaining staff. If the departing employee were participating in a critical project, the company must consider the cost of its completion being jeopardized. The formula to estimate this cost takes 50% of the person's annual salary for his first year of service, plus 10% for each year of service thereafter to account for the continuous development of the employee's knowledge and network base. For a departing five-year veteran, this cost would be $54,000.

- **Cost of the training the company has invested in this employee.** When an employee walks out the door, so does all the training invested in that person. This includes internal training, external programs, external academic education, and licenses or certifications that the company has helped the employee obtain in order to do the job effectively. Competence is expensive to build and expensive to lose. The worksheet calculation accounts for 15 days of education for the employee's first year, plus five days of education each subsequent year, for a $12,250 total.

- **Cost of lost future customer revenue.** Even when companies require employees to sign non-solicitation agreements that temporarily curtail their siphoning former colleagues and customers away from the company, there will be a cost to retain customers who had strong personal relationships with departing sales or service representatives. This cost can be enormous or negligible, depending on the role performed by the person leaving and the approach used in the calculation. For a sales or support person you might include the value of subsequent years of lost revenue from their customers. Another approach for sales employees is to divide the budgeted revenue per sales territory into weekly amounts and multiply that amount by the number of weeks the territory is vacant or partially covered to account for lost sales until the new sales representative is fully productive. This approach can also be used for telemarketing and inside sales representatives. For non-sales staff, you could calculate the revenue per employee by dividing total company revenue by the average number of employees in a given year. Using this approach for SD Inc., the annual revenue per employee would be $366,666 ($44B revenue divided by 120,000 employees). The lost revenue is calculated by multiplying the number of months the position is vacant by the average monthly revenue per employee. If the "Vacant Time" is two months, the lost revenue would be about $61,000 ($366,666/12 x 2). Even though this formula ignores additional lost revenue during the low-productivity "New Hire Training Time" and "Department Training Time," the resulting amount may still seem too high. To acknowledge the variability of this factor depending on the position being vacated in the company, I will just claim half of the $61,000, or about $30,500—a very conservative number.

- **Cost of the impact on departmental productivity**. After the person leaves, the manager and the rest of the department are affected as discussions are held about what critical work must be completed, who will pick up that work, whose normal work will suffer, and what adjustments must be made to departmental deadlines. The calculation also includes the time wasted as department staff discuss their reactions to the vacancy and even consider their own employment options. The calculation assumes five people will each suffer a 10% productivity loss during the 2.5 month "Save Attempt Time" and "Vacant Time," yielding a $6,250 cost of lost productivity.

- **Cost of lost productivity of a backfilling colleague.** Whoever fills in while the position is vacant, whether a single person or a combination of colleagues, will see their own work suffer. The calculation assumes a 25% impact on one backfilling person's productivity in his or her own job while covering two positions for two months. This equates to $2,500 of productivity loss for the backfilling employee. The manager's productivity also suffers a bit while the job is vacant. I assume a 10% productivity hit on the manager, or about $1,170 for the two months.

- **Cost of lost productivity in the vacated position**. The other side of the coin is the lost productivity in the departing person's position. This $5,000 cost is calculated as 50% of the departing person's salary for the two months the position is vacant. Though another person is temporarily performing the work, the backfilling person will be doing the bare minimum.

Even when offset by the $10,000 *savings* of the departing employee's salary for the two months the position is vacant, the above costs triggered by the loss of the good person total $120,400, and that's just the beginning...

2. **Cost of recruiting a new person.** As calculated earlier, it costs about $7,000 to recruit a SD Inc. employee. Note that this cost may cascade to another department if an internal transfer is used to fill the vacated position. At some point, though, an external hire is required, triggered directly or indirectly by the good person leaving. Sooner or later, a new employee requires on-boarding costs, which are considered next.

3. **Cost of on-boarding/training a new hire.** This on-boarding cost is about $31,650 when the following factors are allowed for.

- **Cost of setting up personnel records and system access.** There are costs to set up personnel and employment records for the new employee, to put the person on the payroll, to establish computer and security passwords, to issue an identification badge, to print business cards, to do internal publicity announcements, to hook up telephones, to arrange e-mail accounts, to obtain company credit card accounts, and to lease any other equipment such as cell phones and pagers. The equivalent cost of a day is allowed for these tasks, which is only about $225.
- **Cost of basic training for all company new hires**. The $4,900 total for 14 days of training includes the cost of delivering the training, the cost of various training materials including company or product manuals, and the cost of computer or other equipment used in the delivery of training. The worksheet also shows 100% lost productivity of the new person while taking the training ($2,500), 25% lost productivity of the person backfilling the vacated position while the new hire is taking the basic company training ($625), 10% lost productivity of the manager during this time ($290), and 50% lost productivity in the vacant position while the backfilling person continues to do the bare minimum during this training time ($1,250).
- **Cost of formal departmental training**. Once the company orientation training is complete, additional training specific to the department is required. Assuming five days of formal department training, I include the cost of delivering it ($1,750), although I acknowledge that the cost will be significantly higher for some positions such as sales representatives and call center agents who require four to six weeks of classroom training. Based on the calculations for "Vacant Time," the lost productivity of the new hire, the backfiller, the manager, and the empty position during that training week are included ($1,135, $280, $115, and $570, respectively).
- **Cost of lost productivity during new hire's ramp-up to being fully productive**. Informal training begins after the formal departmental training, as the new person learns the new job, becomes familiar with company policies and practices, learns how to get things done, develops trust, and builds confidence and competence. I assume a "buddy" tutors the new hire for about six months, losing

about 10% of his or her own productivity for that period ($3,000). Assume the new hire is 25% productive for the first two months after formal training programs, 50% productive for the next two months, and 75% productive for the next two months before reaching full productivity. This is an average of 50% productivity over the six months, or $15,000. The cost of mistakes the new employee makes during this indoctrination period are allowed for in the productivity assumptions.

Altogether, the three costs of losing a good person, backfilling, and training the replacement add up to over $159,000 for SD Inc., using the assumptions documented in the worksheet. This means that the KPMG/CATA estimate of $25,000 and the BusinessWeek article estimate of $50,000 are grossly underestimated, even when added together. Human resources departments often estimate the overall cost of losing and replacing a good employee using the following rule of thumb:

Two to three times the person's annual salary.[6]

For SD Inc., the average employee salary is $60,000, so two to three times this salary would be $120,000 to $180,000. My carefully derived estimate of $159,000 passes the reasonableness test by falling within this range.

Why Employees Stay

An example from a recent study by the consulting company Arthur D. Little helps connect sustainable development and retention. The pharmaceutical firm Novo Nordisk, an award winner for its commitment to honesty and shareholder engagement, had a staff turnover rate of only 5% at the end of 1998, compared to an average of 10% for the biotech industry. Reinforcing sustainable development is a natural extension of a strong core ideology. Novo Nordisk launched its Values in Action initiative in 1999 to further align its business with sustainable development.[7]

In *First Break All The Rules*, Marcus Buckingham and Curt Coffman analyze Gallup polls that examined what attracts the best employees to a company and what makes them stay.[8] Gallup identified 12 questions that appear to measure the "core elements" needed to attract and keep the most loyal, productive, and talented employees. One of the 12 questions is: "Does the mission of my company make me feel like my work is important?"

Survey after survey show that the best people stay when they feel valued, are empowered, have career opportunities, and feel the company respects work/life balance issues. They also stay when they feel they are doing something worthwhile.

In his Meaning At Work study in early 1997, Tom Terez conducted 15 focus groups and an extensive series of one-on-one interviews to identify the characteristics of worthwhile work and meaningful workplaces.[9] He heard from hundreds of people whose collective work experience exceeded 3,000 years. Terez synthesized all the factors that contribute to a meaningful work experience into what he refers to as the "22 meaning keys." Listed alphabetically, they are:

- Acknowledgment
- Balance
- Challenge
- Dialogue
- Direction
- Equality
- Fit
- Flexibility
- Information
- Invention
- Oneness
- Ownership
- Personal Development
- *Purpose* (My italics)
- Relationship-building
- Relevance
- Respect
- Self-identity
- Service
- Support
- Validation
- Worth

Terez found that each of us has a set of factors that determines what we need to have a meaningful work experience. It's much like a set of keys we carry with us at all times. For one person, the top three keys to meaning at work might be a sense of community, a sense of purpose, and opportunities to be inventive. Another person's top three keys might be a sense of purpose, abundant challenges, and a good fit in the organization.

Tying it all together are six major themes from Terez's interviews, some of which are surprising.[10]

1. **There's a huge distinction between "meaningful work" and "job satisfaction."** For most people, "satisfaction" looks and feels like conformance to standards. Needs and expectations are met—period.

Meaning goes much deeper. In a meaningful workplace there is less focus on needs and expectations, and more emphasis on hopes, dreams, and fulfillment.

2. **People define "meaningful workplace" in vastly different ways.** The advocates of "five easy steps" must be gnashing their teeth as they scan the long list of 22 keys. This is one case where quick, blanket fixes just won't work. Individualized approaches must be used, given the different combinations of keys that make a workplace meaningful to employees.

3. **Several keys rise above all others in importance.** Topping the list is Purpose—the sense that what I'm doing as an individual, and what the organization is doing collectively, truly makes a positive difference. Also in the top tier, in order of importance, are Ownership, Fit, Oneness, and Relationship-building. In the second tier: Service, Equality, Validation, Invention, and Personal Development. For organizations wanting to foster a greater sense of meaning, these keys offer a logical starting place.

4. **People do NOT cite incentives or high pay as key ingredients of the meaningful workplace**. Incentives came up only once—from a former salesperson who told horror stories of internal competition. As for compensation, people sharply distinguish between "fair pay" (critically important) and "high pay."

5. **Business concepts and strategies—such as reengineering, strategic planning, total quality management and its more recent incarnations, etc.—seldom come up during discussions of meaning in the workplace.** In all the research conversations, no one said or even suggested that "a recent reengineering initiative helped me find greater meaning in my work." Rather, people focused on fundamentals—like purpose, service, dialogue, and respect.

6. **There's an almost desperate eagerness to talk about meaning in the workplace.** People from all walks of work life participated in the Meaning At Work project. With few exceptions, they showed remarkable zeal in sharing their stories. It seemed as if they had been holding back for years—and in fact, many had been doing just that. A recurring comment was, "I wish we could have this conversation back where I work."

Too often the knee-jerk reaction to the challenge of attracting and retaining talent is to throw money or stock options at it. Fair compensation is certainly an important reason why people want to work for a particular company. However, given the similar compensation plans of most competing companies, the McKinsey and Terez studies described above show that values and purpose can be a differentiating factor for talented people choosing an employer.

In his article "The New Spirit of Work," David Dorsey reinforced how important corporate values and the company's perceived impact on society were for retaining employees (my italics).

> "Every company is facing the same two big issues—retaining the best people and improving their productivity," says Craig Neal [Heartland Institute, Minnesota]. Fortunately, he says, both issues have the same solution: *create companies where people can bring their whole selves to work, where they can integrate their work into their lives* .... Richard Barrett [a consultant on spirituality in the workplace] has a simple premise: People and companies do well, financially and otherwise, to the degree that their interests match their values .... *People need to believe in what they do for a living before they can tap into their deepest creative potential* .... In [a 1997 survey], 75% of graduating MBA students said that a company should consider its impact on society in such areas as the environment, equal opportunity, family relationships, and community involvement. *A full 50% said they would take a cut in salary to work for a socially responsible company* .... People who have learned to make a living now want to make a difference.[11]

That difference can be realized by working for a company whose purpose is aligned with essential aspects of sustainable development. Those companies satisfy people's quest for daily meaning as well as for daily bread. European graduates agree with their American counterparts. A 1996 European graduate survey of 16,000 final-year students at 56 universities, business schools, and engineering schools in 14 countries found that European graduates put care for the environment at the top of their agendas—68% said they were prepared to pay the price for a better environment.[12]

The Potential Retention Benefit of a Sustainable Development Vision

Would top talent care enough about sustainable development for it to be a significant retention factor? The 1997 survey of MBA students mentioned in David Dorsey's article, and the *Millennium Poll on Corporate Social Responsibility* referenced earlier suggest some might. The *Millennium Poll* found that corporate social responsibility is fast becoming a global expectation.[13]. Most Americans (53%) say firms need to have a balance between focusing on profits and demonstrating concern for ethical and social issues. Another 35% support an outright commitment to an ethical and socially accountable approach to fulfilling the corporate mission. So almost 90% of Americans, and the majority of the business school students who were surveyed in the polls mentioned above, agree that companies should do more than focus only on profitability.[14] That's not necessarily a fair expectation, but nobody said consumers would be fair. As they see the increasing impotence of national governments in the face of corporate globalization, they begin to hold corporations accountable for "civil society" issues that used to be the preserve of governments.[15]

Another U.S. study in 1997 found that 76% of consumers polled said that—assuming no difference in price or quality — they would switch brands to align themselves with a good cause.[16] A 1999 study by Ernst & Young and Maritz Automotive Research showed that 40% of Canadians would expect to pay more for "greener" vehicles. Of these, 42% would be "willing" to pay $2,000 more for this type of vehicle, 11% said they would be willing to pay $5,000 more, while the balance would pay from 0 to $500 more.[17] That is, more than half would stick to their environmental convictions even though they would incur a financial penalty.

It is likely that some top talent is similar to the MBA graduates, consumers, opinion leaders, and car buyers surveyed in the above studies, which reinforce the influence of environmental and social responsibility factors when selecting a company. Certainly, a job with a company that is actively pursuing ecologically and socially beneficial strategies to help "save the world" does sound like worthwhile, socially responsible, and meaningful work. How many talented employees would be attracted to a visionary company committed to sustainable development? As noted earlier, the *Millennium Poll* suggests it is reasonable to assume that 20 to 39% of opinion leaders (i.e., top talent) would be inclined to reward/punish their own company for its degree of social responsibility, which we can assume would include the decision to stay or leave.

In SD Inc., there are 120,000 employees. Employees leave companies for a variety of reasons, and the company may not regret seeing some of them depart—in fact, they may encourage some to leave. If we assume that each year the company loses just 1% of the employees that it doesn't want to lose and then has to replace them, then the annual corporate cost is about $190.8 million ($159,000 per person x 1,200 people lost). And the real question is, how would a well-communicated and credible corporate sustainable development agenda affect the retention of these good people? Money is definitely important—informal surveys worldwide indicate that 40% of information technology professionals will seriously consider leaving their enterprise for a 20% greater salary.[18] Would they all care enough about their company's environmental focus to stay, despite higher salaries and better job opportunities elsewhere? Certainly not, but there is strong indication from the above retention studies that many would.

Given the survey data, and assuming a competing company's remuneration differential is less than 20%, the worksheet conservatively assumes that 20% of the 1% (1,200) of people leaving SD Inc. would indeed change their minds and stay if SD Inc. had a vibrant sustainable development mission. This leads to avoiding over $38 million of costs, which is like adding $38 million of pure profit to the bottom line (see the "Retaining the Best Talent" worksheet in the Appendix).

Benefit 3: Increasing Employee Productivity

Studies have shown that those who consistently excel at what they do receive far more from work than salary and camaraderie. Today there is a growing recognition that productivity is directly linked to the level of satisfaction and fulfillment that people get from their work. People who excel have a sense of purpose, a feeling that their work has meaning and contributes to a worthwhile cause. (My emphasis)

David McNally[1]

THE TIME HAS COME to dispel the notion that being green is bad for business. If saving the planet isn't reason enough, there's another incentive for companies to contribute to sustainable development—it will boost productivity and, ultimately, profit. As Jim Collins and Jerry Porras say in *Built To Last: Successful Habits of Visionary Companies*, profit and core values go together in the long term.

> Visionary companies pursue a cluster of objectives, of which making money is only one, and not necessarily the primary one. Yes, they seek profits, but they're equally guided by a core ideology — core values and a sense of purpose beyond just making money .... Yet, paradoxically, the visionary companies make more money than the purely profit-driven comparison companies .... Profit maximization does not rule, but the visionary companies pursue their aims profitably. They do *both*.[2]

According to Nicholas Imparato and Oren Harari in Jumping the Curve, current wisdom on performance is that P (performance) equals A (ability) multiplied by M (motivation):[3]

$$P = A \times M$$

Let's assume that SD Inc. has won the talent war and has the best people—they have the ability. The challenge is to motivate them to maximize their performance. Money and awards will appeal to their extrinsic motivation. The purpose and meaning in their work will appeal to their intrinsic motivation. Usually, companies awaken these higher, intrinsic motivations through their vision and mission statements.

The Vision — Commitment Relationship

A powerful mission is both an attractor and an energizer, according to former U.S. Secretary of Labor Robert Reich.

> Xerox Parc guru John Seely Brown said it best: "The job of leadership today is not just to make money. It's to make meaning." When it comes to attracting, keeping, and making teams out of talented people, money alone won't do it. Talented people want to be part of something that they can believe in, something that confers meaning on their work and on their lives—something that involves a mission.
>
> And they don't want that mission to turn into the kind of predictable "mission statement" that plasters many a corporate-boardroom wall. Rather, they want spiritual goals that energize an organization by resonating with the personal values of the people who work there—the kind of mission that offers people a chance to do work that makes a difference. Along with the traditional bottom line, great enterprises have a second bottom line: a return on human investment that advances a larger purpose. A powerful mission is both a magnet and a motivator.[4]

The research by Collins and Porras shows that visionary companies which have been successful over the long term do have core ideologies—core values and a sense of purpose beyond just making money. This core ideology guides and inspires people throughout the organization and is a significant differentiator.

> A detailed pair-by-pair analysis showed the visionary companies have generally been more ideologically driven and less purely profit-driven than the comparison companies in 17 out of 18 pairs. This is one of the clearest differences we found between the visionary companies and comparison companies.[5]

Sustainable development could be considered a core ideology, so lessons learned about core ideologies also apply to sustainable development. For a core ideology to be effective, senior executives must believe in it and must ensure it is deployed throughout the organization. Visionary companies work hard to indoctrinate employees in the core ideology so that it forms a common base of values from which they can make day-to-day decisions.[6] This attention to company-wide education is consistent with the pervasive education and engagement approach I am proposing as a prerequisite for capturing the seven bottom-line benefits of highly sustainable organizations.

It helps if top executives sincerely and obviously espouse the core ideology. A halfhearted start can turn out to be worse than no start at all. Unless senior executives are genuinely committed to the sustainable development journey, they would be doing themselves and their employees a favor by not even starting. They may also find that the basis of their commitment evolves from business benefits to include a more profound concern for ecological and social issues.

The second finding by Collins and Porras also relates to the challenge of sustainable development. Successful visionary companies use bold missions—what Collins and Porras call "Big Hairy Audacious Goals" (BHAGs)—as a particularly powerful mechanism to stimulate progress. They found more evidence of this mechanism in the visionary companies, and less evidence of it in the comparison companies in 14 out of the 18 pair cases.

> Like the moon mission, a true BHAG is clear and compelling and serves as a unifying focal point of effort — often creating immense team spirit. It has a clear finish line, so the organization can know when it has achieved the goal; people like to shoot for finish lines .... A BHAG engages people—it reaches out and grabs them in the gut. It is tangible, energizing, highly focused. People "get it" right away.[7]

BHAGs get employees going. People find them stimulating, exciting, adventurous. They are willing to throw their creative talent and energies into them. BHAGs fit the core ideology.

> BHAGs should be a powerful statement about the company's ideology. To defy the odds, to take on big hairy challenges — especially if rooted in ideology — does much to make people feel that they do something special, elite, different, better.[8]

Sustainable development is certainly a BHAG, or includes a collection of BHAGs, and reflects a strong core ideology. Zero emissions, self-sufficient energy production, zero waste, and helping to restore the social and environmental health of the planet would be powerful vision elements for a company.

Why do visionary companies do better? Theories on organizational development and organizational behavior say people are more satisfied and more committed to organizations that resonate with their ethics and values.[9] The literature on leadership always includes encouragement for leaders to galvanize people with a powerful shared vision, the energy source for aligned employee efforts. The literature on how organizations learn describes how the disciplines of team learning, shared vision, mental models, personal mastery, and systems thinking combine to allow an organization to fully realize the potential of its human capital.[10] Instead of being viewed as costs or even assets, "knowledge workers" are viewed as investors whose currency is the precious commodity called human capital. The conditions that predispose individuals to invest their personal human capital in a job include their self-interested commitment to the organization's vision.

Here is what twelve leadership consultants say about the value of leaders effectively communicating a compelling, motivating vision, and how a higher purpose increases commitment.

1. In his pamphlet *Firing Up Commitment During Organizational Change*, Price Pritchett talks about firing up people with a cause.

   > Here's the simple fact: People don't care about working for a company, they want to work for a movement. Provide employees a grand purpose, a mission with a larger meaning, a cause that transcends the dullness of their everyday duties. Give them a dream they can identify with, and watch commitment climb.[11]

2. In their research leading up to writing *The Leadership Challenge*, Jim Kouzes and Barry Posner found that one of the five practices of effective leaders is to inspire a shared vision.

   > Leaders breathe life into the hopes and dreams of others and enable them to see the exciting possibilities that the future holds. Leaders forge a unity of purpose by showing constituents how the dream is for the common good.... Not everyone we interviewed used the term vision in describing leadership practices. Some referred instead to purpose, mission, legacy, dream, goal, calling, or personal agenda. No matter what the term though, the intent was the same: leaders want to do something significant, to accomplish something that no one else has yet achieved.[12]

Exemplary leaders inspire and excite employees with an ideal and unique image of the future. What could be more purposeful than being the most sustainable company in your industry or in the world, to the benefit of both the company and the common good?

3. Frances Hesselbein emphasizes the unifying value of a shared sense of purpose and a higher goal in her essay "The 'How To Be' Leader" in *The Leader of the Future.*

> This "how to be" leader holds forth the vision of the organization's future in compelling ways that ignite the spark needed to build the inclusive enterprise. The leader mobilizes people around the mission of the organization, making it a powerful force in the uncertain times ahead. Coordination around the mission generates a force that transforms the workplace into one in which workers and teams express themselves in their work and find significance beyond the task, as they manage for the mission. Through consistent focus on mission, the "how to be" leader gives the dispersed and diverse leaders of the enterprise a clear sense of direction and the opportunity to find meaning in their work.[13]

The essay's title reflects Hesselbein's premise that future leaders will focus on "how to be" — how to develop quality, character, mindset, values, principles, and courage. A mission that included sustainability aspirations would provide fertile ground for growing these leadership attributes and would contribute a powerful unifying force for the organization.

4. Peter Senge is an expert on shared visions and their importance in learning organizations. In *The Fifth Discipline* he outlines the value of a truly shared vision.

> Few, if any, forces in human affairs are as powerful as a shared vision. At its simplest level, a shared vision is the answer to the question, "what do we want to create?"... . Shared visions derive their power from common caring .... Genuine caring about a shared vision is rooted in personal visions .... It is not truly a "shared vision" until it connects with the personal visions of people throughout the organization .... When people truly share a vision they are connected, bound together by a common aspiration .... Visions are exhilarating .... Shared vision fosters risk taking and experimentation .... The power of aspiration drives positive visions.[14]

The discipline of a shared vision enables organizations to learn and thrive together. The bond created by an organizational vision that embraces corporate social responsibility strengthens as it aligns with the personal visions of employees.

5. Underlying all this is the powerful notion of "worthwhile work." In their book *Gung Ho*, Ken Blanchard and Sheldon Bowles identify three principles for achieving commitment to the company, enthusiasm, and productivity in the workplace: worthwhile work, being in control of achieving the goals, and cheering each other on.[15] We feel our work is worthwhile if we know we make the world a better place, if everyone works toward a shared goal, and if values guide all plans, decisions, and actions. If we feel we are contributing to the well-being of humanity, we will be more committed to our worthwhile work. Seeing how our work and our company contribute to the sustainability of the world would certainly bolster that commitment.

6. The importance of meaningful work is echoed by Richard Leider in *The Power of Purpose.*

   > Many organizations are rediscovering the connection between values, behavior, and productivity. They are making the connection between spirit and work. Their leaders are observing, as Stud Terkel did, "most people have work that is too small for their spirits."[16]

7. *In Even Eagles Need A Push*, David McNally describes a survey done by Wilson Learning Corporation in which 1,500 people were asked "If you had enough money to live comfortably for the rest of your life, would you continue to work?" While 70% said they would, 60% of those said they would change jobs for more "satisfying work."[17] McNally says that extensive research into why people work has revealed three dominant reasons: money, affiliation, and meaning.[18] He says meaning is the key to productivity.

8. McNally also quotes from Dr. Charles Garfield, author of *Peak Performers*: "Peak performers are people who are committed to a compelling mission."[19] Productive people feel good about the purpose of what they are doing.

9. According to Gail Sheehy, author of *Pathfinders*, we feel better and are more productive when we attempt to make our world better.[20]

10. What if we were to tap into that potential? In *The Inside Edge*, Peter Jensen, an author who has coached champion Olympic athletes and leading business executives, quotes Yogi Berra's wry estimate: "Sport is 90% mental, and the other half is physical."[21] Jensen goes on to cite brain research that shows we are only using 5 to 10% of our brain and

asks what we suppose the other 90% is for. More importantly, he asks whether it can be activated by a higher cause.

11. In *Growing The Distance*, Jim Clemmer talks about how purpose is a prime human energy source.

> Our vision, values, and purpose are at the center of our being. They are the wellspring from which our energy flows. Individuals, teams, and organizations with a strong sense of self, clear direction, and meaningful purpose have a high degree of energy .... High-energy environments brim with passion and deep commitment .... When we align an individual's personal goals with those of family, workgroup, or organization, we tap into huge energy reserves.[22]

Imagine the productive energy released when our personal sustainability purposes resonate with our organization's sustainability purposes.

12. In *Leaders*, Warren Bennis and Burt Namus reinforce the idea that "transformative leaders" use visions to transform intention into reality.

> Effective leadership can move organizations from current to future states, create visions of potential opportunities for organizations, instill within employees commitment to change and instill new cultures and strategies in organizations that focus energy and resources.[23]

So a dozen books by leading authors and consultants—Price Pritchett, Jim Kouzes and Barry Posner, Frances Hesselbein, Peter Senge, Ken Blanchard and Sheldon Bowles, Richard Leider, David McNally, Charles Garfield, Gail Sheehy, Peter Jensen, Jim Clemmer, and Warren Bennis and Bert Namus—echo the claim that effective leaders improve commitment with inspiring visions. Talented people are more committed when working for companies whose missions inspire worthwhile work.

What might a company's vision look like if it included sustainability dimensions? It might be as simple as Ikea's—"a better everyday life"[24]—which explicitly embraces a path that will help achieve a sustainable society in ecological balance.[25] Some Ikea workers develop a passionate and productive commitment to their work as their personal values converge with the values of their company. The mission statement for Tom's of Maine includes the phrase: "To be a profitable and successful company, while acting in a socially and environmentally responsible manner."[26] The founder, Tom Chappell, admits that originally he felt this was the right thing for a business with soul to do. After the success of his business, he now knows it's also one of the most competitive things a business can do.

Or suppose a company embraced a core value similar to that of Scandic Hotels. Their central value is omtanke, which means "profound caring" for their customers, co-workers, shareholders, communities in which they operate, and the environment.[27] They are seeing widespread employee engagement with and commitment to creative, environmentally friendly approaches to running their hotels.... profitably. The vision might also include social responsibility. For example, in his 1995 speech at the Comdex computer show, IBM chairman and CEO Lou Gerstner expressed potential for network computing to change the world in fundamental ways for the better.

> I think we will make our visions reality. I think that as stewards of our industry, we will step up to the challenges of social responsibility. We will improve the world and the way we work, the way we communicate, live, and learn.[28]

Companies will find their own ways to describe their purpose beyond making money for shareholders. It is when they transcend extrinsic results and appeal to a common good that visions are truly inspiring.

The Involvement – Commitment Relationship

Visions drive commitment, but they are not the lone ingredient. The team consulting company Belgard-Fisher-Rayner (BFR) created a commitment model that shows how four factors combine to yield employee commitment.[29]

The four factors, shown in Figure 5.1, are:

- **Clarity**: Employees understand what the goal is—the objectives are clear and they can articulate them to others.
- **Relevance**: Employees see the relevance of the goal to business success—they understand how it is good for the company's customers and helps the company succeed.
- **Meaning**: They see the personal meaning of the goal—what it means to them personally and how it resonates with their personal values as a worthwhile goal.
- **Involvement**: They want to be, and are, involved in the shaping and deployment of the goal. Without involvement, there is no commitment. When it is impractical to involve everyone in shaping a large-scale change, employees may choose representatives to be involved. Giving people the choice to be involved is the key point, even if they choose not to be.

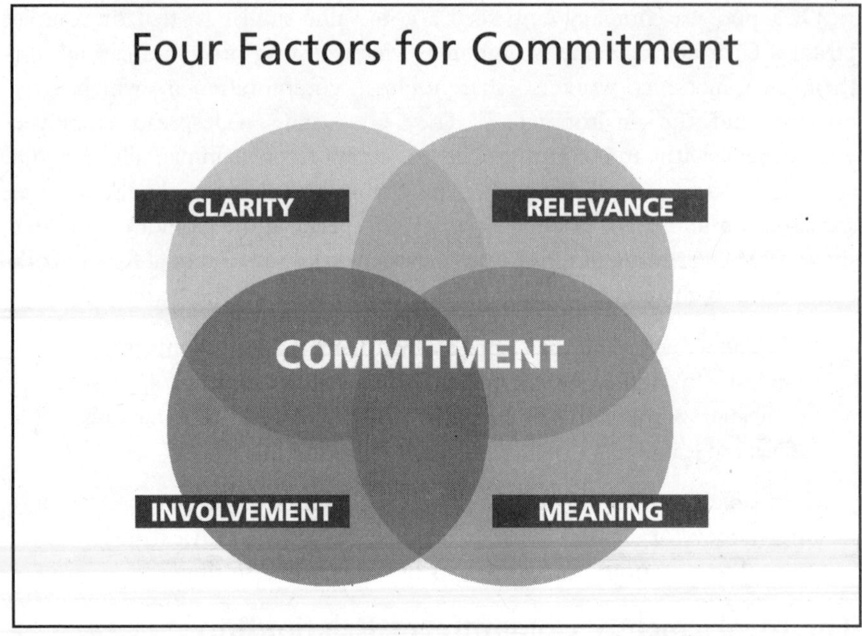

Figure 5.1 Four Factors for Commitment

A high-performance culture/company unleashes the potential of people who are committed to clear, relevant, and meaningful work that they have been involved in shaping. Commitment is very different from "compliance." Commitment engages the energy and creativity of people's hearts, minds, and hands, while compliance only engages their hands. Commitment requires Clarity, Relevance, Meaning, and Involvement, while compliance only requires a worker who will carry out someone else's idea—at most, the Clarity and Relevance factors may be present in compliance.

I have already discussed how visions inspire commitment by satisfying the Clarity, Relevance, and Meaning factors. A purpose is inspirational when it is clear, it relates to the success of the business, and it resonates with employees' personal values as a worthwhile goal. Corporations that adopt a sustainability goal as a higher purpose in their business mission will therefore create an energized workforce of people who only need the Involvement factor to be fully committed to the cause.

Steve Rayner, the originator of the commitment model, derived it from his observations while studying high-performing teams. He found that involvement was a critical ingredient for commitment.

> Certainly involvement was a fundamental element to generating commitment, but involvement as an isolated act without some greater context didn't lead to commitment. There had to be a clarity of the impact the involvement could have, it needed to be seen as relevant toward some goal or improvement that could be tied to a better future, and it had to have meaning to the individuals performing the work. All four of these elements—involvement, clarity, relevance and meaning—were present in the high commitment teams and conspicuously absent in the low commitment ones .... I would say all four elements are essential to generating commitment. Involvement, however, is the foundation that the other elements strengthen. Put another way, without involvement you probably cannot have sustained commitment, even if you had tremendous clarity, relevance and meaning.[30]

Note that our proposal includes engaging all employees in finding ways to strengthen the company's commitment to sustainable development—they are empowered to make suggestions and to take action. Their knowledgeable involvement provides the underpinning for enhanced commitment. The proposed investment in employee education ensures they focus on the best opportunities. An educated and informed employee population that has a clear sense of the company's sustainable development goals, that understands the relevance of these goals to competitive advantage in the marketplace, that is involved in suggesting and implementing environmental and social projects, and that has personal values resonating with the corporate stewardship of the planet, will be committed to the company's success.

The Commitment – Productivity Relationship

So leaders use clear, relevant, and meaningful visions and empowered involvement to inspire commitment. Does this commitment really help the bottom line? To assess the business value of an organization's sustainability vision, it must be shown that people not only feel better, but that their productivity is also higher when they are fulfilled by doing worthwhile work. After vision-involvement-commitment, productivity is the next link in the chain leading toward the bottom line.

How much more productive are employees in visionary companies? Stephen Covey, in *The 7 Habits of Highly Effective People*, says that people who are positively inspired to be proactive and take initiative for something they believe in aren't just 25 to 50% more effective, they are 5,000+% more effective.[31] In *The Tom Peters Seminars*, Tom Peters quotes Nathan Myhrvold, head of research at Microsoft, who says the difference between an average producer/employee and the very best producer/employee can be a factor of 1,000 (100,000%).[32]

Those are big numbers. However, it is unclear if the claims are shoot-from-the-hip hyperbole or based on factual research. The connection between commitment and productivity requires clarification. In fact, Steve Rayner points out that commitment does not necessarily equal increased productivity.

> Commitment clearly enhances the potential for increased productivity, but it does not guarantee it. Productivity is the outcome of a system of multiple parts—including structure, technology, processes, quality, information, teamwork, roles, leadership, development, rewards and commitment. A team can be extremely committed, but lack critical information or be working with poor technology and antiquated processes—the result may be high commitment and desire but relatively low productivity. Having said that, the other side of the coin is that I don't believe you can sustain productivity growth over the long haul without a high level of workforce commitment. In other words, commitment is required for long term productivity growth but commitment alone does not guarantee productivity.[33]

That is, commitment is necessary, but not sufficient, for productivity. Other factors need to combine with commitment in order for the workforce to be productive. Rayner's caution is reinforced by a corporate leadership model used by Hay/McBer, one of the world's largest human resources consulting firms.[34] Their model lists seven critical and intertwined aspects of any business that managers must work to improve so that the business will be successful. "Organizational Climate" is one element that Hay/McBer recognize as important to success, and they list six areas in "Climate" where a specific approach can improve employee productivity. Several of these areas echo the commitment four factors in Rayner's model:

- **Clarity**: Everyone knows what is expected of them and of their organization.
- **Standards**: Management sets challenging but attainable goals to improve performance.
- **Flexibility**: The workplace is free of unnecessary rules and constraints, and it supports new ideas.
- **Responsibility**: Authority is delegated and people are held accountable for results.

- **Rewards**: Performance feedback is frequent and candid, good work is recognized, and rewards are directly related to performance.
- **Team Commitment**: People trust each other, have a common goal, and are proud to be part of the organization.

Sustainable development relates to several of the six areas of Organizational Climate. A clearly articulated vision of sustainable development would contribute to Clarity; the BHAG nature of sustainable development would contribute to the "challenging but attainable" aspect of Standards; and the worthwhile nature of sustainable development would contribute to the pride in Team Commitment. Educating, empowering, and involving employees in sustainable development initiatives aligns with Flexibility and Responsibility.

The impact that the productivity generated by a positive Organizational Climate has on the bottom line is significant. Hay/McBer's research has shown that 24 to 30% of the variance in revenue and profit between organizations can be attributed to differences in Organizational Climate.[35] It follows that the climate of a visionary company with a sustainable development mission would be more positive, resulting in a payoff in hard business results from increased employee productivity.

In summary, leading authors and consultants agree that talented people are more committed when working for companies whose purpose and mission inspire them. Commitment leads to productivity if the climate is positive. Sustainable development includes economic, social, and environmental dimensions—it would be difficult to find a more powerfully inspiring trio of aspirations. The above analysis suggests that corporations taking on a sustainable development goal as a higher purpose to their business mission will create an energized, committed, and motivated workforce that will be more productive. Therefore, if corporations are interested in attracting and retaining the best talent and in unleashing their creative and productive potential through intrinsic motivation, visibly committing to corporate social and environmental responsibility could yield this competitive edge. Good leaders who align employees' efforts with inspired visions of sustainability leadership, who educate and empower their carefully recruited talent, and who provide the necessary support to make it happen, will see the difference in their bottom line.

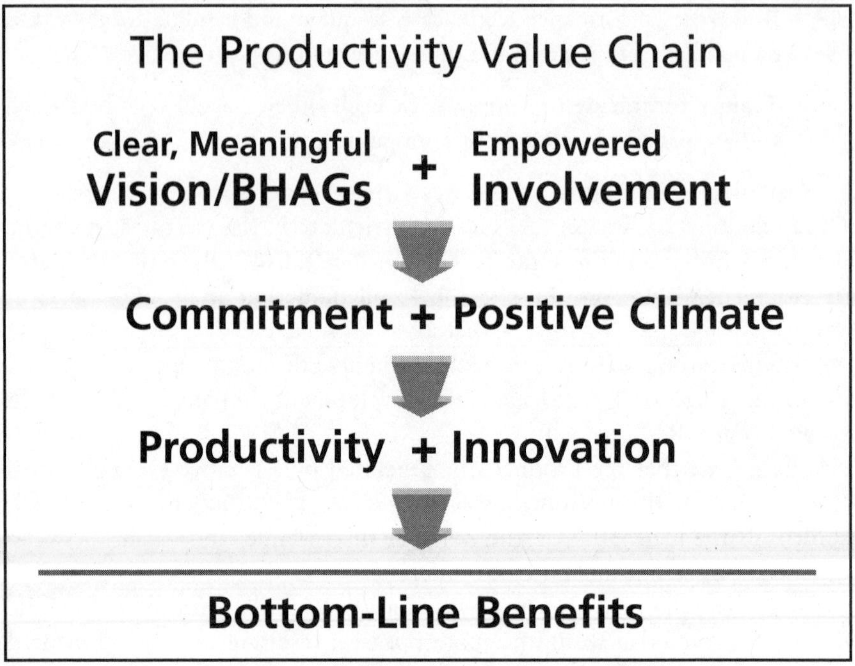

The Productivity Value Chain

Clear, Meaningful **Vision/BHAGs** + Empowered **Involvement**

Commitment + Positive Climate

Productivity + Innovation

Bottom-Line Benefits

Figure 5.2 The Productivity Value Chain

The Bottom-Line Benefit From Higher Individual Productivity

The vision-involvement-commitment-climate-productivity chain to the bottom line has been logically traced. Quantifying the bottom-line impact is next—"Show me the money!"

Collins and Porras discovered that visionary companies had 65-year cumulative stock returns between 1926 and 1990 that were over 6 times (600%) greater than comparative companies', and 15 times (1500%) greater than the general market's.[36] Crudely averaging the difference over the 65 years, the returns were 9 to 23% better each year.

A corporation's adoption of a sustainable development mission would help attain similar results to those of the visionary companies studied by Collins and Porras, but it is not a magic answer. Not all employees' values will resonate with a sustainable development vision. Say those of only 20% do, to be consistent with the percentage of people assumed to be attracted by SD Inc.'s environmental and social responsibility image in the earlier recruiting and retention calculations. Conservatively assuming these employees would then be 25% more productive (instead of 5,000% as Stephen Covey suggests, or 100,000% as Nathan Myhrvold suggests), this works out to an average 5% increase in productivity for the whole workforce (25% of 20%). Note that this is considerably below the 9 to 23% higher returns for visionary companies.

Why am I using such conservative assumptions in the calculation? The returns yielded when using higher assumptions are so huge that they jeopardize credibility. The average of a 25% increase in productivity for 20% of the workforce yields a $360 million annual benefit from productivity improvements. This is like adding 6,000 unpaid employees to the SD Inc. company. The "Increased Productivity" worksheet in the Appendix allows you to see the impact of your own more conservative or aggressive assumptions.

The Innovation Factor

A possible objection to the productivity improvement case is that it is not feasible to expect additional productivity from an already overworked workforce. Since productivity benefits are the second largest contributor to the total benefits of sustainable development, this is a critical gut check.

Productivity comes as much from working smarter as working harder, and creative juices flow when people are excited about their work. Although some employees will exhibit increased commitment by working longer hours, the real payoff comes when employees use the time they are already working more productively. That's the basis of the increased productivity calculations for SD Inc., and the benefits are real.

Innovative breakthrough thinking is a highly valued core competency in leading companies. Environmental considerations can provide strong impetus to innovation. Edgar Wollard, chairman and CEO of DuPont, says: "No corporation can be truly innovative until everyone in the company has adopted an environmentalist attitude."[37] Michael Porter and Claas van der Linde reinforce the importance of competing through innovation versus compliance in their *Harvard Business Review* article "Green and Competitive: Ending the Stalemate."

> Managers must start to recognize environmental improvement as an economic and competitive opportunity, not an annoying cost or an inevitable threat. Instead of clinging to a perspective focused on regulatory compliance, companies need to ask questions such as What are we wasting? and How can we enhance shareholder value? The early movers—the companies that see the opportunity first and embrace innovation-based solutions—will reap major competitive benefits.[38]

Environmental considerations can be a prod to change managers' behavior and create a company culture that encourages continuous innovation and learning.[39] In fact, the creative tension in the gap between the current reality and the company's vision of sustainability generates the opportunity for innovative, high-impact interventions. The Achilles' heel of innovation is believing something is not possible. Unless managers believe savings are possible and measurable, they won't even bother trying to find creative ways to capture them. They especially will not be encouraged to think outside the box if current accounting, managerial, and investment approaches do not include and reward sustainable development initiatives.[40] Managers should be evaluated on their business unit's environmental performance, and environmental and social stewardship should be in every senior manager's job description. That's another reason to integrate environmental management systems with conventional business management systems.

One possible reason why managers don't believe in the bottom-line productivity gains is the narrow attribution of sustainability benefits exclusively to the environmental aspect of the triple bottom line, forgetting that there are also human resources aspects to sustainable development. The social dimension of the triple bottom line encourages empowering employees and fostering a balance of their work and personal lives. This approach energizes employees and underlies the productivity claims. Employees will be more productive if they live balanced lives, feel a commitment to the company and its management, believe in what they are doing, and believe it is good for the world.

No other theme so powerfully captures the "Save the World" factor identified in the McKinsey study as the sustainable development theme. Sustainable development adds unique depth to meaningful and worthwhile work for some people, and the connection to productivity benefits has been well substantiated. The productivity contribution of sustainable development strategies for SD Inc. has been limited to a small fraction of the employee population—around 20%—and to a small element of their motivation. There is ample opportunity to claim higher benefits in this area.

The Bottom-Line Benefit From Higher Team Productivity

So far, only the productivity of individuals has been considered. In the belief that the whole is greater than the sum of its parts, the impact of a powerful sustainable development vision on cross-functional team productivity should also be considered. In *Leadership Is An Art*, Max DePree echoes many of the factors identified in Tom Terez's research on individual productivity, described above, showing that they also apply to how well we actively work with others in our workplaces (my italics).

> What is it that most of us really want from work? We would like to find the most effective, most productive, most rewarding way of *working together*. We would like to know that our work process uses all of the appropriate and pertinent resources: human, physical, financial. *We would like a work process and relationships that meet our personal needs for belonging, for contributing, for meaningful work*, for the opportunity to make a commitment to grow and be at least reasonably in control of our own destinies. Finally, we'd like someone to say "Thank You!"[41]

In most large organizations, a major challenge is developing teamwork between departments that do not know nor understand each other. Often the goals of one department do not align well with the goals of neighboring departments, or departments' measurements and how they are evaluated are poorly aligned. In the worst cases, company departments compete internally, wasting energy that should be used to compete with the company's external competitors. For a company to win in the marketplace, its internal functions must work together despite functional differences. The more opportunities for employees from different departments to get to know each other and work together on common purposes, the better they will develop as interdepartmental teams. Sustainable development programs that multiple departments work on together provide an excellent team-building opportunity, with a beneficial spill-over effect when the departments continue to team on other business solutions.

This benefit is substantiated by a hotel chain's experience, documented by Brain Nattrass and Mary Altomare in *The Natural Step for Business.* Scandic Hotel's environmental dialogue program proved to be an amazingly effective approach to unifying and engaging its workforce.

> Ken Hopper [general manager of one of Scandic's Stockholm hotels] remarks: "I've been involved in Scandic for ten years .... Nothing has ever been close to creating as much excitement as this environmental campaign. It was just huge .... It brought people together in a way we've never ever been able to bring our staff together before and we haven't since. Nothing we've done has mobilized a force that's created such unison."
>
> CFO Kerstin Goransson said that she was surprised by the power the environmental dialogue process had for the whole organization: "I have never ever seen anything else unifying 5,000 people. I could never

> imagine the power of doing something like this that involved everyone. Everyone was engaged and involved. The engagement was total and that surprised me a lot."
>
> As [Roland] Nilsson [CEO] says: "It is the first cooperative activity where they were really unified irrespective of where they worked in the company. I mean it was fantastic. Everyone loves taking care of the world."[42]

Would what worked for service employees in Scandic Hotels work also for more highly trained employees in a high-tech company? Would a unifying focus on ways to generate savings and revenue by corporate social responsibility initiatives also help cross-functional teamwork? Let's suppose it would. Unfortunately, the productivity impact is not quantified for Scandic Hotels, so I need to make assumptions. Assume the resulting productivity from improved company-wide teaming was only 2%, another conservative assumption. It would certainly be greater than zero. This yields an additional $144-million productivity benefit, the equivalent of adding another 2,400 unpaid employees to the company.

The Bottom-Line Benefit From Improved Working Conditions

The above benefits are based on people being inspired and drawn together by opportunities for environmental and social projects that transcend departmental boundaries. There is a third potential contributor to productivity benefits driven by environmental initiatives—increased productivity from improved workplace conditions.

Let's suppose the company decided to retrofit its buildings, or design new buildings, to capitalize on energy efficiencies. That is, lighting systems are converted to more energy-efficient bulbs and small-task lighting, and clever ways are found to bring in natural light throughout the workplace, reducing glare. Workers gain more control over their environment—lighting, temperature, and air flow—using occupancy sensors and work station controls. Using variable speed motors in heating/ventilation and air conditioning (HVAC) systems improves heating, cooling, and air quality. For example, Cisco Systems equipped its buildings' climate-control systems with more costly but more energy-efficient motors. On top of that, Cisco attached a $2,500 variable frequency driver to each of these 500 motors so they don't work any harder than necessary to move heated or cooled air.[43]

Why did the company do all this? To reap the resulting ongoing savings in energy costs, which pay for the upgrades. Surprising many companies that have made these kinds of changes, an unanticipated ancillary benefit becomes evident—their people are more productive in the upgraded facilities. Paul Hawken, Amory Lovins, and L. Hunter Lovins explained and quantified this productivity gain in "A Road Map for Natural Capitalism" in the *Harvard Business Review.*

> Because workers would be more comfortable, better able to see, and less fatigued by noise, their productivity and the quality of their output would rise. Eight recent case studies of people working in well-designed, energy efficient buildings measured labor productivity gains of 6% to 16%. Since a typical office pays about 100 times as much for people as it does for energy, this increased productivity in people is worth 6 to 16 times as much as eliminating the entire energy bill.[44]

Most energy-efficient design practices are cost-effective just from their energy savings; the resulting people productivity gains make them indispensable. Joseph Romm, author of *Cool Companies*, uses nearly 100 case studies to show how firms can add millions of dollars to their bottom line in the process of becoming environmentally friendly. Whether it's converting to energy-efficient lighting or simply educating employees through workplace initiatives, companies that invest in energy efficiency also see significant returns in terms of morale and productivity. Here are some actual cases researched by Romm (italics in original).

- Verifone, a California manufacturer, renovated and daylit one of its buildings. The improvements that saved 60% of the energy would have paid for themselves in 7.5 years. The increase in productivity of more than 5% and drop in absenteeism of 45% brought the payback to under a year—*a return on investment of over 100%.*
- A Wisconsin insurance company moved into a new building with 40% lower energy costs and work stations which give employees personal control over their lighting, heating, and cooling. *Productivity rose 7%.*
- Lockheed built a daylit, energy efficient engineering development-and-design facility in Sunnyvale, California, that saved $300,000 to $400,000 a year on energy bills—and *productivity rose 15%.*
- Control Data's Operations Group in Sunnyvale, California, upgraded their lighting for $15,000. Energy use dropped 65%, saving $7,000 a year. The reduced glare cut the number of input errors, *raising productivity by an estimated 6%*, which was worth $28,000 a year.[45]

Anticipating there might be a temptation to dismiss these improvements as merely evidence of the "Hawthorne Effect," Romm devotes an appendix to proving this assertion wrong. The Hawthorne Effect is a theory about human motivation that is deeply entrenched in the mythology of management theory. It is based on studies conducted from 1924 to 1927 at the Western Electric Hawthorne Works in Chicago, where Harvard Business School professor Elton Mayo examined the effect of working conditions on productivity. In a set of experiments at the plant, he studied the effect on productivity of changes to lighting and to the length and frequency of rest breaks. He concluded that the attention the women received in the study from the researchers outweighed the influence of the other changes. Their productivity went up, regardless of whether the workplace illumination was increased or decreased, because their self-esteem was improved by the attention they were receiving as they participated in the experiments.

Since the Hawthorne experiments claimed there was no clear connection between productivity and the amount of illumination, Romm felt it was important to clarify what was really found. By carefully analyzing the original research notes, he shows the Hawthorne studies incorrectly attributed worker productivity improvements to increased attention the workers received, regardless of whether lighting improved or was made worse. Romm meticulously debunks the myth of the Hawthorne Effect and goes on to cite proof of the opposite: work conditions, not merely attention to employees, were responsible for the productivity rise for the five relay assembly workers studied at Hawthorne.[46] Romm documents further cases which showed productivity improvements of 6%, 7.1%, 13.2%, 14%, and 25% after workplace environments were upgraded.[47]

There is also a health and absenteeism dimension to good building design. The U.S. Environmental Protection Agency (EPA) now lists indoor air quality (IAQ) as the fourth largest health threat to Americans. According to the EPA, indoor air can be a hundred times more polluted than outside air, and the Occupational Health and Safety Administration (OHSA) claims that 25 to 50% of all commercial building have IAQ problems.[48] The EPA estimates that building-related illnesses caused by poor air quality account for $60 billion of annual lost productivity in the U.S., and a wider study valued that loss as high as over $400 million.[49]

Romm estimates that productivity benefits due to workplace design range from 7 to 15%. In addition, there is a drop in sick leave and absenteeism.[50] The earlier estimate by Hawken and the Lovins' was 6 to 16%. Again, to be conservative, I will assume only a 7% gain in productivity for 50% of the employees for SD Inc. Even with no allowance for savings from reduced absenteeism, SD Inc. would reap benefits of $252 million, the equivalent of 4,200 more employees.

The power of environmental initiatives to engage and unleash employee productivity is too big to ignore. The productivity improvements in SD Inc. at the individual and team level, plus improved productivity from better workplace design, add up to $756 million, or 12,600 "free" employees (see the "Increased Productivity" worksheet in the Appendix). Companies ignoring this potential are leaving money on the table.

The first three categories of sustainable development benefits which I have examined are people-related. Next I will consider savings in the manufacturing of products, savings in the operation of commercial sites, increased revenue and market share, and reduced risks. I will look at direct and indirect effects these benefits have on the bottom line, as the whole company is engaged in the exciting quest for sustainable approaches to its success.

Benefit 4: Reduced Expenses in Manufacturing

Through fundamental changes in both production design and technology, farsighted companies are developing ways to make natural resources—energy, minerals, water, forests—stretch 5, 10, or even 100 times further than they do today. These major resource savings often yield higher profits than small resource savings do—or even saving no resources at all would—and not only pay for themselves over time but in many cases reduce initial capital investments.

Paul Hawken, Amory Lovins, and L. Hunter Lovins[1]

Even if a company doesn't really care about the environment, there are substantial savings to be derived within today's operations by eliminating or recycling waste and redesigning products to use less energy, water, and materials in the manufacturing process. These are the "low-hanging fruit" of eco-efficiency, which excite companies in their first blush of enthusiasm for environmental concerns. A quantum leap in capturing these benefits is the strategy I will explore.

Waste = Squandered Corporate Assets

When we step back and look at the amount of waste produced directly and indirectly during normal manufacturing processes, the picture is shocking.

> When people think of waste, they consider their household garbage, exhaust gases from their cars and the containers of rubbish outside businesses or construction sites. If you were to ask how much material is wasted each year, most people would admit that a certain percentage is wasted, but not a great deal. Actually, we are more than 10 times better at wasting resources than we are at using them. A study by the U.S. National Academy of Engineering found that about 93% of the material we buy and "consume" never end up in salable products at all. Moreover, 80% of the products are discarded after a single use, and many of the rest are not as durable as they should be. Business reformer

> Paul Hawken estimates that 99% of the original materials used in the production of, or contained within, the goods made in the U.S. become waste within 6 weeks of sale.[2]

Figure 6.1 reinforces these numbers.[3]

When a company buys raw materials, it owns them. To then throw them out under the guise of normal waste is to squander corporate assets. If the term "waste" were replaced with "squandered corporate assets," corporations would be pressured by their shareholders to pay more attention to this opportunity for cost savings. The business imperative to stop squandering these assets has an environmentally beneficial by-product—a true win/win proposition.

Figure 6.2 shows four ways to save costs and help the environment in the manufacture of products:

1. Substitute less expensive, more environmentally friendly raw materials and energy sources for those currently being used.
2. Reduce the amount of material, energy, and water used per product, even if this means fundamentally redesigning the product or manufacturing process to do so.
3. Reduce, reuse, and recycle scrap material and wasted energy, turning them into useful product instead of throwing them away.
4. Reuse and recycle components and materials from returned products that have been designed for disassembly (DfD).

Savings From Materials and Energy Substitutions

Materials Substitutions

First, let's consider the choice of raw materials from which products are made. Despite notions of market- or customer-driven corporate strategies, the selection of materials used in goods is not a consumer's choice. It is a corporation's choice. To be sensitive to the environment, companies should consider the material flows that are required to produce the raw materials they are purchasing. This "cradle-to-grave" perspective encourages us to look back to the cradle of the raw materials themselves—the energy and materials consumed in extracting, preparing, and transporting the raw materials used in the company's manufacturing processes. Friederich Schmidt-Bleek of the Wuppertal Institute for Climate, Environment and Energy (one of the most respected environmental research organizations in Europe, based at the

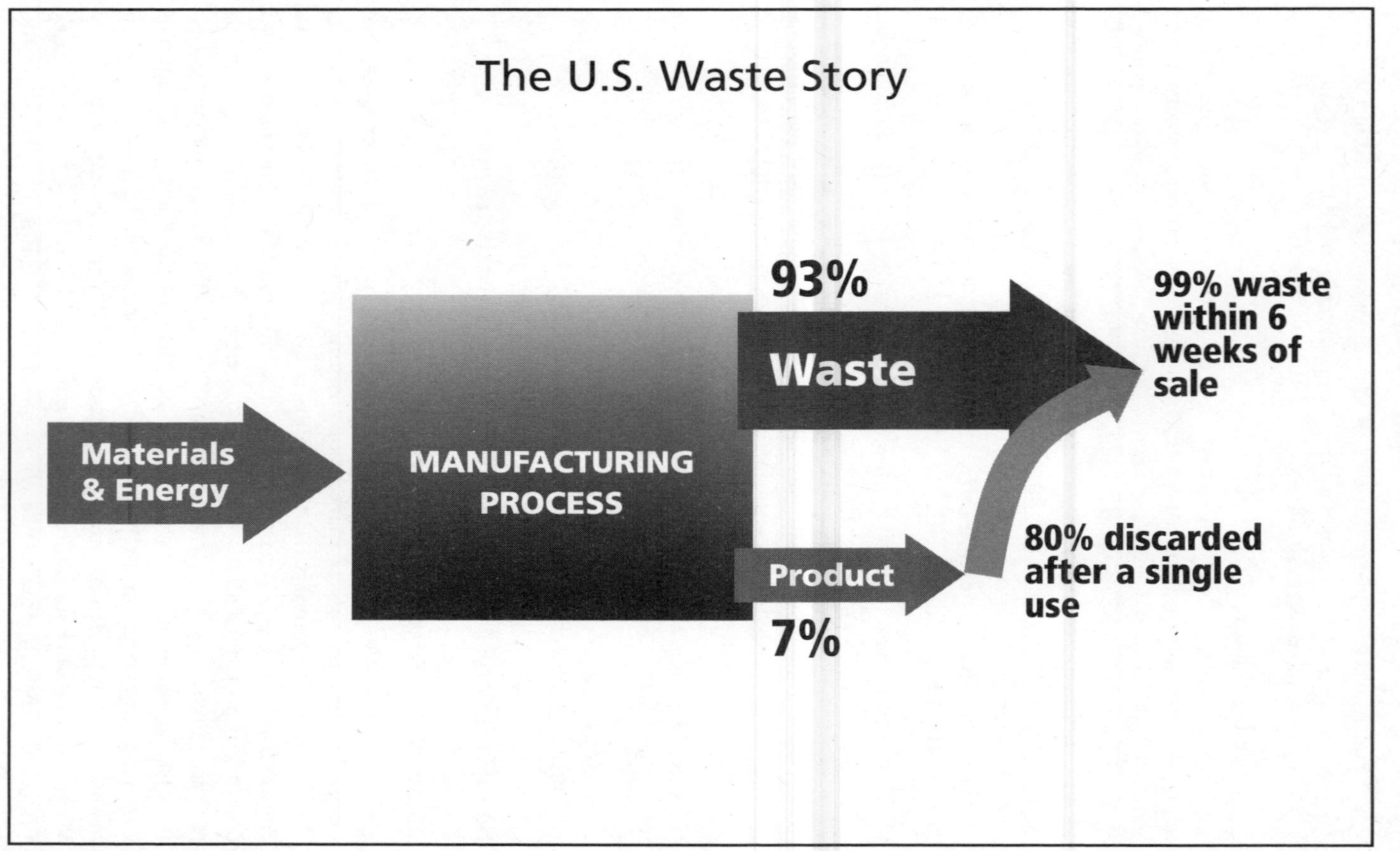

Figure 6.1 The U.S. Waste Story

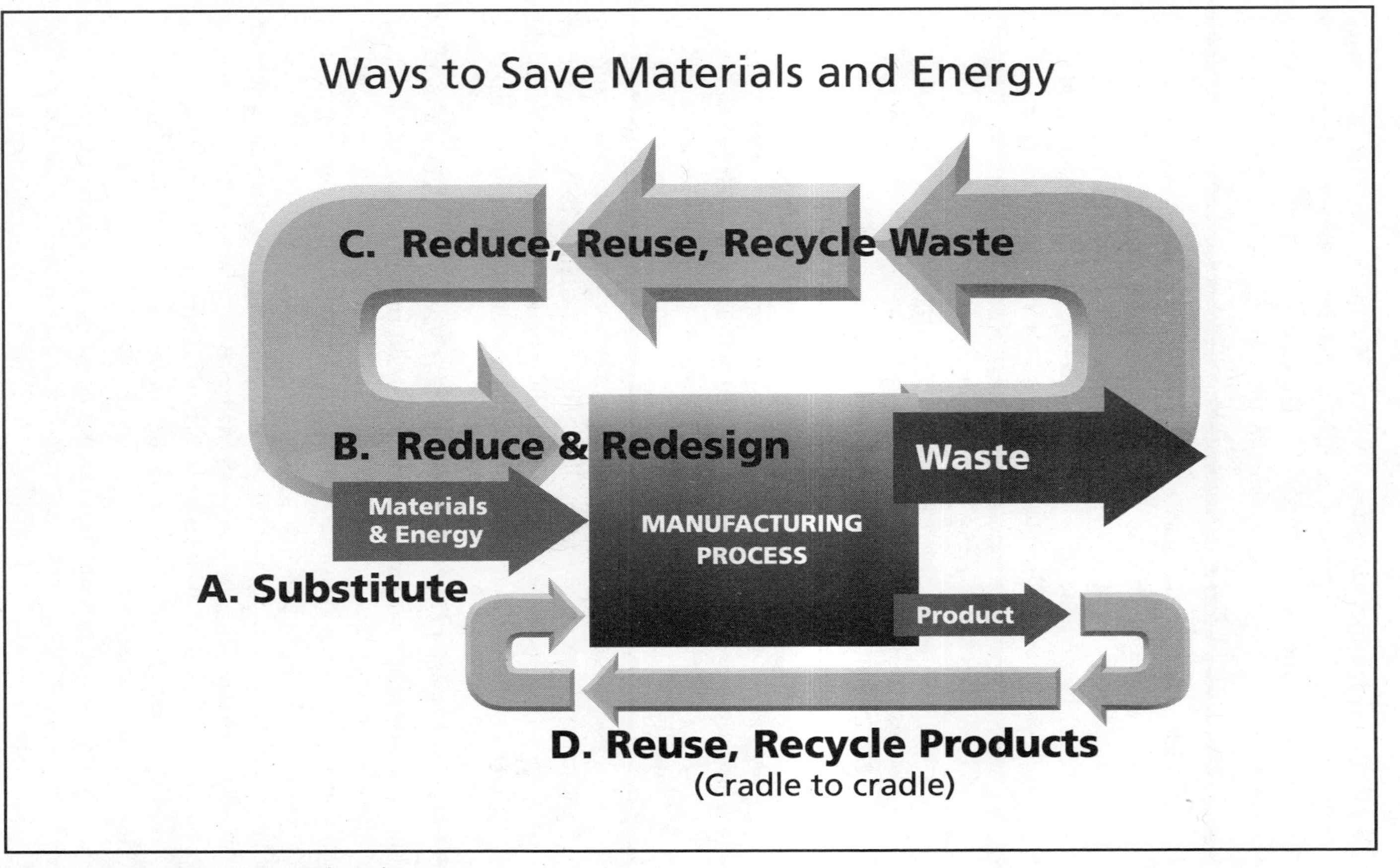

Figure 6.2 Ways to Save Materials and Energy

North-Rhine/Westphalian Science Centre, Germany) has proposed that a measure of "material intensity" be used to determine how much material is used to refine the raw materials and produce a product. This measure is described in the book *Factor Four*, in the chapter succinctly entitled "The Gold Ring on Your Finger Weighs Three Tonnes."

> A kilogram of metal obtained from mines often requires tonnes of ore to be processed. Schmidt-Bleek speaks of the "ecological rucksack" carried by the metal .... In the case of gold and platinum the relation is 1:350,000. Imagine the weight of the ecological rucksack of the gold ring on your finger. It would be 3 tonnes for a ring weighing a mere 10 grams.
>
> Every good and service that we enjoy has an ecological rucksack to carry. The catalytic converter in cars, once heralded as the saviour of German forests, weighs less than 3 kg but carries a rucksack of more than 2.5 tonnes, chiefly owing to the platinum that is used .... Orange juice isn't innocent either. Depending on the country of origin, a litre of orange juice has caused soil and water movements of more than 100 kg. Your daily newspaper may weigh a pound, but its ecological rucksack is likely to be 10 kg. Manufacturing a car typically involves 15 tonnes of solid waste, not counting the water that is used and polluted in the process.[4]

What about computers? In *Mid-Course Correction*, Ray Anderson adds up all the material processed and distilled to produce a ten-pound computer and ends up with a rucksack weighing 40,000 pounds.[5] He also estimates the amount of waste generated to make a semiconductor chip is over 100,000 times its weight.

There are several ways to substitute less expensive, more environmentally friendly, raw materials. First, use materials with smaller ecological rucksacks. Big rucksacks may equate to higher prices, although subsidies in many natural resource and energy industries distort this free market assumption. As these subsidies and tax breaks for natural resource companies are subjected to increased public scrutiny and protest, prices will better reflect the true costs of raw materials. By choosing raw materials that have smaller ecological rucksacks, companies will be in a better competitive position when this happens. They will directly save money as they indirectly contribute to the health of the planet.

Second, designing manufacturing processes to use recycled materials may save money over using new raw materials. For example, the primary source of scrap steel for Chaparral Steel's mill in Texas is old automobiles. To recycle this material, an automobile shredder facility, the largest and most productive in the world, is located next to the mill. The shredder operation provides Chaparral with a competitive advantage in the acquisition of raw material. In 1996, the shredder transformed over 700,000 tons of old cars and other light scrap into raw material. This volume represents about 40% of Chaparral's total scrap needs.[6] (The idea of taking processed goods and recycling them into raw materials is called cradle-to-cradle.)

Third, ensure your suppliers are adopting more environmentally sensitive approaches. For example, Ford and General Motors (GM) have set green standards for their parts suppliers. The two Detroit automakers said they want all suppliers to conform to the international ISO 14001 standard, under which independent auditors evaluate processes to measure energy use, waste disposal, water treatment, recycling, and air pollution. Ford, the first automaker to certify all its plants worldwide under the standards, required suppliers to have at least one manufacturing site meet the ISO 14001 standard by the end of 2001, and all manufacturing sites shipping products to Ford will have to conform by July 1, 2003. GM set a deadline of December 31, 2002, for its suppliers and its own facilities to meet the ISO 14001 environmental discipline.[7] Of course, ISO 14001 does not set environmental standards; it just ensures processes are measured and followed. But it's a start. In addition, a supplier's environmental performance may be evaluated through questionnaires or environmental audits. Quaker Oats, the Body Shop, and Bell Canada are some of the corporations that require such feedback from their suppliers.[8]

Fourth, replace hazardous materials and chemicals with non-hazardous ones. This switch has a sometimes overlooked benefit in the form of labor savings.

- Reduced handling costs due to use of less hazardous materials
- Employees formerly used in hazardous materials handling or hazardous waste treatment can be redeployed to other more productive areas (This could be another contributor to productivity that was not included in our earlier discussion.)
- Environmental Affairs staff spend less time monitoring compliance with hazardous materials regulations
- Increased productivity due to a safer and/or more pleasant work environment

- Decreased turnover due to higher manufacturing employee commitment and morale
- Less management time to manage exclusively environmental matters

Energy Substitutions

As well as being sensitive to the environmental impact of the raw materials used in the manufacture of their products, companies should similarly be concerned about the environmental impact of the energy they use.

> Metals were just the beginning of Schmidt-Bleek's rucksack story. Energy, too, carries a rucksack. Those 3,000 million tonnes of coal that we burn each year carry a rucksack of tailings and water weighing easily 15,000 million tonnes—not to mention the 10,000 million tonnes of CO_2 that is released in the burning process.9

Suppose concerns about climate change, asthma, and other health problems overcame fossil-fuel energy companies' denial that there is a problem. The two big motivators for an apathetic citizenry are threats to health and threats to children. Any threat to children's health is doubly potent. Suppose the public clamor became too great for governments to ignore. Suppose they took the advice of Thomas Casten in *Turning Off The Heat* and aggressively—

- deregulated electricity everywhere;
- eliminated barriers to efficiency embodied in tax, environmental, and regulatory law; and
- eliminated the present subsidies for fossil fuel, estimated to be $4 billion in the U.S. per year, mostly in depletion allowances given as tax credits to oil and gas companies.[10]

In the U.S., in the 50 years to 1998, fossil fuels and nuclear energy received $111.5 billion in federal subsidies, whereas renewables received just $5 billion, excluding large hydro projects, which have their own environmental disadvantages.[11] Governments in developing countries are giving polluting fuels like coal, oil, and nuclear energy at least 10 to 20 times as much subsidy as they put into renewables like wind and solar energy.

Suppose instead that eco-taxes were instituted on fossil fuel use and subsidies were deflected to renewable energy sources. If this happened, companies that converted to sustainable, renewable, non-fossil energy sources would be preparing themselves for a competitive advantage.

There are several ways to substitute more environmentally friendly energy sources for traditional ones. First, consider using renewable energy sources. DuPont, the world's largest chemical company, recently set a goal of sourcing 10% of its energy needs from renewable sources such as solar power by the end of 2010. It uses almost no renewable energy right now.[12] The British supermarket group Sainsbury started using wind power from an on-site wind turbine for one-third of the electricity at one of its Scottish distribution depots, and its eco-friendly flagship store in Greenwich, England, boasts solar panels and wind turbines.[13] Renewable energy alternatives are more environmentally benign and are becoming more cost competitive with nonrenewable or nuclear energy sources. Wind power is now down to 4.2 cents/kWh, making it cost competitive with traditional energy sources. The use of solar power has expanded sharply in recent years: over 1,000 buildings in Switzerland and Germany have been solarized, while Japan installed 62,000 solar generators in buildings by 2000. In the future, deregulated energy utilities will manage a portfolio of technologies, which will include wind and solar power, and cogeneration from many small partners.

Second, exploit the paradox of scale in a deregulated energy industry. Usually scale refers to "economies of scale," implying "big is better." However, when it comes to renewable energy generation, often small is better. Energy technologies are becoming smaller and better suited for local generation and usage. Miniaturization and modularization are being applied to energy technologies, just as they have been to information systems technologies. Some consumers and companies may be able to stay entirely off the grid, using their own sustainable energy alternatives. Better still, they can sell excess energy to the power utilities and may actually make money from their energy flow.

Third, consider using fuel cells. Fuel cells are gaining attention as a pollution-free energy source that generates power through an electrochemical process rather than through combustion of nonrenewable, polluting fossil fuels. Once prices for this technology decline, the sky's the limit for its ability to replace centralized electricity generation.[14] More and more businesses and private citizens are opting off the commercial power grid and choosing instead to install their own mini-power plants. By the end of 2000, Plug Power LLC began selling dishwasher-size fuel cells for the home at $4,000 apiece, and researchers say personal power is poised to enter the mainstream of American life, just as PCs did in the 1980s and cell phones in the 1990s. The new systems provide more reliable power and drastically reduce air pollution, say proponents, because they produce both power and hot water. Hot water, the only "waste" from a fuel cell, can be used for both heating and cooling, making the system two to three times more efficient than conventional power sources. The era of big central power plants is over.[15] Companies can deploy power generators throughout their plants, exploiting whichever renewable or nonrenewable energy source is appropriate for plant needs.

Finally, going even further with system integration as electric utilities are deregulated, it will become more attractive to use wasted heat from company industrial processes to generate electricity. Steam that otherwise would be vented into the atmosphere can be used to turn mini-electrical generators. The resulting electricity can be used on-site by the company, and excess electricity can be fed into the electrical grid to generate a credit on the company's electrical bill from the local electrical utility. Campbell's can make both soup and electricity from the steam in their cookers, and will generate revenue from both.

By implementing energy efficiency measures, the U.S. could avoid wasting $300 billion of energy each year.[16] Wasting resources wastes money and people. Wouldn't downsizing unproductive tons, gallons, and kilowatts of wasted material and energy to cut expenses be more supportive of corporate social responsibility than downsizing people?

Savings From Reducing the Materials, Energy, and Water Used Per Product

> Business strategies built around the radically more productive use of natural resources can solve many environmental problems at a profit.[17]

I have considered ways to substitute more environmentally friendly materials and energy for the supplies currently being used. Unfortunately, because of inequitable subsidies and short-term costing of traditional energy and materials, the costs of the suggested substitutions are usually deemed to be higher today than their less environmentally friendly alternatives. That's not fair, but that's the way it is and will continue to be until the material and energy substitutions can be produced in sufficient volume and subsidies are changed to level the playing field.

In the meantime, the trick is to work on the other end of the equation—instead of trying to replace the material and energy required today with alternatives, reduce the amount you use. Until prices better reflect the size of the material's and energy's ecological rucksacks, wise companies use minimum material design to reduce the material and energy used per product or service. This resource-productivity model reduces the price of production, which increases competitiveness and lays the foundation for a higher bottom-line return.

Reducing the amount of material used also has labor productivity benefits: there are reduced handling costs because there are fewer components or less material to handle, and there is less overtime because of more efficient processes. An extreme example of reducing the material needed for a product or service is to replace printed manuals or catalogues with electronic publications on the Internet.

There are several ways to minimize the amount of energy used in manufacturing. First, insulate. Use the traditional approaches, insulating pipes, furnaces, boilers, and other sources of heat loss. As any home owner would attest, avoiding lost heat conserves energy and lowers the monthly bill. Husky Injection Molding Systems in Bolton, Ontario, attributes $525,000 annual savings to its energy-efficient building design.[18]

Second, replace plant light fixtures with more energy-efficient ones. Many plant executives think they already "did" energy efficiency when the oil shock hit them in the 1970s and early 1980s. Their "been there, done that" attitude is premature. Maybe they did an earlier round of energy-efficiency measures, but doing another with more modern technologies could be profitable. Malden Mills in Massachusetts was already using energy-efficient metal-halide bulbs in the mid-1990s. They found that by doing a further warehouse retrofit using today's much improved technologies, they improved visibility, reduced their electrical energy used for lighting by another 93%, and had a payback period of 18 months.[19]

Another example of savings from light fixture retrofits in a manufacturing setting is provided by General Motors' Oshawa car plant. GM reduced total energy consumption by 26 million kWh per year as a result of its Lighting Retrofit Project. The company replaced the T12 fluorescent light fixtures used in the manufacturing line with high-efficiency T8 fixtures, reducing energy usage by 38%. They also replaced the fixtures used for high bay lighting in the body plant with metal-halide fixtures, reducing energy consumption by 46%.[20] At the National Parts Distribution Centre in Woodstock, Ontario, GM saved over $500,000 annually by converting the lighting system from fluorescent to high-pressure sodium (HPS) lighting.[21]

Third, install energy-efficient pumping motors and piping systems. Pumping is the largest application for motors, and motors use 75% of all industry electricity.[22] Manufacturing requires motors and pumps—lots of them. Interface Inc. discovered that using big, straight pipes with small pumps—instead of small, crooked pipes with big pumps—would cost less, even before counting the ongoing energy savings from the lower electricity use of the smaller pumps, motors, motor controls, and electrical components. By first laying out the pipe route and then positioning the tanks, boilers, and other connected equipment, Interface's engineer discovered he could use 7-horsepower pumps instead of 95-horsepower pumps, a 92% reduction. These embarrassingly simple design changes meant Interface did not need big pumps to overcome the extra friction of longer, twisting routes for the pipe. The icing on the savings cake was reducing heat loss by an extra 70 kilowatts because the shorter, straighter pipes were easier to insulate well, repaying the insulation's cost in just three months.[23]

The whole system cost can be optimized by counting not just the higher capital costs of fatter pipes but also the lower capital costs of smaller pumping equipment, instead of "pessimizing" the costs by looking at the component costs in isolation. These small changes at the downstream end of a process often yield big savings upstream, with environmental side benefits. In any pumping system, saving one unit of liquid flow or friction in an exit pipe saves about ten units of fuel, cost, and pollution at the power station.[24]

Fourth, consider a more holistic approach when evaluating construction and design bids. One of the big challenges in energy conservation is the way most purchasing decisions are made one at a time without regard for the whole system cost. Saving energy requires more than just a piecemeal tuning of existing energy usage. It demands that you look at the big picture of how the components of electrical systems can be combined in smarter ways. Consider distribution transformers. Every office and factory building needs them, and they are relatively inexpensive at only $320 apiece. Most companies try to save a buck by buying the lowest priced, inefficient models. Since all electricity must flow through these transformers, using the cheapest, most inefficient ones wastes $1 billion in electricity per year in the U.S.[25] It's more energy efficient and more cost effective to spend more money on transformers and then save money on energy.

The purchasing department should use similar thinking when it evaluates tenders for wires. All electricity must also flow through wires. Thin wires get hot. To prevent fires caused by overheated circuits, the National Electrical Code defines the minimum thinness of the wire that can be used. Thin wire costs less, so electricians bidding on jobs use the thinnest allowable wire to win the contract. The irony is that if office lighting circuits used fatter wire with less electrical resistance, lower electricity bills would generate after-tax returns of 193%.[26] When doing retrofits or building new facilities, engineers and architects are traditionally compensated for what they spend, not for what they save, which ignores the long-term operating costs and expenses. It is the responsibility of the purchasing department to ensure this approach is reversed and the ongoing operational savings are harvested.

Fifth, look for ways to level the electrical load so that more energy is purchased at off-peak rates. General Motors implemented a Peak Demand Management system in its transmission plant in Windsor, Ontario. By rotating the shutdowns of heating and ventilation systems to avoid exceeding a peak usage, it saved 1.16 million kWh.[27]

Exploiting combinations of these five approaches reaps big energy and financial savings. Earlier, I mentioned that microchips have material and energy ecological rucksacks of 100,000 times their own weight. Natural Capitalism cites examples of high-tech chipmaking plants that have reduced their energy by half or more, with typical after-tax returns of over 100% on retrofit investments.

> A large Asian chip-assembly plant in 1997 cut its energy bills by 69% per chip in less than a year; a Singapore chipmaking plant between 1991 and 1997 cut its energy use per wafer by 60% with half the paybacks under twelve months and four-fifths under eighteen months; another saved $5.8 million per year from $0.7 million in retrofit projects.[28]

Combining these energy conservation methods with increased use of renewable energy creates a powerful energy pincher movement, shown in Figure 6.3.

Saving water used in manufacturing can also yield substantial savings. Fluke Corporation in Seattle found it paid for water four times: when it was metered for the water in the first place, when it treated the water to production standards, when it treated the water prior to discharge, and when it was charged sewage fees. Over two years, Fluke reduced water use from 2.5 million gallons per month to 400,000 gallons per month, resulting in bottom-line savings of $138,000 per year.[29] In 1994, Suncor Energy's Oil Sands Group conserved 2,000 cubic meters of water per day, just by recycling wastewater from its powerhouse into the extraction unit.[30] In addition to reducing water use, the initiative also yielded energy savings and fewer air emissions.

An innovative approach is used by Ethel M Chocolates in Nevada, a division of Mars, Inc.. It has a "Living Machine" that treats thousands of gallons of wastewater a day. The system uses an acre of tanks, marshes, and reed beds where bacteria, zooplankton, plants, snails, and fish process the organic waste into water that is reusable for industrial purposes.[31]

Internal eco-efficiency initiatives usually reap multiple concurrent benefits rather than savings in only one area. For example, Schneiders' meat-packing plant in Kitchener, Ontario, has reduced wastewater by 52%, reduced solid waste by 68%, reduced the consumption of cleaning chemicals by 50%, and

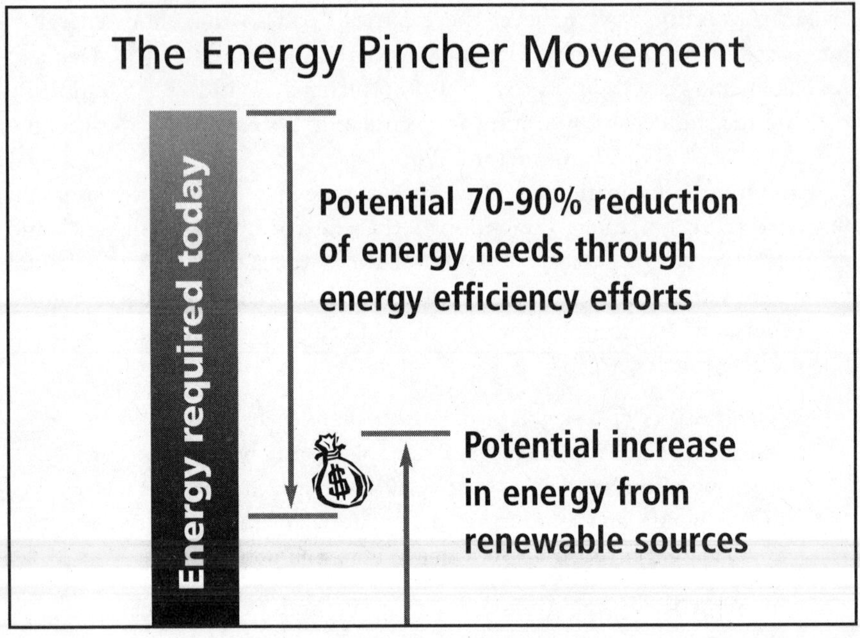

Figure 6.3 The "Energy Pincher Movement"

eliminated the use of foil paper in all processed meat. The president understands the value of small savings in production costs: "If we save 1 cent a pound, we make $10 million profit."[32] Baxter International's 1993 environmental report also succinctly cut to the chase: "The total savings generated from Baxter's environmental program were $48 million in 1993. This added eight cents per share to Baxter's profitability."[33]

Savings From Redesign

In the first stage of a company's journey toward sustainable development, it strives to wring out the waste of energy, water, materials, and other resources throughout its production systems and other operations. It can do this at a profit by replacing old industrial technologies, materials, and energy sources with new ones, and by improving materials, energy, and water efficiencies, as we have seen. However, the biggest savings breakthroughs occur when companies adopt a fresh approach to design that considers industrial systems as a whole, rather than as a collection of isolated parts.[34] Huge savings can be attained by process redesign, rather than process tuning. Continuous improvement of old manufacturing processes eventually will hit a wall where the cost to squeeze out additional savings exceeds the savings that would be gained. That's when designers need to step back, break old paradigms, and ask different questions.

> The old idea is one of diminishing returns—the greater the resource saving, the higher the cost. But that old idea is giving way to the new idea that bigger savings can cost less—that saving a larger fraction of resources can actually cost less than saving a small fraction of resources. This is the concept of expanding returns, and it governs much of the revolutionary thinking behind whole-system thinking.[35]

A wonderful example of this replacement of incremental environmental thinking with quantum leap thinking is offered by Bill McDonough's "no-pipe" approach. Environmentalists encourage working on "front-of-pipe" eco-efficiency instead of "end-of-pipe" compliance and filtering. McDonough goes even further and eliminates the pipe: "You put the filter in your head and design the problem out of existence."[36] The side benefit is that when there is no waste, the environment is healthier and there is no need for government regulations. Gunter Pauli's Zero Emissions Research Initiative claims that with this kind of creative thinking, in 20 years zero-waste will be a standard industry objective, not the exception.[37]

Interface provides an example of substantial water savings from process eco-redesign. When Interface redesigned the way it made carpets, one of its most successful measures was switching to a type of embroidery process to color the products, replacing the use of steam to fix dye to the fabric and the use of high-pressure water to wash away the excess. This move cut water use to about 10,000 gallons per month from 120,000 gallons, within one year. The local water utility was so surprised by the rapid reduction that it sent somebody to see if the meter was broken. At the same time, Interface has seen its sales grow to $1.1 billion in 1997 from $600 million in 1993.[38]

The Microelectronics and Computer Technology Corp. (MCC) in Austin, Texas, reinvented how printed wiring-boards are fabricated. MCC is an R&D consortium that came up with an approach that reduces hazardous waste by 30 to 100%, water use by 50 to 90%, and energy use by 50 to 75%. More significantly, MCC's design saves 20 to 70% of traditional circuit board manufacturing costs, which goes straight to the bottom line.[39]

Savings From Reducing, Reusing, and Recycling Scrap Material

Hazardous waste receives more attention than any other kind of waste. Every country has regulations about its emission and disposal, and all companies must comply. Hazardous waste, including chemicals, can be recycled on-site or off-site, sent to landfills, incinerated, or neutralized by aqueous and other treatments. Amounts released to the air or water or disposed of off-site are carefully monitored. Companies work hard to cut their hazardous waste. Since 1987, IBM has reduced the amount of hazardous waste it generates and manages by more than 80%.[40] In just five years, after measuring and addressing its hazardous waste production, Sunoco reduced its shipments of hazardous waste by an impressive 85%.[41] It costs money to dispose of hazardous waste—haulers are paid to dispose of it carefully—so reduction of hazardous waste saves disposal and dumping fees.

The ultimate way to mitigate the end-of-pipe environmental impact of hazardous waste is to eliminate the use of hazardous liquids or materials in the first place. A good example of this approach is the virtual elimination of the use of CFCs as a circuit-cleaning agent when that chemical's impact on the ozone layer was detected.

Up to 100% of the chemicals used in some manufacturing processes can be recycled, reducing the chemicals "consumed" or "wasted" to zero. If you do not waste materials, you can make more product without buying more raw materials. Waste minimization and recycling efforts at Husky Injection Molding in Ontario resulted in an 85% waste diversion rate and generation of $263,000 in income.[42] Interface Inc. has an objective to eliminate all waste in the manufacture of carpet. This zero-waste strategy led to a corporate-wide treasure hunt that helped keep resource inputs constant between 1994 and 1998. Revenues rose by $200 million, and Interface attributes $67 million of this revenue increase to the company's 60% reduction in landfill waste. Interface is doing well while doing good. Between 1993 and 1998, revenue more than doubled, profits more than tripled, and the number of employees increased by 73%.[43]

Green strategies require no business, employee, or shareholder sacrifices. Toyota, which has revolutionized manufacturing by pioneering a much-copied "lean" production system, aims to cut industrial waste by 100% at its new assembly plant in France.[44] If zero waste is attainable in the manufacture of carpets and cars, surely it is a reasonable goal for manufacturing companies in other industries.

Looking beyond the walls of the company, there are opportunities for synergistic relationships between neighboring companies. System integration with other companies provides another way to reduce the materials used to produce goods and services. Using the waste from one company as the food for another is called "industrial ecology" (see Figure 6.4).

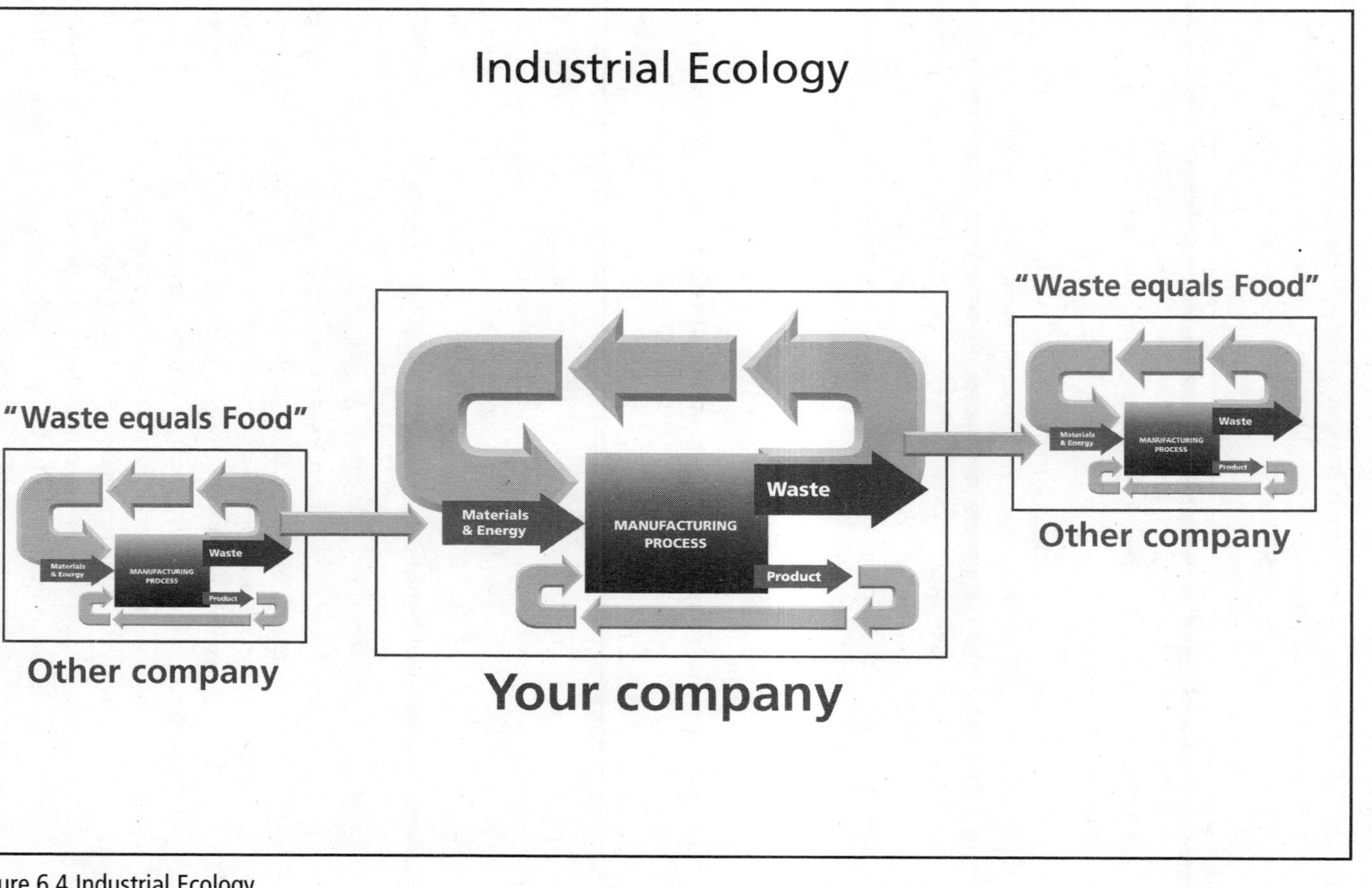

Figure 6.4 Industrial Ecology

> This approach takes a systems approach to eco-efficiency and applies it to multiple corporations working in concert, such as one company's wastes becoming another's raw materials. The best-known example of industrial ecology comes from Kalundborg, Denmark, where a group of local companies — a refinery, a power plant, a pharmaceutical company, and a fish farm, among others — found that they could reduce costs and increase efficiency by using each other's waste as resource inputs.[45]

That is, one manufacturing company sells its leftover scrap to another company that can use the scrap to produce its product—"waste equals food." In Kalundborg, the companies in the eco-industrial park trade various by-products: steam and heat, water, refinery gas, gypsum, biomass, liquid fertilizer, fly ash, and sludge. They invested $60 million over five years on the infrastructure to support these exchanges and have reaped over $120 million in cost savings.[46] This increased efficiency benefits the bottom lines of all participating partners.

Similar synergies are exploited by a Chaparral Steel mill, a neighboring TXI cement plant, and an automobile shredding facility in Midlothian, Texas. The steel mill uses scrap from the automobile shredding facility and sends its millhouse dust, electric arc furnace slag, and mill scale to the cement plant for processing.[47]

As of 2001 there were eco-industrial networks developing across Canada, the U.S., and Europe, referred to as eco-industrial parks, industrial ecosystems, zero emissions clusters, and sustainable technology parks. The BHAG vision for eco-industrial networks is the clustering of symbiotic companies, including "live-work" apartment units to eliminate some workers' daily commute. They will be attractive places to live and work, with rooftop gardens on all buildings, and zero air emissions. The idea is that industrial parks will be real parks. Assembly, disassembly, repair, and remanufacturing facilities will coexist synergistically. Vegetable-based plastics used in hard goods will be completely compostable after they can no longer be reused or recycled. Both active and passive solar energy will be captured, with excess energy converted to hydrogen through the electrolysis of water —the hydrogen then will be used to power fuel cells in buildings and vehicles. A solar aquatics system will treat gray-water human sewage and storm water, with the ponds providing a habitat for migrating birds and the treated water being recycled back to manufacturing plants. Thus, the closed-loop systems in these industrial ecosystems will benefit the companies, the communities, and the environment.[48]

Savings From Reusing and Recycling Returned Products

There are substantial savings to be derived within manufacturing firms from the first three options of substitution, manufacturing efficiencies or redesign, and using waste as raw material. As mentioned before, some describe these as the "low-hanging fruit" of eco-efficiency—they are relatively easy, they are high profile, and they have immediate payback. Most companies are already reaping at least some of these benefits.

Now government "take-back" regulations are beginning to focus on the fourth option—reuse and recycle components from returned products. The concept of "extended producer responsibility" (EPR) makes producers responsible for the environmental impacts of their products even at the end of the products' useful life. As such, EPR shifts to private industry the responsibility for taking back, recycling, and ultimately disposing of discarded material that would otherwise be managed by local governments. This incorporates the costs of product disposal or recycling into product price.

Take-back is a proactive, financially attractive example of corporate social responsibility.[49] Truly voluntary EPR initiatives are implemented when a company is able to make a profit or gain a marketing advantage by taking back its products, components, or extracted materials. Take-back will also change how products are made, as some companies realize the long-term costs of their materials and processes. Chemist Michael Braungart and architect William McDonough illustrate this shift in their Intelligent Products System, described in *Green Development.*

> [The Intelligent Products System] defines three levels of products: consumables, products of service, and unsaleables. *Consumables* are organic products that are eaten or will biodegrade without harmful effects. These products would be designed for decomposition rather than recycling. *Products of service* are durable items like TVs and cars, which would not be sold but would be licensed to people by the original manufacturer… . *Unsaleables* are toxic materials. These are the items that can never be thrown away and cannot serve as food. They will always belong to the original maker and will be stored (at the manufacturer's expense) in protective containers until a safe method of detoxification can be found This system makes manufacturers responsible for the long-term effects of the products they produce.[50]

The real benefit of take-back is the producer mindset it encourages. The above classification redefines unsaleable waste as poison. Once a company realizes it will be reclaiming its products and owning them forever, it gets smarter about how it designs them. It uses design for disassembly (DfD) so that it will be easier to take the product apart to reuse its components. It uses different and fewer fasteners. It stamps plastic components with part numbers and other information instead of using gummy labels that require more labor and time to remove. It gets serious about using non-toxic materials to simplify handling processes. It cleans up its design act.

Once a company understands the value of taking back its own products, it flips from fighting take-back regulations to insisting on them. In business, the best way to make sure you get your asset back after the consumer is finished with it is to lease it, the way people lease cars or computers. There is a subtle but profound difference in what consumers are purchasing. People aren't buying a car; they are leasing personal transportation. They are not buying a computer; they are leasing computing capability.

Interface's Evergreen Lease is an example of this paradigm shift from selling products to leasing services in the carpet industry. It also is a great example of take-back resulting in upstream product redesign. Interface's Evergreen Lease service entitles the customer to clean, fresh carpet for a monthly fee. Interface inspects and replaces worn carpet tiles each month and recycles the fibers and chemicals from the old carpet. Since the 80:20 rule applies—80% of the wear happens on 20% of the area—the savings on carpet replacement are five-fold. In addition, Interface designed its new Solenium carpet to last four times longer and use 40% less material than ordinary carpet, yielding a seven-fold reduction in materials intensity. Combined, these two factors lead to a 35-fold reduction in the flow of materials needed by Interface to maintain a superior floor-covering service. In addition, Solenium carpet is completely recyclable so there is no waste, and it is free from chlorine and other toxic materials.[51] When combined with other product design environmental initiatives, the economic benefits to the company of taking back its original well-designed product can be significant. Similarly, Collins & Aikman Floorcoverings of Dalton, Georgia, refers to its closed-loop recycling program as "mining buildings instead of mining the earth." They pelletize returned carpet and use it as raw material for carpet backing—and have sent no manufactured waste to landfills since 1993.[52]

EPR began because of a shortage of landfill capacity in Europe. As was hoped, its benefits for sustainability have been far-reaching.

> Well-designed EPR programs encourage both source reduction and recycling, and therefore result in reduced energy and materials consumption and reduced toxicity of products. When consumption of energy and materials decreases, the environmental impacts associated

with these activities—such as air and water emissions—also decline substantially. Therefore, EPR can be viewed not only as a mechanism to divert materials from disposal but as an important strategy for sustainability.[53]

Savings From Packaging, Transportation, and Approval Cycles

In addition to the four benefit areas above, there are three more potential savings arenas when environmental mindsets are unleashed in manufacturing and distribution. The first is a reduction in packaging costs through alternate approaches and less waste. For example, in a 30-month effort at reducing packaging waste, Johnson & Johnson saved 2,750 tons of packaging, 1,600 tons of paper, $2.8 million, and at least 330 acres of forest annually.[54]

Secondly, there are savings in resource-efficient transportation and shipping of the finished products. Sources of savings are:

- Reduced fuel costs from more efficient modes of transportation
- Increased cost-effectiveness due to lighter, smaller, and more efficiently packaged products
- Fewer vehicles or loads due to smarter combinations of shipments by batching loads
- More efficient routing algorithms

Thirdly, when a company eliminates or significantly reduces its use of hazardous materials in new products, the products can be brought to market faster, enhancing the company's competitive edge. Why? Research and development people can design manufacturing processes faster since they don't have to build in procedures for handling hazardous materials. It also takes less time to obtain a permit to manufacture the product, since the company avoids all the extra regulatory approvals that are required for hazardous waste handling and disposal. As an aside, a company with a good track record on environmental responsibility will also have a bank of goodwill with inspectors. A company with a reputation for practicing good environmental stewardship may face fewer inspections, receive speedier approvals, and be able to use more flexible techniques to meet environmental regulations.[55]

Tracking Environmental Costs

One other issue you need to consider is the best accounting approach to use in your manufacturing area in order to track and improve environmentally related costs. In *The Green Bottom Line*, Martin Bennett and Peter James suggest three layers of cost and the most appropriate way to account for each of them.[56]

- *Internalized conventional product costs* include the typical costs tracked by manufacturing companies, such as the labor, materials, energy, water, and capital costs that I have been discussing. These costs may be allocated to specific products or processes that generate them using Activity-Based Costing (ABC) or full-cost accounting, or they may be misleadingly spread across multiple products as shared overhead. Management accounting systems are important to the successful running of any business. Their biggest value is in focusing the attention of managers. The use of full-cost accounting systems for internalized conventional costs makes good business, as well as environmental, sense.[57]

- *Internalized environmental costs* include regulatory, operational, image/community relationship, contingency, waste disposal and treatment, recycling, and pollution prevention expenses. An ABC approach makes it easy to trace and track these costs and assign them to the product or process that incurs them, but it may be fought by managers whose superficially profitable products will be revealed as losers if their environmental costs are allocated to them.

- *Externalized environmental and societal costs* are the difficult-to-quantify costs of the business's impacts on the environment and society for which it is not legally liable, such as polluted discharges that contaminate the drinking water, air, or the fish and food eaten by downstream communities and wildlife.[58] Extended producer responsibility (EPR) is an example of how the externalized cost of disposing of a product after its useful life is being internalized by companies that are required to take their products back. Although EPR does not internalize all environmental externalities, it does internalize actual waste management costs into product prices and thus is a step in the direction of sustainability.[59] Externalized costs must be considered if the market's "invisible hand" is to reconcile the basic conflict between making decisions based solely on short-term profit and making decisions based on social and environmental responsibility.[60]

The first two internalized costs are seen as "private" costs, while externalized costs are often called "social" costs. Social costs are hidden and not yet included in many cradle-to-cradle full-life cycle or full-cost accounting methodologies—they are potential future internalized costs, if and when regulatory or consumer pressure becomes great enough. They may have real effects on market share and profitability as consumers become increasingly upset about suppliers who privatize their profits, but socialize their losses.[61] By adopting sustainable manufacturing practices, companies can convert this threat to an opportunity.

The Potential Benefit From Reduced Manufacturing Expenses

It's time to total up the potential savings in manufacturing. As you have seen, the areas for savings in manufacturing are many and diverse. Some require capital investments, some don't. Some have short payback periods, after which ongoing savings are reaped; some payback periods are longer. Depending on the company, some savings are built on existing initiatives, while others are brand new. Given such diverse factors, a line-by-line estimate would be impractical for SD Inc., so I will use a simple macro-level approach.

I will avoid double-counting. Companies are already financially benefiting from their existing environmental programs and projects. These initiatives are the "work in progress" base on which companies will build the momentum for new initiatives. The quantification of additional bottom-line benefits will only include incremental savings. The environmental personnel, fees, and other expenses incurred to obtain today's benefits are assumed to be constant —they will just be focused differently.

Hardware sales are assumed to contribute 50% of SD Inc.'s annual revenue, with the remaining revenue generated from software and services. Hardware materials, energy, and water costs are assumed to be 30% of hardware sales, so hardware costs for SD Inc. are $6.6 billion (50% x 30% x $44 billion).

Now for the big question: How much of this cost of hardware would be saved by a more aggressive blend of eco-efficiency, process redesign, and take-back initiatives? Obviously, the cost of hardware manufacturing saved is somewhere between 0% and 100%. Even a small percent yields a big number, so we'll choose a very conservative factor of 5%, yielding savings of $330 million.

Reducing manufacturing expenses yields real savings and there will be a huge temptation to simply pool them immediately with other general expense savings that flow to the bottom line. The challenge is to protect part of these environmentally related savings for reinvestment in the corporate infrastructure to reap longer-term energy and materials savings. Investment candidates include conversion to renewable energy supplies (solar, wind, fuel cell), further redesign of products and services for easier disassembly when they are returned and recycled to save on raw material costs, and replacing water pumps and pipes with more efficient ones. Company accountants may treat these projects as investment projects requiring capital, rather than maintenance projects requiring expenses, and their rules for capital investment in environmental projects may demand a payback period that is too short. The company may be willing to wait longer for a payback on its investment if it uses part of the money saved from other environmentally related initiatives as capital. The benefits are compounded as these investment seeds are later harvested. I assume 50% of the savings will be reinvested, so only the remaining $165 million is added to our annual profit. See the "Reduced Manufacturing Expenses" worksheet in the Appendix for a summary of the calculations and discussion in this chapter.

Benefit 5: Reduced Expenses at Commercial Sites

The profits from saving electricity could be increased even further if companies also incorporated the best off-the-shelf improvements into their building structure and their office, heating, cooling, and other equipment. Overall, such changes could cut national electricity consumption by at least 75% and produce returns of around 100% a year on the investments made.

Paul Hawken, Amory Lovins, and L. Hunter Lovins[1]

Although many companies begin looking at environmental concerns because of pressure from shareholders and regulatory agencies, they find a lot of unnecessary financial waste in the process. In some cases financial officers become the biggest proponents of cleaning up a firm's environmental act to reap cost savings. Often financial staff and enlightened senior executives become the biggest allies of the Environmental Affairs department because they understand that organizations can improve shareholder value by cutting costs and improving environmental performance simultaneously. These savings are derived not only by reducing the costs of energy, materials, and water in their manufacturing operations, but also from efficiencies in the operations of their other sites. I will use the term "commercial site" to include any non-manufacturing location, including commercial stores, staff and field location office buildings, distribution centers, and storage facilities.

When your office building is also your store, when it's open 24 hours a day, seven days a week, and when your customers live in it, you will focus more attention on ensuring it is run efficiently. That is why hotels are leaders in operating their buildings as a business and a source of savings from eco-efficiency, as confirmed by this estimate for Scandic Hotels.

> CFO Goransson estimates that the combined cost for the total Scandic group for water, energy, and waste is SEK 160 million (over U.S. $20 million) .... The estimated financial benefits generated by the Resource Hunt (Scandic Hotel's all-employee program focused on water, energy,

> and waste efficiency) were in excess of SEK 6 million in 1997, roughly U.S. $800,000, which went straight to the bottom line.[2]

Hotels generate visible revenue and expenses. Office buildings only have visible expenses—all the more reason to reduce those expenses as much as possible. As with manufacturing, the savings in operating office buildings come from waste reduction, energy efficiencies, and water conservation. I will consider these areas, but first I will look at how an enlightened and educated employee population can find savings in a different way.

Savings On Employee Discretionary Consumables

Once a company has decided it wants to improve its sustainable environmental leadership, executives soon realize that they cannot do it alone. As with any change, the engagement and commitment of all employees is critical to success. For example, Scandic Hotels' Resource Hunt was not just a program for environmental experts—it involved all employees, and reaped higher returns because of the engagement of that larger community. Similarly, the 3M Company's Pollution Prevention Pays (3P) corporate-wide program, launched in 1995, rewards creative employees who design pollution prevention projects, encourages sharing good ideas, reports results to all employees, and has saved the company well over $750 million since its inception in 1975.[3] Dow Chemical also found that employees can generate millions of dollars in savings if the program is allowed to build over several years.

> Dow Chemical launched their Waste Reduction Always Pays (WRAP) programme in the early 1980s... . WRAP challenged employees to propose waste reduction initiatives offering greater than 100% per year return on investment (ROI). The first year, 1982, brought 24 projects that met the standard, with a satisfying average ROI of 178%. "Great, we've got the low hanging fruit," the managers thought. "But just in case we missed a few things, let's try it another year or two and see if there's any more benefit." There was, year after year. In 1993 (11 years after the program began), the company adopted 140 employee WRAP recommendations, with an average ROI of 208%! The cumulative record for the programme over more than ten years—204% ROI, and cumulative savings of $110 million.
>
> How was this possible? One reason was that the early strategies provided a platform for the next wave of improvements; some options became feasible only after earlier improvements were made. As the work force got smarter, people learned what to look for and they spotted

> opportunities they would have missed without the experience and success of earlier years. Both employees and managers were increasingly motivated by the profitable payoff from the projects—and the rewards provided to the people who suggested them.[4]

Suppose a company educated its employees to be more aware consumers, and they started to continually look for more enviro-friendly actions in their homes and workplaces. There is some evidence that people would become more careful about consumables at work if they were trained to be more frugal without sacrificing quality. Weyerhaeuser Co., for example, participated in a program based on Vicki Robin's book *Your Money Or Your Life* to teach employees better money management and more conscious spending practices. In a follow-up survey of employees a year after they had taken the workshop, 28% said they were more frugal with company resources than before.[5]

This can show up in areas like purchasing supplies. Corporations make big decisions about buying paper.

> Paper entails a considerable cost to businesses that use it in large volumes. The value of total shipments of paper from U.S. manufacturers in 1994 was $138 billion. This figure includes $55 billion for market pulp and paper in its basic form (large rolls) and $83 billion in value added from converting rolls of paper into products like corrugated boxes, paperboard cartons, envelopes, writing tablets, etc.[6]

Increasingly, purchasing departments are specifying sustainably harvested paper products and choosing suppliers with the most environmentally friendly production of office supplies…at the best price. That's the first step. The second step is to use these supplies responsibly.

The rate at which these supplies are consumed has much to do with the mindset of each employee as a resource-and-supply gatekeeper. In *The Natural Step for Business*, Brian Nattrass and Mary Altomare outline how educating all employees about sustainability can pay dividends.

> All companies have two categories of flows: matter and energy. In realistic terms, over time these are comprised of hundreds of thousands of flow components moving through a business. During a typical day, each employee will make dozens, often hundreds, of decisions involving flows into or out of the corporation. This may range from the mundane, such as the use of electricity, water, paper, coffee and so on, to larger transportation, manufacturing, and inventory purchasing decisions. Thus, every employee is a resource gatekeeper. For real change to take

> place, every employee needs a common language and a shared mental model to contribute effectively to the company's sustainability vision. In addition, they need to be involved in translating that mental model of sustainability into daily practices.[7]

With the cooperation of environmentally sensitized employees, companies can reduce unwanted or unneeded paper. In an experiment at its Swiss headquarters, Dow Europe cut office paper flow by about 30% in six weeks by reassessing whether people receiving printed reports or memos really needed them.[8] Oticon, a Danish hearing-aid manufacturer, also saved about 30% of its paper costs by speeding up its decision-making process so that reports were no longer needed.[9] AT&T saved 15% of its paper costs just by switching the default printing setting on their copiers and printers to duplex mode.[10] Xerox estimates that if employees increased their duplexing rate on a 60-copies-per-minute copier in a small office, they could realize savings of $1,600 a month.[11]

Savings From Improved Waste Handling

The waste from commercial office buildings is similar to that from hotels. With a little effort in sorting, these businesses can obtain considerable saving in waste disposal. For example, in 1996 Scandic Hotel's Resource Hunt program, mentioned above, had a three-year target to reduce unsorted waste by 30%. After just 11 months, Scandic's unsorted waste was reduced by 15%. At the Scandic hotel in Bromma, waste was sorted carefully into 13 categories, cutting 1996 waste removal costs in half. At the Scandic hotel in Slussen, the costs for waste removal have dropped by 50% per year since employees started sorting waste, from about $25,000 per year down to about $9,000. They think they can get it down to $5,000 per year, an 80% reduction from the original $25,000.[12] Think what that kind of saving would add up to for all of a company's commercial sites.

Why is sorting waste a cost-effective strategy? By sorting their own waste, companies can eliminate the cost of intermediate waste companies that sort cardboard, paper, tin cans, chemicals, plastics, food, and glass containers into separate categories. By eliminating the middlemen, they can sell the sorted waste directly to other companies that use it as raw material in manufacturing processes, or they may find they can use it themselves and save handling, shipping, and raw material expenses. For example, organic waste from the company cafeteria can replace expensive fertilizers when it is composted and used on the company landscape gardens, or it can be sold to local farmers as food stock for pigs or to a factory for conversion into biogas to heat homes. The possibilities for waste reduction, reuse, and recycling are limited only by the entrepreneurial imaginations of employees.

Savings From Energy Efficiencies

Retrofitting Old Buildings

Retrofits provide many ways to conserve energy in commercial buildings. In the U.S., the EPA has awarded an "Energy Star" to the 500 most energy-efficient office buildings and K-12 schools. All of these buildings have energy performance that places them in the top 25% of similar buildings nationwide, based on comparisons with other buildings in the EPA database. Those with a low score have an opportunity to improve energy performance, and thus lower operating costs through reductions in energy bills. Thomas Casten outlines some of the ways to achieve the Energy Star designation in *Turning Off The Heat.*

> This [Energy Star] designation will signify that the building has utilized energy-saving technologies like insulated or special reflective glass, on-site power generation with heat recovery, photo voltaic panels that produce electricity from sunlight, solar water heaters, occupancy sensors, and other technologies to reduce its energy waste.[13]

There is a wealth of information and tools to help corporations improve the energy efficiency of commercial buildings. One proven strategy is the EPA Energy Star buildings upgrade process.

> [It] is part of an integrated approach to whole-building energy efficiency. Participants that follow this approach are able to reduce their energy use by 30 percent while achieving an internal rate of return (IRR) of 20 percent or greater on their investment. By planning energy-efficiency upgrades in the order suggested, participants can use the energy savings from initial upgrades to help pay for more costly upgrades later in the process. This strategy can also ensure that large energy systems, such as HVAC [heating, ventilating, and air-conditioning], are the most appropriate size for each facility.[14]

The EPA has several tools at it Energy Star website to help companies track and manage energy use in buildings, to benchmark their buildings' energy efficiency, and to financially assess the cost effectiveness of upgrades.[15] To make success even more certain, the Energy Star Buildings program recommends a five-stage approach.

- **Stage 1: Green Lights**. Installing readily available, proven lighting technologies can reduce a building's lighting energy use by 50 to 70%. Corporate partners in the program agree to survey 100% of their facilities' lighting systems and to upgrade 90% of that square footage to energy-efficient lighting within five years of joining the program. These retrofits must also achieve a minimum internal rate of return of 20% and there can be no compromise in lighting quality.
- **Stage 2: Building Tune-Up**. Conducting simple low- or no-cost adjustments to existing building equipment can result in an energy savings of 5 to 15% and may have a dramatic effect on the scale and type of upgrades needed in later stages.
- **Stage 3: Other Load Reductions**. Reducing the energy demand of a building by improving the energy efficiency of office equipment (such as computers, copiers, and fax machines) and of the building envelope (including windows, insulation, and exterior surfaces) will not only lower electric bills, but will also save on heating and cooling costs.
- **Stage 4: Fan System Upgrades**. Optimizing the fan systems in a building can save 50 to 85% in related energy costs while improving building comfort and reducing unnecessary noise from improperly sized fan systems.
- **Stage 5: Heating and Cooling System Upgrades**. Implementing the first four stages eliminates the heat emitted by inefficient equipment and prevents heating and cooling losses. To further capitalize on these improvements, energy-efficient heating and cooling systems should be "right-sized" to meet the exact needs of a building. Each year, there is $1 trillion misallocated in the U.S. to unnecessary air-conditioning equipment and the power supplies to run it, about 40% of the nation's peak electric load.[16] Since most of this is driven by corporate needs, there is low-hanging fruit just waiting to be plucked by aware executives.

As of June 1995, Energy Star partners included 40% of the Fortune 500 U.S. companies, as well as thousands of smaller businesses.[17] Of course, these steps are not unique to American companies. In 1999 the Toronto Dominion Centre in Toronto was the site of North America's largest lighting retrofits, worth about $40 million and expected to cut power bills by $5 million annually.[18]

What's the payback when multiple stages are implemented? One EPA Energy Star partner is IKEA in North America. As of November 1999, it has saved over 3 million kWh of usage. This translates into annual savings from lighting load reduction, air conditioning reductions, and reductions from lower lighting system maintenance of more than $500,000, with a simple payback period for all projects of 1.9 years. The environmental benefits are also substantial.

> Environmentally, IKEA in North America has avoided more than 4,000,000 pounds of annual carbon dioxide emissions, over 17,000,000 grams of annual sulphur dioxide emissions, and almost 7,000,000 grams for annual nitrogen oxide emissions equivalent to planting 982 trees, removing 482 cars from U.S. roadways. and preventing the combustion of 313,500 gallons of gasoline.[19]

Computing companies are reaping the benefits of energy conservation efforts, too. From 1990 through 1999, IBM conserved about 8.6 billion kWh of electricity (enough to power 1.43 million average homes in a year); saved $529 million in energy costs; and avoided approximately 5.7 million tons of CO_2 emissions (equal to taking 1.41 million cars driving 10,000 miles off the road) as a result of energy conservation actions.[20]

Sometimes the savings are on a moving target—electricity rates increase and companies expand their real estate. One impressive project was undertaken at Ryerson Polytechnic University in Toronto. Through a creative series of retrofits, Ryerson achieved energy savings of $1.2 million per year and reduced its peak load from 35 million kWh to 24 million kWh. Its 1996 electricity cost of $2.2 million was about the same as it was in 1989 despite cumulative rate increases of 27% during the same time period and a 28% increase in campus real estate.[21]

The Intergovernmental Panel on Climate Change (IPCC) estimate of the potential for global energy savings in the residential/commercial sector is about 25% by 2025.[22] The authors of *Factor Four* estimate the potential for increased energy efficiency is higher. They include the combined effect of energy efficiencies and the use of non-fossil fuel sources of energy.

> Using existing technologies, we can reduce present electrical consumption by 75% in homes and industry .... A company called Southwall makes windows that gain heat when placed on the south side of a building in a Saskatchewan winter. We can build houses that require no internal heating devices whatsoever.[23]

The "Factor Ten" club of prominent environmentalists, formed in 1994, goes even further.[24] It says that sustainable levels of material flows in Organization for Economic Cooperation and Development (OECD) countries will not be reached until material intensity is reduced by a factor of 10—a 90% reduction in energy and materials, rather than the 75% reduction proposed by Factor Four. The good news is the Factor Ten club feels this goal is technologically achievable within one generation. The bad news is that even if something is achievable, it won't actually happen without fresh thinking.

In the quest for energy efficiency, we should focus on saving energy before seeking new sources. There is more energy in the attics of North American homes than in all the oil buried in Alaska.[25] Paul Hawken claims we can save 90% of the energy used in buildings if we only use technology in clever ways.

> State-of-the-art technologies — fans, lights, pumps, superefficient windows, motors, and other products with proven track records — combined with intelligent mechanical and building design, could reduce energy consumption in American buildings by 90 percent. State-of-the-art technologies that are just being introduced could reduce consumption still further.[26]

This is reminiscent of the energy pincher (shown in Figure 6.3) created by lowering energy needs while increasing the use of renewable energy. Energy-efficient buildings are no longer a technical challenge—we know how to retrofit old buildings to save enormous amounts of energy. Amory Lovins describes in *Factor Four* how old wooden-frame buildings, glass-walled office towers, university buildings, and masonry row houses can be retrofitted to save 70 to 90% of their energy consumption—and the payback occurs within months or a few years.[27]

The federal government in Canada has undertaken an innovative approach to funding retrofits. Specifically, National Resources Canada (NRCan) has initiated the Federal Buildings Initiative (FBI—an unfortunately confusing acronym) to help federal departments and agencies reduce energy and water consumption and greenhouse gas emissions in their buildings and other facilities.[28] The FBI addresses three common barriers to improving energy efficiency:

1. Inadequate capital budgets for energy efficiency projects
2. The need for reliable information on current energy technology and practices
3. The lack of required skills to manage retrofits

The FBI is proving commercial buildings can be retrofitted with no net cost to the owners by using savings from reduced energy costs to pay the contractors. Under the FBI's innovative financing arrangement, clients have the option of overcoming tight capital budgets by transferring the up-front expense and risk of projects to pre-qualified energy management firms. Following retrofits, departments or agencies pay the lower utility bills that result, and then they pay their energy management firm the savings (the difference between pre- and post-retrofit bills) that result until the firm has recovered all project costs. From that point, energy savings are retained by the department. The FBI initiated retrofits of 6,500 federal buildings and other facilities by 2000, reducing greenhouse gas emissions significantly and generating annual savings of $26 million. FBI projects are helping the environment by reducing the risk of climate change and promoting healthier, more productive workplaces.[29]

For example, in 1989 NRCan helped the National Research Council of Canada sign a five-year, $1.6-million contract with Rose Technology Group Limited (RTG) (now Vestar). Under the terms of the contract, the National Research Council did not have to put up any money. Instead, the energy service company would finance the needed improvements and later recoup its investment from the resultant savings in energy. The project focused on four buildings with a total floor space of 657,000 square feet. As part of its service, RTG first conducted an energy audit. By reviewing three years of utility bills before undertaking the retrofit, and adjusting for weather and occupancy, the company established an energy-use baseline for the buildings. The most important improvements involved installing a centralized energy management control system, improving the lighting in buildings, and retrofitting air-handling units. These led to savings of $400,000 a year, and the project had paid for itself even before the contract expired.[30]

Sometimes energy-saving retrofits can just be added on the outside of a building to passively trap and use solar heat. An example of this approach is the use of Solarwalls to heat portable classrooms.[31] A Solarwall is 6 meters wide by 2.5 meters high and is mounted on the south-facing outside wall of a school portable. As the sun warms the Solarwall, it heats the air in the narrow space between the Solarwall and the siding of the portable. The warmed air then rises in the space and is pushed by tiny solar-powered fans into the classroom. The resulting convection currents draw more outside air through tiny pinholes in the Solarwall. This air picks up heat as it goes through the same cycle. Using Solarwalls is expected to save one-third of the portable's electrical heating bill. A retrofitted Solarwall will pay for itself in five to seven years—in half that time if it is incorporated into the manufacture of the portable. This is another example of a cost-neutral way to save money and energy and reduce carbon dioxide emissions through building retrofits.

Most nonrenewable energy is generated from fossil fuels. Burning these fuels creates carbon dioxide (CO_2), which scientists link to climate changes. Damages from extreme weather conditions cost insurance companies huge unforeseen payouts. No wonder 60 of the word's largest insurance companies signed a statement in 1996 urging governments to reduce carbon emissions, as they saw weather-related claims climb from $17 billion in the entire decade of the 1980s to $66 billion in the first six years of the 1990s.[32]

If residential and commercial buildings can reduce their use of fossil fuels by 25 to 75% of their 1990 level of use, there will be 25 to 75% fewer CO_2 emissions caused by that sector, benefiting the environment. There is no secret to how that reduction could be made. It requires design, insulation, super-windows that keep heat out or in, and energy-efficient appliances—all existing technologies. What's stopping us is not the need for a technological breakthrough. What's stopping us is a nearsighted insistence on unreasonable payback periods for retrofits, and a lack of awareness of the total benefits that can be achieved.

Doing It Right In New Buildings

New commercial buildings can produce even more impressive energy savings. Amory Lovins describes the ecologically built Rocky Mountain Institute, high in the snow-covered mountains of Colorado where the winters are long and cold. The building was built so energy efficiently that its greenhouse grows luscious tropical fruit year-round, uses passive solar heat for 99% of its heating, and has a monthly electricity bill of less than $5—before the credit from the energy utility for the extra electricity that the building feeds back into the utility's grid.[33] Expressed differently, this is a 100+% savings in energy.

The ING Bank's new 538,000-square-foot "organic" headquarters building in Amsterdam is an example used by Paul Hawken, Amory Lovins, and L. Hunter Lovins to illustrate that it doesn't cost more to design energy-efficient buildings.[34] Energy-saving systems paid for themselves in the first three months—the annual energy savings are $2.9 million per year, easily offsetting the extra $700,000 in construction costs. The building uses less than a tenth of the energy of its predecessor, a fifth of the energy used in a typical conventional office building in Amsterdam, and 92% less energy than an adjacent bank building constructed at the same time. Every office has natural air and natural light; heating and ventilation systems are largely passive, and no conventional air conditioners are used; indoor and outdoor gardens are fed by rainwater collected on the roof; absenteeism is down 15%, and productivity is up. The building took three years to design because the bank insisted that all employees and contractors understand and provide input for every detail—the workers even chose the site, ensuring it was close to most of their homes. The building uses local materials and is architecturally innovative, with curvilinear form, plants, artwork, and flowing water.[35] It works for the people, the bottom line, and the environment. The authors of *Natural Capitalism* go on to say:

> Although many developers assume green buildings must cost more to build, green design can actually *decrease* construction costs, chiefly by saving infrastructure expenses and by using passive heating and cooling techniques that make costly mechanical equipment unnecessary.[36]

A new building can even generate revenue by selling excess electricity back to the grid. How? If a building uses the latest energy-efficient design techniques and technologies, it will save 99 to 100% of its heating energy and 97 to 100% of its air-conditioning energy.[37] By tiling the building's roof with solar panels/shingles, a company could generate more electricity than the energy-efficient building requires and could become a net exporter of energy back to the local utility. This generates additional revenue and profit, which can flow straight to the bottom line, as was illustrated in figure 6.3.

Energy self-sufficiency has been attained in residential homes, which have much in common with commercial sites. Canada Mortgage and Housing Corporation (CMHC) sponsored the construction of a "Healthy House" in Toronto in 1998. It is a 1,700-square-foot, semidetached, three-bedroom family dwelling with four floors of living space on a vacant, infill lot in the Riverdale area of Toronto. Its total annual operating costs are under $300.[38] Of particular interest is how solar energy is used in combination with energy-efficiency features.

> Solar panels generate electric energy which can be stored for later use .... Energy efficiency is achieved through airtight wall and roof construction, thermally efficient windows and doors and high levels of insulation and weather resistance in the building envelope .... Triple-glazed, thermally efficient windows are strategically located to make maximum use of solar gain and minimize heat loss in winter. Solar radiant floors have been specifically designed to retain solar heat during the day and radiate it to the interior at night. Heat radiates not only from floors, but from ceilings. Sunlight is collected through solar panels and heat is retained. If required, warm water is circulated through pipes

> in the floors to supplement solar heat. The heating bill is estimated at $80 per year .... [In the summer], heat gain is controlled by window shading and moderated air flow. Efficient electrical appliances and gray water heat exchangers provide less internal heat gain and less need for air conditioning. Excess heat is radiated to the ground surrounding the house. Waste water system provides evaporative cooling through a heat exchanger.[39]

"All the really important mistakes are made on the first day," as the design adage says. Paul Hawken, Amory Lovins, and L. Hunter Lovins quote Joseph Romm in *Natural Capitalism* about how 80 to 90% of the life-cycle ecological costs of a typical building are made inevitable early in the design phase, long before the building has been built.

> Although upfront building and design costs may represent only a fraction of the building's life-cycle costs, when just 1% of a project's upfront costs are spent, up to 70% of its life-cycle costs may already be committed. When 7% of project costs are spent, up to 85% of life-cycle costs have been committed.[40]

It pays to think smart early...and to think differently. In *Green Development*, the Rocky Mountain Institute outlines the four key approaches required by development teams to enable improvements in savings:

- Whole-systems thinking, where one solution coincidentally solves multiple problems
- Front-loaded design, just mentioned above
- End-use/least-cost considerations (considering operational costs over time as well as initial design and construction costs)
- Teamwork among the developers, architects, construction workers, real estate brokers, tenants, and community members

None of these approaches can work alone—they are mutually reinforcing and all are required for the full potential benefits to be realized.[41]

Savings From Employees Taking Responsibility for Energy Savings

As mentioned earlier, educated, caring employees can make a difference to energy conservation in their day-to-day discretionary activities at commercial sites. Employees can save energy by turning off lights when they leave offices and conference rooms, using stairs instead of elevators when going up or down just a few flights, using the power-saving settings on their computers, and turning off their computers when they are out of the office. It is estimated that as many as 75% of computers and printers are left on all the time, even though they are used only infrequently. If employees simply turn them off at night and on the weekends, their energy costs can be cut by up to 75%.42 U.S. engine maker Pratt and Whitney, for instance, saved $200,000 per year ($50 for each monitor) with this measure.[42]

How else might educating employees help save energy? Suppose an employee arriving early one morning notices the lights were left on all night in his building module. He knows from his training that normally the lights would have been automatically turned off at 6 p.m. and turned on at 7 a.m. by a computerized lighting control system. Arriving before 7 a.m., he finds the module ablaze with light. He makes one phone call and the situation is corrected. Apparently the lighting-control program had been inadvertently erased during an electrical system upgrade the week before, and building management was not aware of the problem. If the early arriver had assumed it wasn't his problem, energy could have been wasted for months.

Employee awareness can be heightened by simply providing feedback to employees. In a housing project in the Netherlands, half the utility meters were installed in the basements as usual, and half were installed in the front halls where the residents could see them daily. In the houses where the meters could be readily seen, 30% less energy was consumed.[44] Perhaps there would be similar results if electrical meters were strategically and aesthetically located near the entrances to modules within office buildings?

Education yields awareness, and awareness enables responsibility and action. Educating employees and turning them loose on an eco-efficiency quest would be a fun way to improve the bottom line.

Savings From Water Conservation

Low-flow toilets and shower heads can reduce household water consumption by 50%. What works at home works in hotels. It only took Scandic Hotels about one year to pay back the $4,000 to install water-saving devices on taps in all hotel rooms, cutting water use in half without sacrificing guest comfort.[45] What works at home and in hotels would work at business or commercial buildings. A toilet is a toilet, regardless of where it is. There is no reason why toilets on company sites could not be low flow, saving water costs.

Sewage costs are usually based on the what-goes-in-must-come-out theory—they reflect how much water is used. If there is a reduction in the amount of fresh water purchased from the local utility, there is a corresponding reduction in sewage charges. Companies can reduce their need to purchase water simply by treating it themselves and reusing it in a closed loop system.

> John Todd of Living Technologies in Burlington, Vermont, has used biologically Living Machines—linked tanks of bacteria, algae, plants, and other organisms—to turn sewage into clean water. That not only yields cleaner water at a reduced cost, with no toxicity or odor, but it also produces commercially valuable flowers and makes the plant compatible with its residential neighborhood. A similar plant at the Ethel M Chocolates factory in Las Vegas, Nevada, not only handles difficult industrial wastes effectively but is showcased on public tours.[46]

Savings From Lower Landscaping Costs

A naturalized landscape that doesn't use pesticides and greatly reduces water consumption is a daily reminder to employees and passersby that the company cares. About 40 to 80% of a water utility's peak demand in the summer is driven by landscape watering, which can be reduced by about 50% by relatively modest improvements: using water-frugal grasses; growing flora indigenous to the region; and converting lawns into diverse native grasslands, bushes, and trees.[47]

As an added benefit, planting trees can offset the greenhouse gases created by employee travel. Dan Morrell of Future Forests has a beautifully simple formula for determining how many trees to plant. Seven trees will offset five flights between New York and London. Five trees will reabsorb one automobile's emissions for a year. Plant three trees, and you can enjoy ten hours of carbon-neutral train commutes each week for three years. The reality is much more complicated than that, and it depends on the species of tree, soil type, rainfall, longitude, latitude, and all sorts of other factors. Future Forests averages it out so that the figures stack up but don't complicate the message. They will plant trees for a company, on the company's premises or elsewhere, and they have more than 10,000 people and 52 companies signed up, including Avis, Tower Records, and Mazda.[48]

Interface Carpet Inc. has a similar program with Trees For Travel. Interface's CEO, Ray Anderson, suggests additional landscape ideas in *Mid-Course Correction*.[49]

- Leave as much habitat and vegetation as possible undisturbed by construction
- Landscape to promote biological diversity

- Design to minimize the impact on local environment
- Compost organic matter
- Mulch lawn clippings
- Put up bird boxes and start an employee-run nest box monitoring program
- Plant a butterfly garden near an area that employees use often
- Join the Wildlife Habitat Council
- Start an employee vegetable garden
- Create a series of nature trails for employees and their families or even for the whole community
- Xeriscape by using plants adapted to local rainfall conditions
- Use gray water to water the landscaping
- Highlight native plants that are adapted to the local environment and do not require a lot of maintenance
- Employ an organic approach to pest management to minimize the use of chemical pesticides
- Install storm water protection ponds to minimize volume and temperature spikes on local waterways from rain showers
- Create bird sanctuaries in migration paths

Savings From Reduced Office Space and Less Business Travel

By exploiting the potential of e-business and e-mail, computers and the Internet can significantly reduce the environmental impact of doing business. Computers and telecommunications eliminate the need for many office workers to commute every day. Some estimates indicate up to 20% of the workforce will be home-based by the year 2004.[50] The Stanford Institute for Quantitative Study of Society predicts that at least 25% of the workforce—32.3 million people—will telecommute or work from home by 2005; and JALA, an international group of telework and telecommuting consultants, forecasts 51 million U.S. workers telecommuting by 2030.[51]

Working from home offers benefits for employees, the environment, and businesses. The employee eliminates the time, expense, and hassle of commuting and may also experience a more enjoyable and relaxed working environment. Work/life balance improves for many employees. Telecommuting is good for the environment, which benefits from a reduction in vehicular emissions. It should also mean less road congestion, less blacktop, and more green spaces. In fact, the *Washington Post* on July 20, 1999, had a story about a legislative proposal to provide incentives to companies that encourage their employees to telecommute. The measure is designed to reduce traffic and improve air quality in the nation's five most congested areas by encouraging employees to work from their homes. Companies in cities such as Los Angeles and Washington DC would earn pollution credits for their efforts in reducing smog. The credits, determined by the vehicle miles eliminated by telecommuting, can be kept, bought, or sold by the businesses.[52]

Companies also benefit. Many companies have found that programs encouraging employees to work from their homes have reduced office lease costs by millions of dollars. It is estimated that 40% of 133 million workers nationwide perform duties that could be done by telecommuting, so the potential for savings is significant.[53] The icing on the cake is the potential for increased employee productivity. A Gartner Group study shows that telecommuting improves productivity by 10 to 40%.[54] At some point, even parking space costs can be saved if enough employees work from home.

As well as saving paper and office space, computers and telecommunications eliminate the need for many office workers to travel long distances for business meetings. For most, teleconferencing via the phone is already here. Video conferencing, which uses digital video cameras connected to home and office personal computers, has also become widely available and effective, with potentially huge pollution savings. For a meeting between two parties 600 miles apart, teleconferencing entails less than 1% of the carbon emissions of airline travel.[55]

The Potential Benefit From Reduced Expenses at Commercial Sites

As with the potential savings in the manufacturing area, it is difficult to make a detailed calculation for SD Inc.'s potential savings at commercial sites, but the checklist in the "Reduced Expenses at Commercial Sites" worksheet in the Appendix summarizes the assumptions and calculations used in this discussion.

Since energy costs are only about 2% of total costs in most industries, executives don't pay much attention to them.[56] What they overlook is that energy savings go straight to the bottom line and so represent a far greater percent of profits. If the cost of selling, general, and administrative (SG&A) expenses were about 15% of total revenue in SD Inc., and energy costs were 2% of that, they would amount to $132 million (2% of 15% of $44 billion). Let's lump water and consumables costs into that amount, to be extra conservative.

How much of this annual expense could be saved by an energized and informed employee population, backed by committed executives? Let's assume 20%, another conservative number considering the examples cited above. Therefore, the money saved by energy and material conservation at commercial sites would add about $26 million to SD Inc. profit (20% of $132 million).

Benefit 6: Increased Revenue/Market Share

The idea behind product differentiation is straightforward: companies create products or employ processes that offer greater environmental benefits or impose smaller environmental costs than those of their competitors. Such efforts may raise the business's costs, but they may also enable it to command higher prices, to capture additional market share, or both.

Forest Reinhardt[1]

SAVINGS ARE GOOD. Revenues are exciting. Business strategy is driven by revenue and shareholder value more than by cost and efficiency. A powerful rationale for sustainable development is enlightened self-interest, fed by the prospect of increased revenue, markets, and profits. Over time, societal expectations change. Companies should anticipate those changes and develop new practices, new products, new services, and new markets in advance.[2] Doing this before competitors do is the key to profits.

Environmental differentiation in the marketplace can be crucial to competitive product positioning. Forest Reinhardt, in a *Harvard Business Review* article, outlined three conditions necessary for environmental product differentiation.

1. Customers are willing to pay more for the product, recognizing the extra initial cost is offset by other savings.

2. There must be credible communications about the product's environmental benefits.

3. The company has to be able to protect itself from competitive imitators long enough to make a profit on its investment.[3]

Some conditions may be present today. All are possible tomorrow.

For example, CIBA Specialty Chemicals, a Swiss manufacturer of textile dyes, is charging more for dyes that require less salt to fix the dyes to fabric.

The increased cost of the dyes is offset by customer savings on salt, savings on treatment of bathwater containing salt and unfixed dye before flushing it, and lower rework costs because of higher quality dye fixation rates. CIBA can charge more for its dyes and capture some of the value of customers' lower environmental costs. Patents and complex chemistry protect CIBA's unique product so it can recoup the cost of years of research.[4] Similarly, a company might be able to charge a premium for more energy-efficient products if it educated customers about the savings they could expect on their energy bills by using the products.

The issue here is differentiation. When market leaders take action, their competitors often follow suit.[5] As soon as competitors have similar environmentally sensitive offerings, any competitive differentiation is lost. The half-life of competitive differentiation is becoming increasingly shorter as reverse engineering and corporate intelligence improves. That's why continuous innovation is essential to maintaining competitive advantage.

The payoff for a company that features the reduction of its product's energy requirements and environmental impact is improved brand image and brand equity. More specifically, this increased mind share will be furthered by:

- endorsements by external environmental agencies;
- increased "noise" around the products' environmental attributes; resulting in free publicity/reduced advertising costs for products due to environmental attributes.

Increased Mind Share From Endorsements by External Agencies

In marketing, mind share is an important concept. The marketing adage "Being first in mind is everything" emphasizes how important it is for your company to be the first one customers think of when they need your kind of product. When they think of sodas, do they think of Pepsi or Coke? When they think of personal computers, do they think first of Compaq, Dell, or IBM? Mind share is about perception, not product. It's about being first to associate your company with a word that resonates with your customers' needs and values. If your potential customers are looking for a product made by a caring, socially responsible company, do they think of you? If they are looking for an environmentally friendly version of a certain product, do they think of you? As consumers become more interested in these issues, you will benefit from positioning your brand positively in their minds.

In August 1999, to encourage product recognition associated with environmental factors, the U.S. Environmental Protection Agency (EPA) launched a new public-service television campaign promoting the government's Energy Star label for efficient, low-pollution consumer products (see Benefit 5 for more on Energy Star), similar to the Blue Angel eco-label program in Germany. The EPA wanted to highlight the relationship between energy use in the home and air pollution from power plants. "By purchasing Energy Star qualified products, individuals can play an important role in cutting the emissions that both pollute our air and contribute to climate change," said EPA administrator Carol Browner. The EPA originally estimated that if all consumers purchased Energy Star products and equipment over the next 15 years, the nation's energy bills would be reduced by $100 billion and annual pollution savings would be equivalent to taking 17 million cars off the road.[7] Six months into the program, the EPA raised its estimate to $200 billion savings if all consumers, businesses, and organizations in the U.S. made product choices and building improvements based on Energy Star standards over the next decade.[8]

Another factor that can boost a company's environmental image is publicly tracking its progress in cutting waste and boosting energy efficiency. This transparency enables third party organizations like ethical investment companies, environmental non-governmental organizations (ENGOs), regulatory bodies, communities, and industry trade associations to compare and track companies' progress on the sustainability journey. Japanese companies are embracing open reporting as a way to demonstrate environmental conscientiousness at a time when concern about pollution is rising across Japan following a series of public health scares. Major electronics firms NEC Corp. and Fujitsu Ltd. are among the companies that have released environmental balance sheets. Toyota, Japan's largest automaker, also has detailed its environmental activities, including overall spending on "green activities." The public relations payoff comes when companies are able to show the community that they are tuned to the environment issue.[9]

If these campaigns successfully educate the public to be more careful about the energy efficiencies of their appliance and computer purchases, then it will be important for companies to feature the energy efficiency qualities of their products. Unfortunately, there are few tricks for reducing a given system's energy consumption once it is built, other than just turning it off when it's not in use. Consumers' energy efficiency comes down to purchasing energy-efficient products in the first place, from companies whose brand imagery radiates their corporate social and environmental responsibility.[10] That's why designing products to be energy efficient is vital for earning the public's trust.

Sometimes the third party doing the assessment is a consumer magazine. The impact of a magazine's product ratings can be significant. In 1994, *Consumenten Bond*, a Dutch consumer rating magazine, reviewed 24-inch stereo televisions on four environmental dimensions: energy consumption, recycling, materials, and use of hazardous materials. Nokia and Aristona were rated "best buy," while Sony TVs were rated "reasonable."

> In the month following the test, Sony's market share in The Netherlands for this specific product fell by 12% while Nokia's increased by 57% and Aristona's by 100%. In terms of gross revenue, Sony stayed the same, Nokia gained 73% and Aristona 113%.[11]

The example highlights how a product's environmental qualities influence sales and thus the bottom line of a company. Businesspeople love scorecards. Suppose executives were asked to self-assess their sustainability approaches against a five-stage Sustainability Continuum, based on ideas from Carl Frankel's book *In Earth's Company.*

- **Stage 1: "Regulatory Compliance."** Obey the law and meet all environmental regulations; contain pollution spills and emissions
- **Stage 2: "Public Disclosure."** Publicize environmental policy statements and annual environmental reports with publicity campaigns; prevent pollution
- **Stage 3: "Beyond Compliance."** Voluntarily commit to bettering regulatory emissions requirements, with oversight at the board level; exploit eco-efficiency "low-hanging fruit" for short-term energy and material efficiencies; focus on end-of-pipe solutions and "greening up" of existing products and packaging
- **Stage 4: "Corporate Sustainable Development."** Model a socially responsible business, based on sustainability and value-based principles; focus on front-of-pipe solutions such as zero waste, using only renewable energies, whole-systems thinking and "deep green" design for the environment; view sustainable development as a business opportunity; lease rather than sell; provide services rather than products
- **Stage 5: "Global Sustainable Development Leadership."** Proactively model corporate stewardship of the long-term "global problematique;" shift the business paradigm to include social as well as environmental aspects of sustainable development; encourage

> responsible consumption; look outward by promoting technology transfer to smaller companies and developing countries to address their environmental problems; practice industrial ecology where one company's wastes become another company's raw material[12]

It is useful to tap into the competitive motive. Executives' self-assessments of where their company and their competitors stand on this spectrum would spark a lively and informative dialogue within the company, between companies in the same industry, and with the public. So would public assessments by third parties. That's why the development of common Environmental Performance Indicators (EPIs) for public reporting is receiving so much attention. EPIs would include annual or per-product measures of:

- Energy consumption and efficiency
- Toxic releases into water
- Water consumption
- Hazardous and non-hazardous waste
- Packaging
- Air emissions
- Expenditures on compliance and environmental management systems
- Energy, water, and paper consumed by office employees
- Travel by company employees
- Stakeholder interaction
- Health and safety[13]

The EPIs would be publicly reported annually and would contribute to improved corporate image and reputation as third parties compared, benchmarked, and ranked competing companies.

> The image a company projects through its presence and action helps sell its products and services to customers. Strong environmental performance, communicated through the use of EPIs, can provide quantitative evidence that you are managing environmental issues responsibly. The simple act of measuring and reporting this information, both the good and the bad results, will assist you in promoting your company as willing to be responsible and accountable for your actions

> and open to scrutiny. A positive environmental reputation improves customer relations, and addresses the concerns of community, the general public, and environmental groups.[14]

Related to EPIs are techniques that help a company understand how stakeholders feel about projects that have environmental or social impacts. Using focus groups and questionnaires, a company can determine what stakeholders value and can then quantify the overall stakeholder opinion about a certain project. This analysis may identify factors that are not normally included in EPI lists but are important when assessing the potential downside of proceeding with an environmentally risky project. The authors of *The Green Bottom Line* describe a Stakeholder Value Analysis (SVA) toolkit, which includes a Multi-Attribute Decision Environment (MADE) tool to quantify a wide array of less tangible stakeholder-valued criteria, a sensitivity analysis model, and a model for financially quantifying a wide array of environmental attributes.[15] The sophisticated methodology is especially useful when making difficult environmental investment decisions.

Measurements are critical for three reasons. First, they clarify exactly what sustainable development is and monitor social and environmental progress against specific attributes. Second, they help engage senior management, especially if the measurements are consistent with traditional investment measurements. Third, they enable clear and consistent reporting to internal and external stakeholders by providing a range of common measurements. Common environmental performance indicators are gaining acceptance. Good social responsibility measures need more development.[16]

Various groups are working to develop generic EPIs from which each industry or organization could voluntarily select an appropriate set. In 1993, nine leading North American corporations formed the Public Environmental Reporting Initiative (PERI) and published a set of draft environmental reporting guidelines.[17] The Coalition for Environmentally Responsible Economies (CERES) was launched in 1989 and has published environmental principles and reporting guidelines that are now endorsed by more than 50 companies.[18] The Canadian National Round Table on the Environment and the Economy (NRTEE) is also developing a set of eco-efficiency indicators.[19] Perhaps the biggest commitment, though, is to the Global Reporting Initiative.

> The Global Reporting Initiative (GRI) was established in late 1997 with the mission of developing globally applicable guidelines for reporting on the economic, environmental, and social performance, initially for corporations and eventually for any business, governmental, or non-

> governmental organisation (NGO). Convened by the Coalition for Environmentally Responsible Economies (CERES) in partnership with the United Nations Environment Programme (UNEP), the GRI incorporates the active participation of corporations, NGOs, accountancy organisations, business associations, and other stakeholders from around the world.
>
> The GRI's Sustainability Reporting Guidelines were released in exposure draft form in London in March 1999. The GRI Guidelines represent the first global framework for comprehensive sustainability reporting, encompassing the "triple bottom line" of economic, environmental, and social issues. Twenty-one pilot test companies, numerous other companies, and a diverse array of non-corporate stakeholders commented on the draft Guidelines during a pilot test period during 1999–2000. Revised Guidelines were released in June 2000.
>
> By 2002, the GRI will be established as a permanent, independent, international body with a multi-stakeholder governance structure. Its core mission will be maintenance, enhancement, and dissemination of the Guidelines through a process of ongoing consultation and stakeholder engagement.[20]

It is worth noting that paralleling this shift to increasing transparency and including social and environmental measures in public reports at the corporate level is a movement at the national level to replace the Gross Domestic Product (GDP) with the Genuine Progress Indicator (GPI). The GDP has become the foremost indicator of economic progress, but it is a flawed indicator because it lumps together all products and services bought and sold without distinguishing between transactions that add to well-being and those that diminish our quality of life. That is, the GDP treats crime, divorce, and natural disasters as economic gain; it ignores the non-market economy of household and community; it treats the depletion of natural capital as income; it increases with polluting activities and then again with cleanups; and it takes no account of income distribution. The GPI corrects for these factors, builds on the GDP, and takes into account 20 aspects of our economic lives ignored by the GDP. It is a much better measure of all three economic, environmental, and social dimensions of sustainable development and should replace the narrow GDP as a true measure of national progress.[21]

Returning to the corporate level, the trend toward standard sustainability measurements makes it easy to do internal and external benchmarks of environmental performance and to credibly communicate progress to all stakeholders. It also ensures results. A common business axiom is "What gets measured gets done." The real value to companies of doing good comes when they are seen to be doing good, or at least to be doing better than their competitors. As it markets environmentally superior products produced in demonstrably more sustainable ways, a company's competitive advantage will feed its growing pride in its accomplishments.

Differentiation implies some measure for comparison—it's hard to tell who's ahead when you're not keeping score. It's not enough to do well. To gain competitive advantage, you have to do visibly better. By using the standard measures described above, companies can show this advantage.

Increased Mind Share From "Noise" About Environmental Products

Strangely, few companies help create "noise" around the environmental attributes of their own products. Companies seldom trumpet their investments in "design for environment" (DfE) efforts to build environmental considerations into the entire product-design process. An example cited in *In Earth's Company* is the IBM PS/2 E personal computer, which was introduced in 1993.[22] A fully loaded PS/2 E (the "E" stood for environment) operated at a maximum of just 24 watts, significantly lower than the Energy Star's 30-watt requirement for bare-bones units. It had many eco-features including design for disassembly and the use of recycled content. It used energy-efficient PCMCIA technology—credit card-sized cards for fax/modems. It was so energy efficient that it did not need a fan for cooling. IBM applied strategic environmental management principles in the PS/2 E design and development process, resulting in benefits to the manufacturing company, the consumer, and the environment. I worked for IBM in 1993, but until I read about the PS/2 E in Carl Frankel's book, I had not known about its environmentally friendly attributes. The internal company hype about the environmental attributes of the product was as quiet as the external "noise." It's understandable that consumer awareness was low.

Instead of hiding the environmental characteristics of a product or being silent about them, the company should issue press releases about how environmentally friendly the product is, feature the product at trade shows, hype it in trade magazines, talk about it in advertising, feature the environmental characteristics on the product packaging, and generally make it clear to consumers that choosing the product will benefit the environment. Environmental characteristics are an important criteria for some consumers, and companies should make it easy for them to know which products are eco-friendly. No noise, no knowledge. No knowledge, no sale.

If companies were smarter, they would capitalize on free publicity and reduced advertising with some showmanship about the environmental attributes of their products. Car companies are starting to do this. The novelty of fuel-efficient cars and fuel cell-powered vehicles attracts the press. So does a little theatrical staging. Greenpeace got more publicity from a demonstration in which it used a solar-powered PC to protest nuclear energy than the computer company did. Companies that are the first to feature the environmental attributes of their products—how about a solar-powered PC on a remote island hideaway?—will benefit the most from free publicity.

The Funnel: Differentiate or Die

To emphasize the opportunity for competitive advantage by switching to sustainable strategies, Karl-Henrik Robert, the founder of The Natural Step, uses a funnel metaphor to illustrate how companies are being squeezed by declining resources and increasing customer, competitor, and regulator pressures.

> Many big transnational companies have already suffered economically from public stigmatization due to unethical ecological and/or social behavior. There are also many examples of big transnational companies that have benefited from taking a clear social and ecological stand and from the international dissemination of such standards, thus leveraging the companies' impact for the public good. In addition, there are many examples of business corporations that have suffered economically from increased resource costs, increased costs of waste management, new rules from international business agreements, etc. Part of the economic pressure that many firms are beginning to encounter is due to increased competition from proactive business corporations that are learning how to anticipate and avoid problems far in advance of their competition.[23]

Interface's 1997 *Sustainability Report* echoes this warning.

> We believe that institutions that continuously violate these [sustainability] principles will suffer economically. The walls of the funnel will continue to impose themselves in the form of environmentally concerned customers, stricter legislation, higher costs and fees for resources and waste, and tougher competition from companies who anticipate the narrowing limits and adjust accordingly. The failure of institutions and business to begin to address sustainability not only leads to hitting the funnel wall—wasted effort, energy, money and resources—but further constricts the funnel itself in the long run.[24]

The Funnel
Unsustainable Business
DECREASING: resources, waste disposal options, diversity and health of living systems, corporate image, top talent
Margin for action to avoid hitting the walls
INCREASING: regulations, prices for resources and waste disposal, risks, market pressures and competitiveness, populations, "green consumer" demands, gap between rich and poor
Sustainable Business
Sustainable Business Strategies
Sustainable Practices
Restorative Practices

Figure 8.1 The Funnel

The companies who get to the "sustainable practices" neck of the funnel first (see Figure 8.1) will be the winners. The "early-mover advantage" is a competitive weapon because it gives these early movers longer timetables to develop innovative technological solutions, which can then be licensed to laggards as international regulators tighten standards, urged on by the early movers.[25] It's not a question of if the funnel will tighten; it's a question of when. The losers will disappear from the corporate map of the world as if they had committed commercial suicide.[26]

For retail companies, ensuring good relations with their local communities is critical to attracting clientele. From the time the company applies to locate in the community until it is in full operation, local residents can determine the success of the enterprise. If they sense that the quality of life and the quality of the environment in their local community will be adversely affected by the company, local residents will resist project start-ups, facility expansions, or ongoing developments. An active sustainable development program helps ensure good public relations with the local community.

If a corporation were to rework its processes, products, and services to reap the short-term low-hanging fruit and long-term benefits of sustainable business practices, it would be better positioned than its competitors when government environmental regulations become tighter, raw materials become more scarce, the talent wars heat up, etc.. It would navigate the ever-constraining walls of the "funnel" better than its competitors.[27] By anticipating relevant environmental factors whose increase or decrease could impact its business strategies and by taking preemptive action, the company will strengthen its competitive position. Instead of using competition as an excuse for inaction, the triple bottom line of sustainable development sparks the business case for action and investment.[28] Consequently, the funnel will become a noose for unprepared companies.

Increased Market Share From Attraction of "Green" Consumers

The payoff for differentiation is increased market share as "green" consumers seeking "green" products are attracted to a company's products and services. Sustainability may become a new form of value that society will demand.[29] Government purchasing policies that favor green products, and other economic incentives for environmentally sound products and services, certainly get corporate attention. Green products reduce their impact on the environment in one or more ways: they are produced by a resource- and energy-efficient manufacturing process; they use recycled materials in the product or packaging; they consume less energy or water in their usage; they create less waste by lasting longer or being biodegradable; and/or they produce health benefits for consumers.[30] That is, they are eco-designed to minimize their environmental impacts over their life cycles.

"Designer beef" is an example of a green product—the consumer gets the health benefit of meat from cattle not exposed to herbicides or hormones, while the environment benefits from fewer pollutants.[31] The market for organic produce is growing 20 to 30% per year, in spite of a price premium; it now totals over $9 billion.[32] In 1999, sales of organically grown food doubled in the U.K., even at premium prices, which reinforces that green consumers are becoming a market force.[33] Interestingly, this is the only part of the food business that is growing.

There is some risk associated with a company offering green products, especially if it offers both a green product line and a conventional product line. Some environmentalist consumers may flag the company's efforts as insincere, pointing to the company's retention of a non-green product line. On the other hand, the green product line could create a significant green halo effect, benefiting the company's entire portfolio of products.

> If corporate concern for the environment is consistent with the other signals the company is sending to customers, then the environmental goods the company is providing get bundled with the quality of the company's products, the company's statements about the importance of ethical behavior, the customer's own concern about the environment, and the customer's relationship with the company, in the same way that environmental benefits and private consumption benefits are intertwined for consumers of organic vegetables or "designer beef."[34]

How big is the green consumer market? Estimates vary. Forest Reinhardt's analysis of survey data suggests that green goods and luxury goods seem to attract similar buyers: better educated and wealthier consumers.[35] After assessing the results of several consumer surveys done in the 1990s, Carl Frankel concludes that the proportion of actual green consumers who are prepared to pay more for green products is probably fairly steady at 10% or less of the population.[36] He discounts surveys that yielded higher estimates by citing the "halo effect" in human research, which can cause respondents to give what they perceive the surveyor would think was the "right" answer in an attempt to please the researcher. He also concludes that the 60% of Americans who say they care about the environment are professing an opinion on a transitory issue rather than expressing a deeply held ideology.[37] That's the bad news.

The good news is that there is evidence that environmental considerations have settled into the public consciousness as a second-tier consideration for the everyday consumer. John Elkington warns that what seems like a soft, spongy consumer shift in values can turn almost overnight into concrete-hard opposition—"soft" values like concern for future generations are superseding traditional "hard" values like the paramount concern for the financial bottom line.[38] Frankel graphically describes green consumers as the superficial whitecaps on a powerful sea change in environmental consumer power.[39] He points to the growing interest in alternative therapies, organic food, and "natural" products. The chicken-and-egg dilemma of supply-and-demand for environmentally friendly products is being solved by innovative and farsighted companies. Once the barriers of availability, convenience, and price are breached, the green consumer wave will swell and wash away unprepared suppliers.

Would customers pay more for green products? Maybe. Future Energy Research Corporation, a U.K. manufacturer of environmentally friendly fuels from biomass waste, found that 71% of home owners are interested in buying their electricity from renewable energy sources, and as many as 45% would be willing to pay more. One in five householders questioned said they would pay a premium of as much as £5 ($7.78) per quarter for electricity produced from renewable sources.[40] As cited under Benefit 2, a 1999 study by Ernst & Young and Martiz Automotive Research showed that 40% of Canadians would pay more for "green" cars. Of these, 42% would be willing to pay $2,000 more for this type of vehicle, 11% said they would be willing to pay $5,000 more, while the balance would pay between 0 and $500 more.[41]

Doug Miller, president of the polling company Environics International, has identified four quadrants of consumers based on his company's 1999 fourth annual International Environmental Monitor Survey.[42] The quadrants, in Figure 8.2, show the relationship between the level of environmental and social activism and the consumer's willingness to pay for green products—it shows what consumers do, versus what they say.

> The data shows significant elasticity of demand as soon as the issue goes "top of mind" for consumers. A key element for business is timing: research says there will be another "green wave" over the next 20 years driven by consumer preferences, and forward-thinking firms will be well poised to serve changing demands and emerging markets.[43]

Other surveys say consumers would not pay extra for green products. However, by applying creative approaches to manufacturing and design, environmentally friendlier products and services need not be more expensive

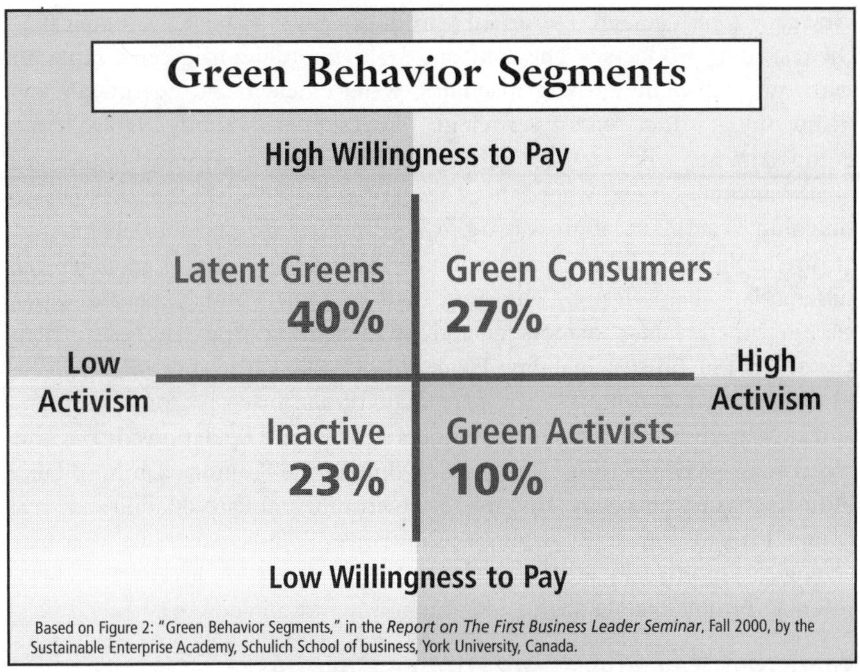

Figure 8.2 Green Behavior Segments

nor lower in quality. That's when consumers will choose the greener product. In 1997, 76% of consumers polled said that — assuming no difference in price or quality — they would switch brands to align themselves with a good cause.[44]

It is also important to ask the right question about costs. Are the costs in question the initial costs or the lifetime costs? A $15 to $20 compact fluorescent light bulb clearly costs more than a 75-cent incandescent light bulb if only the purchase costs are compared. However, the compact fluorescent will last ten times longer and save two to three times its cost in electricity over its lifetime.[45] It's actually cheaper, and the mindset that sees this longer term perspective is gradually penetrating consumer purchasing decisions.

This is encouraging news for those companies adopting sustainability principles in their business strategies. More encouragement is provided by the possibility of higher margins. Electrolux research has found that over 90% of its appliances' lifetime environmental impact occurs after they leave its manufacturing plant and are operated by customers.[46] Customers seem to be aware of this and are willing to pay a premium for long-term environmental benefits and operating savings. In 1996, Electrolux found that its environmentally improved or environmentally beneficial product line (e.g., solar-powered lawn mowers, chain saws lubricated with vegetable oil, high-efficiency appliances, etc.) returned a profit margin that was 3.8% higher than the rest of its products.[47] The company is also appealing to green consumers with water-efficient washing machines, water-efficient and energy-efficient dishwashers, and energy-efficient stoves with subdividable oven compartments. By 1998, sales in Electrolux's Green Range of environmentally friendly appliances accounted for 16% of total sales (based on volume) and 24% of gross margins.[48]

In the hotel industry, Scandic hotels have proven that companies can differentiate themselves by engaging their customers and employees when creating their values statements and by benefiting from the value their customers put on sustainability. From almost going bankrupt in 1991–93, Scandic regrounded itself in the core value of *omtanke*—profound caring—and embraced sustainability in its business strategy and operations. It has now soared past its competitors. For the first time in the Scandinavian hospitality industry, a hotel chain has made environmental sustainability a real competitive advantage. By seizing this initiative, Scandic has shown that true ecological approaches are not a cost, but a source of green customers, revenue, profits, market share, and competitive advantage.[49]

Increased Revenue From Higher Customer Retention/Loyalty

There is financial benefit from increased customer retention due to greater product loyalty as a result of innovation and environmental performance. Patagonia has parlayed its credible commitment to conservation into a hard-to-imitate brand of outdoor clothing for high-income customers who care about the environment.[50] The Body Shop has built a loyal following from its environmental and social initiatives. Neither of these companies sell cheap products, but loyal customers come back because they identify with the values of the company from which they are buying.

That point is worth emphasizing. Loyal customers are attracted to the company as much as the product. Company values matter as much as product features, as shown by the Scandic Hotels example. This is reminiscent of the ability to attract and retain employees whose values resonate with a company's corporate social and environmental responsibility. Employees value sustainable development. So do customers.

New Markets

Focusing on corporate social responsibility can not only expand existing markets, but it can also open up entirely new markets. The gap between rich and poor is widening, and poverty can be one of the biggest obstacles to sustainable development. Conventional wisdom says the world's four billion poor people are desperately trying to survive, and environmental protection is not likely to be high on their list of priorities. However, in 1999 Environics researchers quizzed nearly 30,000 people in 27 countries, both rich and poor, and found that in poor countries more than half of respondents believe that their health has been harmed a great deal by pollution; in rich countries, this view is held by only about a fifth of those surveyed. When asked if they were willing to pay a 10% premium for a greener cleaning product, two-thirds of respondents in Venezuela and half of those in China, India, and Egypt agreed strongly; in Britain, France, and Japan, barely a fifth thought it worth their while.[51] That creates an opportunity for companies to creatively help the poor, while at the same time using initiatives in underprivileged markets to incubate sustainable technologies of the future.

How? Stuart Hart, director of the Sustainable Enterprise Initiative at the University of North Carolina, describes how areas of abject poverty may be the counterintuitive new frontier for business growth in the 21st century.[52] He describes how subsidiaries of Unilver, Arvind Mills, Citigroup, and Johnson & Johnson are actively developing strategies for markets at the bottom of the pyramid. In India, a Unilever subsidiary has created a new, lower-polluting detergent with a drastically reduced ratio of oil to water for washing clothes in rivers and public water systems. The company has developed new manufacturing, distribution, packaging, and pricing systems to enable the new detergent to be successful. Arvind Mills sells ready-to-make Ruf and Tuf jeans kits for $6 (versus the usual cost of $40 to $60 for a pair of finished jeans) to a network of 4,000 tailors in India, which has made Ruf and Tuf the highest-selling brand of jeans in India. Citigroup has partnered with the United Nations to provide microloans of under $15 and has a goal to provide basic credit to the 100 million poorest families in the world. Johnson & Johnson is helping to distribute solar-powered ultraviolet water purifiers to villages in the developing world, at a cost of about 10 cents per villager per year. These four companies are using these frontier markets as proving grounds for technologies that will later replace unsustainable products and processes in the industrialized world—a paradoxical South to North technology transfer.

Usually business does not focus on poverty alleviation, income distribution, basic infrastructure, or basic literacy. However, Carl Frankel, one of North America's leading authorities on business and sustainable development, has described additional noteworthy social efforts by responsible companies. He writes about Eskom's Electricity For All program in South Africa, which goes beyond just electrifying homes.

> What Eskom has set out to do is integrate these new users of electricity into the industrial economy. It does so through an Energization Package that provides basic infrastructure services to individual households, such as a water pump with electricity, and then tops that off with community-support services such as projectors and videos for schools.
>
> It also functions as a job creation program. Eskom hires residents from nearby neighborhoods to construct and maintain the local electricity system. Over 6,300 people work in construction and materials manufacturing for the program and an additional 1,000 are employed in marketing and administration functions in newly electrified areas.
>
> There is also indirect job creation. Electricity flips the switch on all sort of new business opportunities; Eskom estimates that between 10 and 20 new enterprises are launched for every 100 homes electrified.
>
> It's one thing to start a new business, another to make a success of it. Again Eskom is lending a helping hand. The company provides technical and financial support to small businesses. It has also created a small business development franchise that aims to support electricity-intensive franchisers in emerging markets. By supplying technology, creating infrastructure, and building capacity, the company is making a genuine and significant contribution to social and economic development in South Africa—and securing the foundations for a future business for itself in the process.[53]

Frankel also describes how Hewlett-Packard and Cisco Systems are looking for ways to make a digital dividend by tackling the digital divide.[54] HP's new venture, World e-Inclusion Services, targets the world's poor with the aim of applying information technology to address five types of need: health and telemedicine, education, broadening access to markets, boosting employment, and expanding access to credit. Similarly, Cisco is partnering with the United Nations Development Program by funding a Netaid.org website in support of the "eAction" program, which fights extreme poverty by enabling people to volunteer their time, make cash donations, and purchase fair-trade arts, crafts, and food. The intent of the HP and Cisco projects is to use information technologies to help reduce social and economic disparities, and at the same time provide access to new markets.

These initiatives in very poor markets have social and environmental benefits. The challenge of making them profitable requires breaking old business paradigms and leads to new ways of collaborating with consumers who are wise to the local culture and circumstances that must be respected.

Companies develop techniques for contending with markets where people have no normal infrastructures like postal addresses, plumbing, phones, or electricity. The creative and innovative solutions forced by these conditions provide a platform for innovation in developed markets, which can lead to leapfrogging competition.

This is sustainable development business strategy at its purest: making money by improving social conditions using state-of-the-art technology founded on high ecological principles. While raising the bottom of the world's population pyramid is the responsibility of all institutions, the private sector has the resources, leverage, and power to play a central role in this endeavor. Poverty provides the greatest threat, and poverty alleviation the greatest opportunity for business. The markets opened up are where tomorrow's companies will be competing for market share. The first companies in will have the competitive edge when sustainability moves past the tipping point and becomes ubiquitous.[55]

Increased Profits From "Dematerialization"

What if repeat customer business was built in to a product? What a compelling approach to customer loyalty that would be. Customers automatically renew their business with you when they lease services instead of buying products outright. Changing the business model from purchase to service will allow the supplier and the customer to make money the same way. Dematerialization—selling services instead of products—is also the ultimate in environmental sensitivity, since product take-back is automatic.

> The business model of traditional manufacturing rests on the sale of goods. In the new model, value is instead delivered as a flow of services—providing illumination, for example, rather than selling light bulbs.[56]

That is, the focus is no longer on producing products, increasing throughput, and making large energy- and capital-intensive investments. Instead, it shifts to bundling services, selling end-use value, and ensuring cradle-to-cradle product stewardship. Under Benefit 4, I described Interface's Evergreen Lease.[57] Other companies are adopting the service model and decoupling growth from material resources. Elevator giant Schindler, for example, prefers leasing vertical transportation services to selling elevators, because leasing lets it capture the savings from its elevators' lower energy and maintenance costs. Dow Chemical and Safety Kleen prefer leasing dissolving services to selling solvents because they can reuse the same solvent scores of times, reducing costs. United Technologies' Carrier

Division, the world's largest manufacturer of air conditioners, is shifting its mission from selling air conditioners to leasing comfort.[58]

A variation on this theme is "shared savings," used by chemical companies to sell chemical performance instead of chemicals. "Performance fees" are paid each month when "performance expectations" are met. A good example is the Pay-As-Painted program under which Chrysler pays its paint supplier, PPG, a fixed amount for each vehicle that leaves the paint shop with a finish that meets Chrysler's performance expectations for a quality finish.[59] Similarly, Ford has subcontracted to PPG/Chemfil the Total Fluids Management and Total Solvent Management programs at its Taurus assembly plant in Chicago. Ford pays PPG/Chemfil a fixed monthly fee for managing the inventory, tracking, distribution, and environmental/quality control of chemicals, which remain the property of PPG/Chemfil until used by Ford.[60] DuPont has a similar arrangement with Ford in the U.K., and saved about 8% in costs each year in the first two years, while increasing its market share in the automotive painting business from 25 to 75%.[61] General Motors also has a Chemicals Management Program with its chemical supplier, BetzDearborn, at a truck and bus assembly plant in Janeville, Wisconsin.[62]

The idea of selling services instead of goods is used by computer companies, too. Large companies have made innovative contracts that involve leasing computing, not computers. This approach works with smaller businesses, as well. In August 1999 the New York Times reported that for a $165 monthly charge per user, Centerbeam Inc. is offering business customers fully loaded PCs, a wireless network, and a high-speed phone line. Founded by Sheldon Laube, the former chief technology officer for Novell and Price Waterhouse, Centerbeam will provide all management and backup services, and the PCs will be upgraded at least every two years. Laube says, "The whole idea is you don't buy computers any more. You buy a service from us and we buy all the pieces and worry about making them work."[63]

Interestingly, leasing also reverses the motivation behind the throw-away society. Instead of using planned obsolescence to boost sales, manufacturers are encouraged to make more durable products with a longer lease lifetime. The longer the product lasts, the more profit for the companies. They get rich by reducing the amount of material used to make our possessions and by manufacturing our possessions to last longer. The steady flow of monthly leasing payments stabilizes the peaks and valleys of volatile sales. It reduces the need to maintain manufacturing capacity to meet peak demand, another source of waste and risk. When they become service providers, manufacturers' long- and short-term incentives become perfectly attuned to what customers want, the environment deserves, labor needs, and the economy can support.[64]

Product longevity gives corporations a competitive advantage when it enables longer warranties on any products that are still sold instead of leased. Happily for the environment, longer durability avoids waste and overflowing landfill sites. This is another win-win proposition for corporations and the environment.

New Revenue Opportunities From Environmental Services

Stuart Hart points out that business not only has a responsibility to do no harm by not polluting, but it also has an opportunity to profit by being restorative.

> The achievement of sustainability will mean billions of dollars in products, services and technologies that barely exist today. Whereas yesterday's businesses were often oblivious to their negative impact on the environment and today's responsible businesses strive for zero impact, tomorrow's businesses must learn to make a positive impact. Increasingly companies will be selling solutions to the world's environmental problems .... Those who believe that ecological disaster will somehow be averted must also appreciate the commercial implications of such a belief: over the next decade or so, sustainable development will constitute one of the biggest opportunities in the history of commerce.[65]

Consulting companies already understand there's big money to be made in sustainability services. Arthur D. Little has specialized in environmental consulting for years. The auditing firm KPMG has launched Sustainability Advisory Services (SAS) through a unique agreement with the Body Shop International to combine KPMG's globally known expertise for auditing with the Body Shop's acknowledged expertise in social reporting. This service will address a new and growing marketplace that in the U.K. alone is expected to be worth some $33 million in fees within three years. Internationally, KPMG currently employs some 150 professionals worldwide in the area of environmental reporting and has completed reports for leading companies such as Royal Dutch Shell and ICI. It is now adding to this expertise with SAS, which will help companies develop and assess their performance in social and environmental management.[66]

There are software opportunities as well. On August 24, 1999, Reuters reported that Fujitsu had begun selling software and related services in Japan, allowing companies to improve the management of their environment-related activities. Fujitsu said it expects cumulative sales of over $400 million from the new business by 2003. The software series will enable uniform compilation and management of environment-related information, such as data on the use of chemical substances in manufacturing processes or data required to design easily recycled products. The software will also help companies draw up so-called green accounting reports on their environmental record for investors and consumers. Green accounting measures environment-related spending and tracks progress in cutting waste and boosting energy efficiency.[67]

The Potential Benefit From Increased Revenue and Market Share

So what's the bottom line from the increased mind share, market share, revenue, and profits? Let's assume that our hypothetical SD Inc. gains favorable publicity for its environmentally friendly operations, products, and services. More revenue is generated from new green customers, and these customers loyally continue to purchase the company's products; the company adds a new revenue stream by leasing its products instead of selling them; the company launches a services business to help other companies improve their sustainable development; and the company charges a premium for its more environmentally friendly products. See the "Increased Revenue and Market Share" worksheet in the Appendix for a detailed calculation that outlines each of the benefits described above.

Given these diverse new revenue opportunities, let's conservatively assume SD Inc. generates just 5% more revenue. That's not a big percentage, but it's big bucks. Just 5% of SD Inc.'s revenue of $44 billion is $2.2 billion. Assuming the percent of this incremental revenue that flows to the bottom line is the same as that of today's revenue, 7% of this increased revenue would be added to the profit line (today's $3 billion of profit is 7% of today's $44 billion of revenue). That yields about another $150 million of profit (7% of $2.2 billion).

BENEFIT 7:
REDUCED RISK, EASIER FINANCING

For many businessmen, environmental management means risk management. Their primary objective is to avoid the costs that are associated with an industrial accident, a consumer boycott, or an environmental lawsuit. Fortunately, effective management of the business risk stemming from environmental problems can itself be a source of competitive advantage.

Forest Reinhardt[1]

EVEN WHERE WE CANNOT precisely quantify the financial benefits of environmental action, we can at least recognize the risks of inaction. In January 1999, KPMG undertook a survey to establish the profile of risk management practices in Canada's leading organizations.[2] The business leaders were drawn from Canada's top 500 companies as ranked by the Financial Post. KPMG's survey found:

- 95% of executives define risk as any potential threat to meeting objectives.
- Market risk, strategic risk, and risk of recession are cited as major risks in 1999 and 2000.
- 85% of executives believe an effective risk management strategy is either very important or critical to achieving the goals and objectives of their organization.
- Most executives indicate their existing risk management function entails the identification, mitigation, and minimization of risk. Only 9% indicate their risk management function is proactive, and just 7% indicate the function is used to anticipate surprises.
- 92% of organizations undertake contingency planning; 67% perform regular crisis management reviews.

- 55% of executives adjust their required rate of return on investments for risk.

Innovest, an investment research firm specializing in environmental finance and investment opportunities, uses its proprietary EcoValue'21 analysis method to show there is a significant and growing correlation between industrial companies' eco-efficiency and their competitiveness and financial performance. According to EcoValue'21, large-scale investors, lenders, and insurers assess six basic financial risks when they are considering investing in or insuring large projects or companies.[3]

1. Market risk
2. Balance sheet risk
3. Operating risk
4. Capital cost risk
5. Transaction risk
6. Eco-efficiency and sustainability risk

Other investment firms use other frameworks. I will use a slightly different list of five risk categories to integrate all of them and to show how sustainable approaches to a company's manufacturing processes and operations can reduce each risk.

1. Lower market risk
2. Lower balance sheet risk
3. Lower operating risk
4. Lower capital cost risk
5. Lower sustainability risk

Lower Market Risk

There are several risks to the revenues of companies that do not practice sustainable development. Some threats are customer driven and some are precipitated by government regulations. I will describe four market risks and how sustainable development practices reduce each.

- **Lower probability of regulatory bans or restrictions on sales.** Regulatory agencies are looking harder at some products that have been linked to environmental degradation, like pesticides, dioxins, furans, CFCs, lead, and elemental chlorine. Manufacturers can lower this risk by finding environmentally friendly substitutes for any of their products likely to be banned by more stringent regulations.

- **Lower risk of reduced market demand for core products or services**. A corollary to the threat of regulatory restrictions is the threat of customers no longer wanting or needing your product or service. For example, a waste hauler may experience a drop in revenue if companies reduce their waste or if the hauler's disposal practices are discovered to cause ecological harm. An industry may counter unfavorable public perception of its products' effect on people and the environment by investing in advertising to ensure its image is a positive one—the chemical industry's Responsible Care campaign is an example.[4] In addition to developing more environmentally benign products, companies can launch service and consulting businesses to offset lower revenue from sales of products likely to be banned.

- **Lower chance of core product/service quality being reduced by environmental degradation**. If your business depends on a healthy environment and the environment is deteriorating, your business is at risk, even though your own operations may not be causing the devastation. Recreation and tourism are threatened by coastal pollution and forest degradation, often accelerated by pollutants coming from remote sources. Local fisheries are threatened by the devastation of fish stocks by other countries' factory ships. Climate changes ruin historically healthy farming areas. Companies can lobby aggressively to try to reduce the root causes of environmental degradation, but they may also need to explore alternate sustainable business opportunities in the short term.

- **Lower chance of customer boycotts or reduced product acceptance**. As consumers become aware of what some companies' operations and products are doing to the health of the planet, they may take action. There have been backlashes against forest products made from old-growth forests, phosphate detergents, and non-recyclable consumer goods. Companies usually react to these consumer pressures, but it is less expensive to anticipate and avoid these situations. Companies in the manufacturing, mining, oil, forestry, fishing, and food industries are the most susceptible to activists. They can reduce the risk of consumer boycotts by adopting sustainable business practices. They should also initiate open dialogues with the communities where they operate, with concerned customers, and with upset activists to negotiate solutions that work well for all parties.

Boycotts or reduced acceptance can be a huge factor in business decisions, so I will include a few more examples. Forest Reinhardt, a business professor at the Harvard Business School, describes how Alberta-Pacific Forest Industries was almost stopped from logging a vast tract of government-owned aspen and spruce forests in northern Alberta. Aboriginal residents, local farmers, and environmental activists from around the world protested the pollution from the planned mill and the devastation of traditional clearcutting methods. The whole project was in jeopardy until the company redesigned the mill to drastically reduce chlorine and other pollutants, introduced better forest management practices, established meaningful dialogue with the community, and provided recreational access to the woods. The costs of these changes were small, especially compared to the high stakes of having to log in Indonesia or Brazil, where the political and exchange rate risks are much greater. Alberta-Pacific's small investment in the environment helped it reduce market risk, achieve more stable long-term costs, and profit from more sustainable use of the forest.[5]

Most businesses believe "it couldn't happen to us" when it comes to being the target of consumers' environmental action. That's what IKEA, the world's largest retailer of home furnishings, thought. Brian Nattrass and Mary Altomare describe how the company was blindsided in the mid-1980s.

> In 1981, Denmark established a new law regulating the maximum emissions allowed from formaldehyde off-gassing of particleboard, which is a component of many IKEA products. According to [Karl-Olof] Nilsson [in IKEA's Group Staff Environmental Affairs], although the law seemed very strange to IKEA at that time, they simply requested that their suppliers follow it. The Danish authorities decided to test compliance with the new law and found that furniture companies were paying very little attention to it. Being one of the largest companies operating in Denmark, and with headquarters located there, IKEA became the focus of a new and aggressive public campaign. The government tested products from IKEA and found that some products had formaldehyde emissions above the legislated limit. A television program drew dramatic attention to the issue. IKEA was sued for violating Danish laws and assessed a fine. The fine, however, was minimal compared to the damage done to IKEA's image and sales, which temporarily dropped by about 20 percent in the Danish market.[6]

IKEA worked with its suppliers and its suppliers' suppliers to correct the problem. It also began to be criticized for its packaging waste, its use of PVC plastic, and the environmental impact of its famous full-color catalogs. It worked hard to correct these problems, but just when the company thought it had turned the corner on this issue, IKEA hit its second environmental wall.

> In 1992, IKEA faced yet another and totally unexpected formaldehyde crisis. This time it was in IKEA's largest market, Germany, with one of its biggest sellers, the globally popular Billy bookshelf, which represented many millions of dollars of revenue per year to IKEA. Tests conducted by an investigative team from a large German newspaper and television station found formaldehyde emissions for the Billy bookshelf to be just slightly higher than the legislated requirement. This time the culprit was not the particleboard itself—which was the part of the bookshelf that was actually regulated by law—it was the lacquer on the bookshelves. The regulatory details did not matter to the press. The impact of the coverage mattered a great deal to IKEA. Glenn Berndtsson, current head of IKEA's quality division, recalls: "It was in all the newspapers and all the television stations throughout the world: 'the deadly poisoned bookshelves.' From Hong Kong to Australia, we had to put a stop on all sales of Billy bookshelves. We stopped production worldwide."[7]

How much did this corporate nightmare cost IKEA? A lot!

> Berndtsson estimates that the direct cost just to track the bookshelves and correct the situation was between U.S. $6 million and U.S. $7 million at that time, not counting the cost of diverted manpower, lost sales, lost production by suppliers, or the costs and time it took to persuade customers to return to IKEA to buy the bookshelves. Altogether, this one incident cost IKEA and its suppliers tens of millions of dollars to correct.[8]

MacMillan Bloedel took a similar hit when Greenpeace and other environmental activists decided to pressure its customers to stop buying from a clearcutter and heavy chlorine user. MacBlo lost 5% of its revenue almost overnight when Scott Paper and Kimberley-Clark in the U.K. stopped buying its products.[9]

Now the pervasive Internet has radically increased the volume of consumer word-of-mouth and activist demands. PricewaterhouseCoopers' magazine, *Risky Business*, described a 1999 survey by *CEO Magazine* and

Hill and Knowlton Corporate Watch, which revealed CEOs' nervousness about how a company's reputation can be damaged by rogue websites.

> The top Internet-related concern for CEOs was the risk of unhappy customers and disgruntled employees venting dissatisfaction online. CEOs are right to worry. The Internet has created a fundamental shift in the way companies must interact with their critics. Rumor mongering, stock fraud and consumer activism are not new. But a decade ago, a dissatisfied customer might have complained to perhaps 10–20 people about his negative experience. Today, that same individual can set up a web site and reach millions. "You can spend millions of dollars to build a strong brand. One person on the Internet can destroy what took a team of people years to build," says James Alexander, co-founder of eWatch .... Ultimately, the Internet is the core driver of the increased importance of corporate reputation and its management.[10]

The Internet makes it easy to communicate internationally and to organize individuals into large and significant global groups. This has dramatically changed the power dynamic between corporations and citizens. A company can lose its reputation overnight as a result of poor market risk management. Risks related to corporate social responsibility are important potential flash points, as individual and institutional stakeholders flex their new-found ability to rally support for activist causes.

In a wired world, companies can mitigate risk by actively engaging in two-way communication with their communities and consumers, either via the Internet or in face-to-face dialogues. By being open and transparent, they can learn, forge new relationships, spur market growth, and reduce risk exposure by building a foundation of trust. Too often corporations withdraw, become defensive, or offer "no comment" when they find themselves doing damage control. By engaging in open and honest discussions with all their multilevel external communities, especially before unfortunate events happen, companies will be in a much better position to reduce market risks.

Lower Balance Sheet Risk

The five risks in this category show up as liabilities on the balance sheet, if they are accounted for at all. Depending on the industry you are in, some are more likely than others to apply to your company. It is prudent to think through which risks might affect your company and how you might use sustainable practices to lower that possibility.

- **Reduced remediation liabilities**. Polluted land needs to be cleaned up and this can be expensive. The U.S. Superfund is spending billions of taxpayers' dollars to restore sites contaminated by toxic waste, but the government's preferred approach is to force the polluter to pay for the cleanup. A company can forecast how big its remediation liability might be by multiplying the forecasted magnitude of the contamination by the likelihood of its occurrence.[11] If several parties might be held accountable for the damage, then you need to determine the portion allocated to your company when sizing up the magnitude of the risk profile.[12] Legal fees often outweigh cleanup fees, as the guilty parties attempt to minimize their liabilities. Preventing land contamination in the first place is a strategic investment and reinforces the wisdom of treating the environmental management center as a profit center.

- **Lower insurance underwriting losses**. Companies carry insurance to protect themselves against losses from rare occurrences like fire, theft, or big accidents. However, if you are an insurance company and accidents happen more frequently than your actuarial department anticipated, you have to scramble to raise your rates to recoup losses from unexpectedly high payouts. In the last decade, insurance companies have become increasingly concerned by damage claims from storms and floods. In 1998, violent weather displaced 300 million people and caused upwards of $90 billion worth of damage, representing more weather-related destruction than was reported through the entire decade of the 1980s.[13] According to Swiss Re, the world's second-largest reinsurer, the figures soared to over 105,000 deaths and costs of about $100 billion in 1999, but fell back to 17,000 deaths and about $38 billion in damages in 2000.[14] Given the connection between greenhouse gases and climate change, Swiss Re and other European reinsurers are pressing hard for international policies to reduce fossil fuel dependency and increase use of more climate-safe technologies.[15]

- **Less chance of impairment of real property values**. Old, leaking, buried storage tanks and toxic waste ponds on company property reduce the property's value. Manufacturing buildings saturated with toxic waste are worth less and can even flip from the asset side of the ledger to the liability side. Companies practicing sustainable development have less risk of delays, disruptions, or cancellations of divestitures because of environmental liability concerns, and they will have lower financial and staff costs from unanticipated due diligence requirements. Lower asset values not only impair the sale price of the company, but also reduce the asset base against which the company can borrow investment capital for growth. By practicing sustainable operations and cleaning up its premises, a company can reduce this risk.

- **Less probability of damage assessments**. Who wants to be the next Union Carbide, recovering from a Bhopal disaster? Suppose a high-tech manufacturing facility and its chemical farm were hit by a tornado. Who is liable for the resulting damage and pollution outside the perimeter of company property, far beyond what would be mitigated by even the most progressive contingency plans? The resale value of any contaminated company property is also significantly affected—no one wants to buy the risk and cleanup responsibility. Reducing dependency on toxic chemicals reduces the possibility of high-profile disasters, the sullying of the company's reputation as a result, and the liabilities on the company balance sheet.
- **Less risk of "toxic torts."** There is a risk of employees bringing a civil action against employers for workplaces deemed to be dangerous to their health, such as ones insulated with asbestos. Outside groups may file damages against polluting companies or their executives. From 1990 to 1995, a record number of Canadian corporate executives were convicted of environmental offenses (2.5 executives per year). Total annual environmental fines in excess of $1 million are not uncommon in the resource sector.[16] So-called intangibles around ethical issues can suddenly become very tangible when a lawsuit is initiated, and even if the company wins the case, the legal costs can be very high. Companies that eliminate toxic substances in their workplaces and manufacturing processes reduce the risk of toxic tort liabilities.

Lower Operating Risk

Another category of risks may lead to additional expenses. If any of these risks came to pass, they would be covered with money from operating budgets, which might be an unpleasant surprise. If the expenses were sudden and severe, they could jeopardize the company's survival.

- **Reduced costs of cleaning up spills and accidents**. Severely contaminated land is treated as a liability on the balance sheet, whereas a company normally treats the cost of cleaning up accidental spills and releases and the costs of associated fines and penalties as expenses. Most major companies pay for these costs from their operating budgets instead of insuring against these spills.[17] Companies that do pay environmental insurance premiums would add those costs to cleanup expenses. By practicing sustainable development and eliminating the offending substances from their operations, companies lower or eliminate the risk of these expenses being incurred.

- **Lower risk to worker safety from handling hazardous materials**. By definition, hazardous materials are dangerous. Employees handling hazardous substances risk injury, and employers must spend significant amounts to address that eventuality. For example, Chevron is investing more in sprinkler systems, rapid response teams, maintenance, and other systems to reduce risk, as well as working on the human factor by increasing emphasis on safety training programs.[18] These typical company efforts to reduce accidents cost money; so do the worker insurance premiums paid by the company and time lost by injured workers. All these expenses can be eliminated by eliminating hazardous materials from the workplace.
- **Less burden of expensive regulation-driven process changes**. "Pay me now or pay me later." This saying captures the notion that sooner or later companies will be forced to change manufacturing processes that violate evolving environmental legislation, as happened when CFCs were eliminated as a cleaning agent in high-tech manufacturing plants. Companies that want to protect their right to continue operating may face significant unplanned compliance costs, which could be avoided by phasing in the redesign of their processes to remove their dependence on the offending substances.
- **Less chance of reduced process yields**. In natural resources industries, yield is an important factor in success—the more product that is obtained for a given extraction expenditure, the more profitable the company will be. Agriculture, forestry, fishery, and farming industries are susceptible to climate change and environmental regulatory pressures, which may increase what they have to spend to yield the same amount of product. Companies that become eco-efficient are more likely to counter this challenge as they reduce the energy, water, and materials they require to produce their products.
- **Lower impact if raw materials and energy prices increase**. Eco-efficiency also reduces a company's dependence on raw materials that may become more expensive as their own yields suffer. Energy prices

may increase as governments deregulate the energy market or levy environmental taxes on high energy users. Again, companies that become eco-efficient are more likely to weather these price increases as they reduce the amount of energy, water, and materials they require to produce their products.

Lower Capital Cost Risk

Three risks may lead to capital investments instead of higher operating expenses. They may require significant capital outlays to upgrade manufacturing or waste treatment processes.

- **Less product redesign to meet new industry standards or regulations**. A company must redesign a product containing newly regulated substances or a process that violates newly implemented environmental regulations. For example, refrigerator manufacturers had to redesign their products to use refrigerants other than CFCs, and pulp and paper mills are having to meet stricter effluent standards than ever before. Products and processes that are designed using design for the environment (DfE) principles avoid the risk of these significant capital expenditures.
- **Lower cost of input substitution to meet new industry standards or regulations**. Sometimes regulations require companies to use substitute recycled materials for raw materials, at least to some degree. Important customers may order paper products and require that they contain a certain amount of post-consumer recycled fibers. The government may impose a regulation which requres that the plastics used in your products contain recycled plastic or materials other than plastic. Styrofoam packaging may have to be replaced with material that is more eco-friendly. These are not simple changes and may require purchasing new equipment or building new production lines. These expensive retrofits can be avoided by considering the most environmentally friendly materials and processes during the design phase of new products.
- **Lower waste treatment and pollution control expenses**. On-site facilities to treat hazardous waste, reduce harmful emissions, or treat wastewater before flushing it into the municipal sewer system can be expensive. You can avoid these capital investments by not using harmful substances in the first place.

Lower Sustainability Risk

Competitive and regulatory pressures can jeopardize a company's success. In particular, companies will be threatened as sustainability practices are adopted by competitors and as governments require more product stewardship. The next three risks are in this general sustainability category, with expense and revenue implications.

- **Less competitive disadvantage created by energy or material inefficiency**. It's one thing to be expensive; it's another to be more expensive than your competitors. If your competitors are practicing eco-efficiency and benefiting from lower energy and material costs, and you are not, you are at a competitive disadvantage. The earlier discussion of energy, material, and water efficiencies in manufacturing and commercial sites (Benefits 4 and 5) suggested ways to turn this risk around on your competitors.
- **Lower impact of mandatory product take-back, recycling, and life-cycle stewardship costs**. There is a risk that companies will be required to take back their products, and maybe even their competitors' products, instead of having customers throw them away when they are finished with them. Product collection and disassembly logistics can be expensive if the company did not design the product for these contingencies.
- **Less exposure to potential future taxes and regulatory restrictions**. Activists are lobbying for eco-taxes on non-renewable energy, especially carbon taxes on fossil fuels. The more a company can wean itself from dependency on products or services likely to be subject to eco-taxes in the future, the safer its financial health will be.

Understanding and attending to these five classes of risk yield financial returns, whether these are measured as a return on investment or as total stock market returns. It's good business.

> The strategic self-interest of corporations involves being astute about the current reality in which their operations take place and being aware of trends, opportunities, and risks that will affect their operations and profits in the future.[19]

Lower Cost of Capital: It's Easier to Attract Investors

A derivative of the benefit of lower risks in the above areas is the ability to raise capital in the marketplace more easily, as the impact of these risks spills over into market valuation. Innovest has just completed a review of eco-efficiency using its EcoValue'21 environmental rating model. After an analysis of five years of data on over 300 Fortune 500 companies, the report quantifies how companies with better environmental performance achieved superior stock market performance.

> Superior eco-efficiency turns out to be a remarkably robust—and empirically demonstrable—proxy for superior, more strategic corporate management, and therefore for superior financial performance, and shareholder value-creation. In the long run that out-performance premium appears to be in the range of 230 to 240 basis points per year for a broadly diversified portfolio such as the Standard and Poor's 500. The out-performance margin increases to over 400 basis points for portfolios concentrated in high risk areas such as petroleum and chemicals.
>
> In the longer term, the out-performance potential will become even greater. As the capital markets become more fully sensitized to the financial and competitive consequences of eco-efficiency considerations, they will come to reward superior corporate performers even more heavily. Once this occurs, the out-performance gap will widen significantly, and investment performance gains of 500 basis points and even more will become achievable. It is that value potential which the EcoValue'21 platform was specifically created to uncover and exploit.[20]

In fact, computer-sector companies with above average EcoValue'21 ratings outperformed companies with below average ratings by over 2500 basis points of total stock market return over 18 months.[21]

EcoValue'21 just considers environmental factors. The Jantzi Social Index created by Michael Jantzi and Associates, a leading Canadian provider of social and environmental research for institutional investors, is a more complete benchmark of companies practicing sustainable development. The index carefully screens companies on their business practices, community relations, diversity, employee relations, environmental practices, human rights, and product safety, and tracks a portfolio of stocks in 60 companies that a socially responsible investor might purchase. These companies outperformed both the Toronto Stock Exchange (TSE) 100 (by 82 basis points) and the TSE 300 (by 158 basis points) from the beginning of 1995 until the end of 1999.[22]

Investors are attracted to companies by the prospect of increased returns due to lower risk, lower costs, higher revenues, and higher profits. Three critical drivers of profitability potential are corporate agility or adaptability, the durability of a firm's competitive advantage, and the quality of its strategic management. A company's environmental and social performance is an increasingly potent proxy for, and predictive indicator of, all three of these drivers.[23]

How much better do these companies perform? The Innovest EcoValue'21 and Jantzi Social Index measured the improved performance in stock price basis points, as shown above. A 1990 KPMG study expressed the out-performance as a percent.

> Research shows that firms that took their environmental impact seriously performed about 5 percent to 10 percent better on the stock market over the past 10 years.[24]

It gets even better than that. The Environmental Value Fund (EVF) found the companies with the best environmental track records outperformed others by 10% in just five years.[25] The EVF used a Sustainability Index based on ozone depletion and global warming impacts, material efficiency, toxic releases, energy intensity, water use, environmental liabilities, and quality of the environmental management system.

> EVF applied the selected criteria to the world's largest 500 companies, and found that the average rate of return in this group of companies over the last five years was 12%. In contrast, the top 20 companies in the group [according to the Sustainability Index] had a rate of return of 14% over the same period. Finally, the best 74 companies according to the criteria that EVF eventually invested in have had an annual rate of return of 22% over the past five years.[26]

A similar study by the Sustainable Development Group showed the average share price of strong practitioners of sustainable development outperformed the Toronto Stock Exchange 300 index by 10.9% from August 1995 to August 1997—just two years.[27] Investors will soon be taking notice of the Dow Jones Sustainability Group Index, set up in 2000 to track the performance of 200 companies that rate highly on environmental and social responsibility.[28]

So much for the myth that investors must accept some financial sacrifice when making a deliberate choice to invest only in environmentally or ethically commendable companies.

> Pro-environment activities will not adversely affect share price; and socially screened portfolios by and large achieve similar results to portfolios selected from the full universe of available stocks. The results

> would appear to refute the argument that pro-environmental activities adversely affect bottom line performance.[29]

However, we should understand that sustainable development is not a silver bullet. Only when associated with strong leadership, sound business strategies, financial fitness, innovation, employee motivation, and quality products will environmental drivers make a difference. There are no guarantees in business, and certainly there is no guarantee that other factors will not erase the positive possibilities from pro-sustainability initiatives.

> But positive bottom line and cash flow impact will not necessarily lead to improved shareholder value in terms of increased share price which can be affected by a variety of other issues such as interest rates, technological innovation and exchange rate differences .... What [studies] do seem to suggest is that improved environmental performance does not appear to act as a brake on profitability or share price performance as compared with non (or less) environmentally conscious companies.[30]

Other observers have serious concerns about how some analytical approaches try to relate environmental and financial performance by simply using a set of performance indicators and checklists:

> This approach is severely limited because the performance indicators are neither tailored to nor reflective of the issues faced by the individual company or industry. They reflect past and present environmental concerns and may miss important upcoming issues. Neither are such indicators prioritized or weighted in accordance with their potential financial significance. Moreover, the coverage and quality indicators tend to be limited by the data in public databases. The information on environmental management doesn't signify management effectiveness nor does it distinguish between proactive or reactive organizational responses. However, the severest limitation of this approach is the absence of any direct linkage between indicators and any measure of shareholder value or financial risk. This approach leads to parallel measures of environmental and financial performance, rather than an integrated evaluation.[31]

Regardless, there are a growing number of sustainable development-based rankings of companies, which affect them as they go to the stock market to raise money. Companies also go to banks. Lenders consider many factors. The most important environmental factor affecting the interest rate is the element of risk. Most major banks employ senior environmental managers to assess the cumulative environmental risk associated with lending money for mortgage holdings, land acquisitions, etc..[32] For example, the Royal Bank and the Canadian Imperial Bank of Commerce (CIBC) evaluate a company's environmental risk prior to investing or lending money.[33] They consider a good environmental management system a key indicator of reduced risk, and environmental audits will likely eventually be an integral part of a loan application.[34] Why? Because if the bank has to foreclose on its loan, it may suddenly find itself the owner of the property, financially liable for any environmental damage done by the failing company.

Banks have clout. As the Swiss Bank Corporation says:

> It is becoming increasingly apparent that the banking industry's main contribution to sustainable development will be to assess companies' ecological quality as well as their financial creditworthiness. This applies equally to credit rating, investment banking and investment recommendations.[35]

To prove the point, Swiss Bank was one of four banks that provided Kvaener, a leading international engineering company, with a revolving credit facility of several hundred million U.S. dollars in 1995, at a rate that was "a few basis points" cheaper than the standard rate, partially because of Kvaener's good environmental record.[36]

The Potential Benefit From Reduced Risk

It's total time. The sum of the financial benefits of reduced risk is a fruit salad of cost avoidance, lower insurance premiums, reduced legal and regulatory costs, preferred rates on loans, greater investor appeal, and avoidance of lost revenue from consumer activist actions. Depending on the accounting techniques used, these would be accounted for in the operating expenses listed on annual income statements, or in the liabilities listed on balance sheets. Some of the risks may not be allowed for at all, acknowledged with a simple blanket note to shareholders in the annual report explaining that "it is difficult to predict with certainty the amount of capital expenditures that will ultimately be required to comply to future standards."[37] Or a company may lump environmental liabilities with other potential liabilities and dismiss them all.

> The company is subject to a variety of claims and suits that arise from time to time in the ordinary course of its business, including actions with respect to contracts, intellectual property, product liability and

> environmental matters. The company does not believe that any current action will have a material effect on the company's business, financial condition or results of operations.[38]

They could be right—nothing may happen. Or like Ikea, Shell, or MacMillan Bloedel, they could be wrong. In an extreme case, a disaster could wipe out the business. Quantifying the benefits of risk reduction is extremely difficult. Even if it's not possible to quantify all the risk factors, however, just thinking through which ones are important is beneficial.

An excellent methodology for financially quantifying multiple risks associated with sustainable development is described by Robert Repetto and Duncan Austin in a report for the World Resources Institute, *Pure Profit: The Financial Implications of Environmental Performance.* They used a scenario-planning approach to aggregate the financial exposure of 13 U.S. pulp and paper companies to several pending environmental issues.[39] The generic approach that Repetto and Austin used could be applied to any industry sector or company:

- **Identify salient future issues**. Identify future environmental, social, and economic forces that are likely to have significant financial impact on the company within the time frame of the assessment (e.g., the next ten years). Consult with experts from government agencies, industry, environmental and social activist groups, consultants, and scientists. Research published literature. Use a matrix of the forces for change (e.g., market prices and availability, regulations, changes to taxes and subsidies, liabilities, and other risks outlined earlier) and the stages of the product cycle (e.g., supply of raw material, manufacturing process, product output, post-consumer take-back) to identify the key "value drivers" over the range of the product cycle.

- **Build scenarios around each**. Define the range of plausible outcomes associated with each issue. Develop two or three scenarios for each issue.

- **Assign probabilities to each scenario**. Especially do this for the best- and worst-case scenarios.

- **Assess company exposure to these issues**. Have industry or company experts rank each issue based on the magnitude of its potential impact on earnings, its timing (the sooner it happens, the greater its impact), and its probability.

- **Estimate financial impacts contingent on the scenarios.** For the forecast period, first build baseline financial forecasts using industry and company trends. Use a valuation technique (e.g., McKinsey's entity discounted cash flow model, or Stern Stewart's Economic Value Added model) to equate the value of the company to the sum of the discounted present values of all its separate cost, revenue, investment, and financing streams. Then, for each scenario, quantify the outcomes in terms that can be used in a financial analysis (e.g., impact on prices, production costs, revenues, expenditures, investments required, and balance sheet liabilities) for each year in the forecast period. If appropriate, do this for individual company locations. Reduce these year-by-year amounts to discounted present values using an estimate of the weighted average cost of capital. Add these present values to obtain the net financial impact for the combined scenarios, and express this as a percentage of the company's current market valuation.

Using this approach, Repetto and Austin's assessment of 13 pulp and paper companies' exposures in 1998 to 2010 ranged from +2.9% to -10.8% of the companies' current market value, with 12 of the 13 companies affected negatively and most of the companies potentially facing a loss of 4 to 8% of share value. Some companies were poorly positioned for the issues in the scenarios and would face relatively high capital costs to meet regulatory standards or to mitigate other risks. This would put them at a competitive disadvantage if they covered the costs with price increases, or would make them unable to afford other capital expenditures if they absorbed the costs.

This is an important point. Companies sometimes mislead themselves, believing that their relative competitive position will be protected if potential regulatory or other risks actually happen, since their competitors will be subject to the same statutes to a similar degree. Think again. The above study showed a wide range of financial impact on companies in the same industry, depending on how well positioned they were for the impending environmental issue. That's why Repetto and Austin favor a scenario-based comparison of companies, rather than a checklist approach, when assessing their attractiveness as an investment.

It would be impossible to do a credible scenario-based hypothetical projection of the impact of selected risks on SD Inc. I will use a more simplistic methodology. Since risk will ultimately hit either expenses or revenues when and if it happens, I will bundle the financial benefit of reduced risk into savings and cost avoidance. Previously I estimated SD Inc.'s selling, general, and administrative (SG&A) expenses to be 15% of total revenue, or

$6.6 billion based on revenues of $44 billion. Assume just 5% of the SG&A expenses are risk-related, and 5% of that amount would be reduced by more proactive company social and environmental initiatives. This yields about $16.5 million of reduced expenses. Compared to a potential 5 to 20% revenue loss as experienced by MacMillan Bloedel and IKEA from just market risk—proportionately, a $2.2 to $8.8 billion revenue loss for SD Inc.—this is an extremely low and simplified estimate. That's why the scenario-based methodology outlined above deserves serious consideration by financial folks to ensure the risk reality in their situation is more thoroughly accounted for (see the "Reduced Risk" worksheet in the Appendix).

Conclusion

> *Environmental problems are best analyzed as business problems. Whether companies are attempting to differentiate their products, tie their competitors' hands, reduce internal costs, manage risk, or even reinvent their industry, the basic tasks do not change when the word "environment" is included in the proposition .... Companies aren't in business to solve the world's problems, nor should they be. After all, they have shareholders who want to see a return on their investments. That's why managers need to bring the environment back into the fold of business problems and determine when it really pays to be green .... Imaginative and capable managers who look at the environment as a business issue will find that the universe of possibilities is greater than they ever realized.*
>
> Forest Reinhardt[1]

Real Bottom-Line Benefits

As stated earlier, a Mercer/Angus Reid poll found that the most important issue occupying the attention of Canadian CEOs in 1999 was profitability. "Increasing profitability" was chosen by 30% of the Canadian chief executives polled as their first concern, the highest of any priority selected.[2] The only ways to increase profit are to reduce expenses and increase revenue. More pervasive environmental strategies help reduce recruiting, retention, manufacturing, and operating expenses. They also increase revenue by helping to increase employee productivity, expand markets for existing products and services, spark opportunities for new products and services, lower business risks, and contribute to long-term competitive advantage.

> Numerous case studies show that companies leading the way in implementing changes that help protect the environment tend to gain disproportionate advantage, while companies perceived as irresponsible lose their franchise, their legitimacy, and their shirts .... Not surprisingly, University of Oregon business professor Michael Russo, along with many other analysts, has found that a strong environmental rating is a "consistent predictor of profitability."[3]

There is a causal chain linking environmental education, environmentally oriented business processes, marketing strategies, and improved business results. In a 1998 article, Scott Johnson used a modified version of Robert Kaplan and David Norton's "balanced scorecard," which they outlined in the *Harvard Business Review* in 1996.[4] Johnson's four-point balanced scorecard for business links environmental performance to strategic performance in this causal chain.

- *Learning, innovation, growth, and people.* This part of the scorecard assesses how well the company trains employees in life-cycle analysis, life-cycle costing, design for the environment, and overall environmental principles. It then looks at how effectively management empowers employees to take action in their departments with this knowledge.
- *Internal business processes.* This element of the scorecard evaluates how well the company designs processes to reduce environmental costs.
- *Customers and external stakeholders.* Thirdly, the scorecard assesses whether the processes produce environmentally superior products that benefit customers.
- *Finances.* Finally, as the acid test, the scorecard asks how the first three steps led to increased revenue and market share, reduced expenses, and higher profits.

The links in this value chain have been explored in this book. The opening hypothesis was that the bottom-line benefits of more pervasive attention to sustainable development strategies could be identified and quantified. Assumptions made have been supported by research and are deliberately conservative, to ensure credibility. Even so, the total benefits for the hypothetical SD Inc. company are over $3.36 billion of increased revenue and savings, and $1.15 billion of increased profit as the savings flow straight to the bottom line (see the "Total Bottom-Line Benefit" worksheet in the Appendix). CEOs concerned about profitability, take heed.

Not all benefits would be realized in the first year. You must be prepared to take a longer term perspective.

> As with other business problems, the environmental strategy that maximizes short-term cash flow is probably not the one that positions the company optimally for the long run. That's true of all business strategies in general, of course, but it especially applies to the environmental arena because benefits from environmental investments are often realized over long periods.[5]

Three years may be too short a period to accomplish the changes, yet ten years would seem like forever. Suppose the ramp-up of potential savings took five years. In the first year, only 30% of the full benefits would be realized, with 50% in the second, 70% in the third, 90% in the fourth, and 100% in the fifth. Even so, the percent return on the annual environmental education investment ranges from hundreds to thousands. The net present value of the $11 billion total five-year benefit is $9 billion (see "Total Bottom-Line Benefit" in Appendix). Not bad. That's why treating sustainability as a profit center makes so much sense.

"Yeah, but ..."

If the business case is so good, why are smart executives not taking advantage of it? There are four potential reasons.

1. They are not aware of the business case.
2. They are aware of the business case but don't believe it.
3. They believe the business case but are uneasy about setting themselves up for accusations of "green-washing."
4. Their entrenched mental model dismisses the sustainability consideration as irrelevant to business.

They Are Not Aware Of The Business Case

First, there is a very real possibility that the productivity benefits, expense savings, revenue increases, and profit improvements of sustainable development have not been effectively communicated to business executives. You may find that your fellow executives are distracted by the urgent problems of the day, not focused on the important issues of tomorrow. Sustainability seems like a future or irrelevant and abstract issue to some. Just the word "environmental" may have a left-wing or anti-business connotation to many executives. Their mindset about environmental initiatives has been historically rooted in compliance issues, not productivity improvements or new revenue streams, so it is no surprise that they might be uncomfortable with the elements in the business case. They are convinced that environmental report data cannot be readily translated into a measurable contribution to bottom-line profitability in the company's annual report. In fact, traditional accounting methods may not discretely identify environment-driven costs and may just lump them into overhead, or neglect them. Many companies have not instituted the proper infrastructure to evaluate environmental costs against a baseline.

Therefore, it is critical that you use the language and values of mainstream business when you attempt to catch the attention of executive colleagues who are driven solely by bottom-line considerations. The worksheet in the Appendix deliberately uses the business language of quantified benefits to bridge the gap. It helps show the direct relationship between sustainable development initiatives and business results, although not always apparent, is very real, both in the short term and the long term.

They Are Aware Of The Business Case, But Don't Believe It

The second reason why executives have chosen not to aggressively pursue environmental strategies to yield business benefits is that they don't believe the benefits. Why not? First, they may be suffering from a blend of the "NIH" syndrome, the "ten dollar bill" syndrome, or other defensiveness mechanisms. The Not-Invented-Here (NIH) syndrome inhibits you from adopting someone else's good ideas, especially a competitor's, that you didn't come up with first on your own. Admitting that another company's environmental innovation has value implies that you were not smart enough to see it first, a problem that is especially prevalent with managers whose job it is to discover savings in their own areas. The "ten dollar bill" syndrome is a corollary to this. Michael Porter and Claas van der Linde used the example of accountants carefully walking around $10 bills lying on the floor because they assumed that if the money were real, someone else would have already picked it up.[6] They may also be so convinced they have already cleaned the floor that they are blinded to the remaining financial "litter" still waiting to be picked up. Just because environmental benefits become evident, it doesn't mean that managers were stupid for not recognizing them earlier, or that the benefits are any less real because they haven't already been taken. Learning and thriving require some degree of humility.

There is another credibility hurdle for the business case. Each line item in the worksheet makes sense, but when the multiplication factors are applied, the resulting benefits seem too large to be believable. One way to reduce this objection is to claim low, conservative factors, as I did with the SD Inc. calculations used in the worksheets. Another way is to plug in your own factors. That's the real value of the worksheets—senior management can substitute its own numbers and percentages in the productivity, savings, and revenue calculations.

They Will Be Accused Of "Green-Washing"

Another underlying concern inhibits companies from publicly trumpeting their more aggressive corporate social responsibility strategies: executives are uneasy about being accused by environmental activists of paying lip service to environmental concerns and co-opting environmental language for their own selfish gains. "Green-washing" occurs when companies pretend they care and claim they are environmentally and socially responsible, but their track records do not yet validate their claims. This duplicity may be deliberate or may be the accidental result of different perspectives, strategies, and actions by the environmental management and other departments in large, complex companies.[7]

The willingness of business to exploit the green label epitomizes the very worst and most deceitful characteristics of the so-called free market economy. Sometimes, instead of genuinely changing business practices, processes, and products, the response of corporations has been to cash in on the green bandwagon in a cynical exploitation of the latest market fad.[8] Companies need to be aware that once they have used warm platitudes and slick promotional literature, they are committed. Company environmental data and trends will be watched carefully to ensure that specific actions follow words and slogans in advertising. IKEA North America is an example of a company that wants to ensure its products can withstand environmental scrutiny and that its employees are ambassadors for its actions before it goes public.

> It is not part of IKEA North America's plan to advertise itself as being environmentally friendly. According to their business plan, their overall goal is to be an environmentally responsible company without necessarily advertising themselves as such. According to Didi Malabuyo, Assistant to the Sales and Marketing Manager for North America, who has been centrally involved in the relaunch activities [for their internal employee environmental education], it is essential that the IKEA employees believe in the company's efforts and that must be demonstrated not just in words, but also in actions. Once employees are convinced of IKEA's intentions and actions, it will become natural to convey this information to the customer.[9]

Certainly the benefits of increased market share and revenue from a company's sustainable development efforts should only be sought after the company has educated its employees and proven to them that it is serious about sustainable practices. If employees can't be convinced, give up trying to convince customers. In ads, you should be careful to talk about how the company is working to improve the environmental performance of its operations and its products, rather than portraying it as having already completed the journey. No company has reached the target. Few will, and they will be branded as trying to divert consumer attention from saving the Earth if they overstate their case.

Even legendary socially responsible companies can get into trouble. In the mid 1990s, Ben & Jerry's Ice Cream got called on the carpet for claiming that its Rainforest Crunch ice cream was made with nuts collected by Amazon "forest peoples." It turned out that the nut supplier, Community Products Inc. (which Ben Cohen, the "Ben" in Ben & Jerry's, also owned), bought 95% of the nuts from commercial vendors. In a similar fashion, the Body Shop was skewered when a magazine article questioned its claims about animal testing, alleged that the company used petrochemicals in some of its "natural" products, and charged that its Trade Not Aid program accounted for less of its supplies than it had claimed. The Body Shop denied all the magazine's charges, but these experiences reinforce the notion that walking the talk is the name of the game.[10]

When they smell green-washing, environmentalists use reprisal tactics ranging from litigation to lobbying to visible public protest. Responding to these tactics takes executives' energy and focus away from business issues. They have seen what happens to companies in other industries when rhetoric gets ahead of actions, resulting in the company being taken to task by an aroused public:

- Monsanto made a big splash when it stopped manufacturing polluting chemicals and herbicides and created genetically modified seeds that did not require pesticides ... almost. The specially engineered seeds do require large amounts of Round-up, which Monsanto conveniently manufactures. Consumers are awakening to possible ecological and economic repercussions of dependence on genetically modified seeds from a corporate conglomerate. Monsanto's legal bills are growing, especially in Europe, as it fights patent laws, trade laws, consumer activists, suspicious farmers, and an irate public.

- In the auto industry, Ford has positioned itself as a pioneer in reducing the environmental impact of mankind's most polluting invention—the car. However, Ford also produces some of the least fuel-efficient sports utility vehicles and is receiving criticism because of this duplicity.

- The oil companies are scrambling to put an environmental spin on their operations. The ecological disaster caused by the *Exxon Valdez* oil tanker wreck in Alaska was a setback. Royal Dutch Shell and BP are exploring renewable energy alternatives, while carbon dioxide from the burning of their fossil fuels is increasingly linked to global climate change and the increasing incidence of severe weather phenomena. Again, credibility is an issue. Chevron has probably spent five times as much as its skimpy list of environmental initiatives were worth to buy magazine and TV ads in which to boast of its actions.[11] No wonder polls typically find that a mere 10 to 15% of U.S. adults view corporations' eco-claims as trustworthy.[12]

- In April 1990, a two-page ad appeared in numerous national U.S. magazines. It featured a drawing of the Earth and the headline "HANDLE WITH CARE." It is unfortunate that 42% of the worst-polluting chemical companies in the U.S. were members of the Chemical Manufacturers Association, which sponsored the ad.[13] The integrity of the chemical industry's Responsible Care campaign was severely tested by the track record of its members.

So companies are not anxious to put an environmental spotlight on themselves. Few global corporate executives want to subject themselves and their companies to bad publicity or to external pressure to pay even more attention to the environmental and social impact of their operations, products, and services. That is why it is critical that environmental initiatives be proactively framed and staged properly, both internally and externally. This can be done. When approached wisely, credible and balanced publicity about enlightened corporate sustainable development strategies and actions can yield enormous benefits without risk of public backlash. If done with straight talk and sincerity, publicity will give a company the competitive advantage of a positive differentiating factor in the marketplace.

Executives Are Locked In An Old Mental Model

As Forest Reinhardt points out in *Down To Earth*, common sense seems to indicate that doing more than is lawfully required for the environment and society would incur higher costs, causing customers to abandon the company in search of lower prices.

> Logically, if environmental externalities create differences between private costs and social costs, companies that try voluntarily to take social costs into account will lose more money than those that look exclusively at private costs.[14]

Reinhardt goes on to say that traditional, commonsense intuition blinds executives to the full benefits of sustainable development. When the productivity gains, the talent retention advantages, the savings, the risk reduction, and the increased revenue opportunities which I have quantified in this book are explicitly revealed to smart executives, the light will shine on a world of beneficial possibilities. Conventional business wisdom presupposes extra costs are required to improve environmental performance. Conventional business wisdom is wrong.

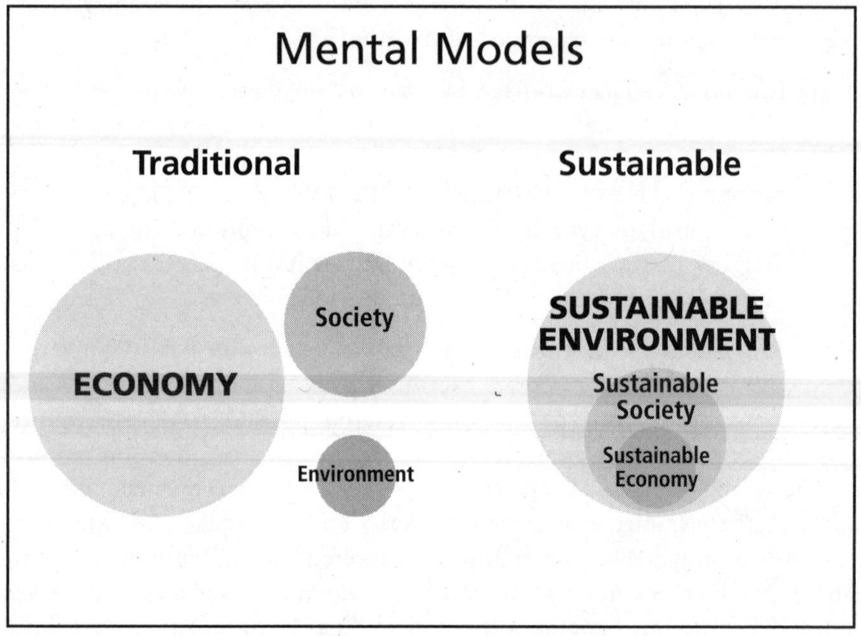

Figure 10.1 Mental Models

To wake us up, we need new paradigms or models of our reality. To feel responsibility for social conditions and the environment, corporations' "mental model" of the economy's relationship with society and the environment needs to be almost reversed. The traditional business view places the environment and society as separate entities, outside economic considerations and minuscule in relative importance (see Figure 10.1). Conventional business intuition mistakenly sees priorities in economic, environmental, and social policy as competing.[15] A more accurate frame of reference would reverse this perspective and acknowledge that the global economy is a small sector within global society, which in turn is within the global environment that is necessary for life as we know it.

The economy is not separate from the natural world. Society and the economy need a healthy environment. The new mental model in Figure 10.1 shows this is not an "either/or" trade-off. It is an integrated "both/and" situation. The concentric circles reinforce that a sustainable economy can only exist within a sustainable society within a sustainable environment. Or they are like the three-legged stool; if one leg is missing, the stool collapses. Global corporations are a part of the global ecology and are dependent on it. No environment, no consumers in society, no business.

Eco-efficiency is a transitional seed. If well-planted and well-tended in the sustainable economy seedbed, its roots will creep into the larger sustainable environment patch. It will prompt deeper thinking and deeper questions in boardrooms about company products and operations. Questions such as "How do our products and services improve the environment and society?" Questions that would have been rejected like a virus if asked earlier. The bottom-line business case for sustainable business helps executives save face as they "get it" and recognize their role in the stewardship of environment and society.

A sustainable economy is a means to a greater end—it is the prerequisite for the restoration of a sustainable environment and sustainable society. As described earlier, these three elements constitute sustainable development. Executives' growing, deepening, creeping commitment to sustainability will gradually transform the corporation, making the rhetoric of their early "green" initiatives seem like a superficial representation of the power of the new reality, instead of vice versa. As Peter Sandman, a leading U.S. expert in environmental risk assessment, says: "Rhetoric changes first, behavior changes next, and attitudes change last."[16] When the attitudes change, magic happens.

The radical restructuring of industrial society from within—authentically reinventing the underlying structure of our relationships with consumerism, one another, and the natural world—is a daunting journey. As Machiavelli said, "There is nothing more difficult to take in hand, more perilous to conduct, or more uncertain in its success, than to take the lead in the introduction of a new order of things." Sustainable development is a first step on that journey. Smart businesses will take the next steps, will be the successful leaders, and will thrive as they lead themselves, other companies, regulatory agencies, governments, and consumers on the transformation journey.

The Sustainable Development Profit Center

The role of the environmental affairs department is too narrow and needs to be changed.

> The world of the environmental professional is undergoing substantial change. The compliance-oriented environmental manager who fails to effectively communicate the link between environmental and economic

> performance to management may be facing extinction. Threats of noncompliance and potential jail terms, while still a possibility, do not carry the impact they once did. Today, a more successful approach is to encourage the use of environmental performance to gain competitive edge. A developing field of environmental performance evaluation provides the "connective tissue" for linking environmental performance to competitive advantage.[17]

If a business unit manager, even more than the environmental affairs or corporate community relations manager, supports social and environmental strategies, real results happen. A business unit manager has authority over capital investment projects, product development, and marketing. As an executive with bottom-line responsibility for the profit and loss of a business, he or she has the authority, the resources, and usually the credibility to shift the business.[18] Such managers would be even more effective if they had the support of an expert and specialized group: the Sustainable Development Profit Center.

The formation of a Sustainable Development Profit Center would be clear evidence of a shift in executives' mental model. Here is a simple illustration of why this would pay off. The Environmental Protection Agency (EPA) says that commercial buildings in the U.S. waste 30% of the energy they use, costing $25 billion per year.[19] Suppose the money required to stop a company's contribution to this waste were treated as an investment, instead of a cost. How would the rate of return on the investment in energy efficiency compare to other investments? Vanguard, one of the largest investment managers in the U.S., partnered with the EPA to make this analysis (see Figure 10.4).

> Investors relate risk and reward. The higher the volatility or risk of a given investment, the higher the reward or return that is demanded by investors. What Vanguard says ... is that U.S. Treasury Bills, with a very low volatility, are bid down to an average annual return of 5%, while highly volatile or risky small business stocks must pay returns over 20% per year to attract investors. The EPA's analysis is that energy efficiency investments have a low risk comparable to corporate bonds. This makes sense. As long as the building is occupied, comfort and lighting will be required, so energy efficiency technologies save energy every year, and the amount of money saved varies only by the price of energy. According to the EPA, these technologies produce 20–30% returns on investment. This is the type of investment that will always be desired—high return and low risk.[20]

Still the question arises—if large resource savings are available and profitable, why haven't they all been captured already? The answer is simple: scores of common practices in both the public and private sectors systematically reward companies for wasting natural resources and penalize them for boosting resource productivity. For example, most companies expense their consumption of raw materials through the income statement but pass resource saving investment through the balance sheet. That distortion makes it more tax efficient to waste fuel than to invest in improving fuel efficiency.[21]

Rates of Return Comparison

Investment Type	Annual Rate of Return	Risk Index *(Year-to-year volatility)*
US Treasury Bills	5%	5%
Long-term Corporate Bonds	8%	11%
Common Stocks	15%	21%
Small Company Stocks	23%	32%
EPA "Energy Star" (Investment in energy efficiency in commercial buildings)	20-30%	7-12%

Figure 10.4 Rates of Return Comparison

The mindset of a profit center would catch these distortions. Without it, even if companies look beyond the initial purchase price when considering energy-conserving wire, fixtures, transformers, and motors, they may only use crude payback calculations instead of discounted cash flow. As recently as a few years ago, the median payback period demanded by companies on energy conservation capital investments was 1.9 years. That's an incredible requirement to show an after-tax return in investment of around 71% per year—about six times the marginal cost of capital.[22]

Transferring environmental initiatives from a department that is perceived as a defensive cost center to one that is viewed as an offensive profit maker can be a vital factor in the success of environmental projects.[23] That is, the "green wall" between the environmental and business staffs would be removed, with the recognition that energy and resource conservation generates profit, not overhead. Instead of laying off engineers to save money when times are tough, companies would use these engineers to innovate and save resources. Upsize the environmental management profit center staff, downsize waste, and make big profits. This is what BASF has done. It has appointed an "environmental opportunities" manager who consults with line managers, using his specialized knowledge to help identify savings and environmental business opportunities.[24] It is critical to integrate strategic environmental management with day-to-day business processes and line operations, as well as with overarching corporate strategy.

> When environmental management crosses the great divide and begins to participate in the central business of business, which is to make money, it gains new momentum, indeed a whole new purpose. It leaves the mop-up crew and joins the ranks of "core competencies." This is a significant step, indeed a *sine qua non* of a more sustainable business paradigm.[25]

Only 18% of executives surveyed in 1994 said they treat their environmental management departments as profit centers, and that number is probably high.[26] To ignore environmental drivers is to remain blithely oblivious to an important element of competitive advantage.[27] However, McKinsey consultants Noah Walley and Bradley Whitehead caution against unrealistic win-win rhetoric that claims simplistic environmental initiatives will automatically improve profit. They rightly point out that some costs of compliance with emissions reduction regulation can far exceed any payback potential, and that companies must evaluate these projects by assessing their impact on shareholder value.

> Only a focus on value rather than compliance, emissions, or quarterly costs can provide managers with the information to set priorities and develop appropriate business responses .... In a world where you cannot do everything, only a value-based approach allows informed trade-offs between costs and benefits .... Managers must set clear priorities based on shareholder value and the amount of discretion they have to deal with the environmental problem at hand; they must make environmental decisions in the context of the company's needs and

> strategy; and they must be able to exercise different options as an uncertain future unfolds .... To prepare a strategy, managers must decide where they want to be on the spectrum from strict compliance to environmental leadership.[28]

This opportunity-oriented and value-based business strategy requires an assessment of *all* business trade-offs when making sustainable development investment decisions. That's what a Sustainable Development Profit Center would do. Quantifying the seven factors outlined in this guide will help you gain the broader perspective you need to ensure you calculate all benefits when you make a business decision.

Changing the Rules of the Game For Your Advantage

Even the best companies will only be sustainable if the institutions and markets surrounding them have been reshaped to support and promote sustainability.[29] Corporate leadership in sustainability will require active lobbying of national and international governments and agencies for more sustainability-friendly policies.

> Around the world, governments tax labor and investment while they subsidize the use of natural resources. The use of public land for grazing and logging, and public support for irrigation, agricultural subsidies, and fossil fuel infrastructure—all these programs work against sustainable development. Business leaders working for change can only go so far before they run into these barriers. At that point they can stop, or they can lobby for changes in public policy that will reward further investment in sustainable development. True leadership on this issue encompasses private investment decisions and public positions as well.[30]

Suppose SD Inc. worked hard to successfully slip through the sustainability funnel ahead of its competitors. It could increase its lead if it joined similarly positioned companies to lobby for government legislation, forcing competitors to take similar measures at greater expense. As the convergence of private and social costs occurs, the rules of the game will change.

For an enlightened government regulatory approach to work, the regulators must set measurable performance standards, have access to information to verify compliance, and be able to enforce the tough rules with all relevant competitors. It is important that the consumption of precious natural resources not be perversely subsidized by governments, and that polluters be punished. The required five-step approach is:

- Stop subsidizing the wrong things, and shift taxes from labor and profits to resource use and pollution
- Pass tough regulations to support the right things
- Ensure there are enough inspectors to catch violators
- Prosecute the polluters
- Publicize who is best and who is worst

By lobbying regulatory agencies to take these steps, a business will have moved from outright obstructionism to wait-and-see to enlightened and proactive leadership in the regulatory arena. Competitors have to scramble to catch up; their associated costs will be higher and they will be at a disadvantage. This is one game where being the leader is much more attractive than being led.

In summary, I have explored manageable, low-risk, and cost-justified measures to reap benefits from more pervasive sustainable development strategies. You have seen that engaging the whole company in sustainable development initiatives can lead to significant business benefits. The worksheets in the Appendix help companies identify and quantify the financial benefits of seven potential benefit areas. By injecting your own parameters into the worksheet, you can prove to yourself that sustainable development will yield hard-nosed business benefits for your company—reduced hiring and retention costs, improved productivity, reduced expenses at manufacturing and commercial sites, increased revenue and market share, reduced risk and easier financing, increased shareholder value, and increased profit.

Executives who devote serious attention to using sustainability performance as a competitive weapon will be well positioned to financially outperform their competitors in the 21st century. To capitalize on the opportunity, the initiatives have to be joined to corporate strategic hot-buttons. Finding those strategic imperatives and linking environmental and social improvements to their success will ensure the needed focus from senior executives.

You don't need to pursue all seven benefit areas that I have discussed. Just a few will build the momentum, and a Sustainable Development Profit Center's first task would be to determine which ones will pay back the soonest and the most. The Center can then reinvest a percentage of the savings in the other areas to create a multiplier effect. The adage "What gets measured gets managed" reminds us that a set of environmental performance indicators should be added to the measurement systems of the business.

Once sustainable development indicators are tracked within the same business cycle as other traditional business measurements, change will magically happen.

The benefits are there for the taking. Smart executives will take them before their competitors do. Companies that lag will be history, trapped in the hoax of perpetual, unsustainable growth. Companies that lead will win.

Appendix
Sustainability Advantage Worksheets

THE FOLLOWING WORKSHEETS are used to illustrate the quantification methodology and are referred to throughout the book. In fact, the book is really a comprehensive description of the assumptions and logic behind the business case embodied in the worksheets. Conversely, the Appendix can be viewed as a précis of the book.

The hypothetical Sustainable Development Inc. company, or SD Inc., is used to illustrate the business case. The real power of the worksheets is realized when you use them to assess your own company's triple bottom-line business case for more proactive environmental and social leadership. I encourage you to tailor the worksheet assumptions and other entries to reflect your company's situation.

If it is helpful to use an on-line version of the worksheet as a starter set, a copy is available from New Society Publishers' website. A soft copy can be downloaded in either Lotus 1-2-3 or Excel format.

Assumptions about the "SD Inc." Hypothetical Company

Revenue (millions) **$44,000**
Profit (millions) **$3,000**

Employee Population **120,000**
  Employees **108,000**
  Managers **12,000**
Average Employee Salary **$60,000**
Average Manager Salary **$70,000**

In the following worksheets, assumptions used in the calculations which are not obviously explicit are shown with this notation: (*Assumption:...*)

Education Investment Required to Achieve Benefits

Costs for One Day of Education for the Whole Company		
Cost to develop and deliver the education		$42,000,000
(Assumption: Whole company receives the education	120,000	
times the cost to develop and deliver one day)	$350	
Cost of lost productivity of an employee while on course		$17,753,425
(Assumption: Annual salary/365	$164	
times the number of employees)	108,000	
Cost of lost productivity of a manager while on course		$2,301,370
(Assumption: Annual salary/365	$192	
times the number of managers)	12,000	
Total cost of one day of education for the whole company		**$62,054,795**
Year 1: Cost of 2 days of sustainability education		**$124,109,589**
Year 2: Cost of 1 day of sustainability education		**$62,054,795**
Year 3: Cost of 1 day of sustainability education		**$62,054,795**
Year 4: Cost of 1 day of sustainability education		**$62,054,795**
Year 5: Cost of 1 day of sustainability education		**$62,054,795**
Cost of 5-year investment in sustainability education		**$372,328,767**
NPV of 5-year investment in education		**$319,939,628**
(Assumption: Internal cost of money)	6%	

Attracting and Hiring the Best Talent

Cost of Recruiting a New Person

External advertising or internal job posting cost		$5,000
Candidate screening costs		$500
Interviewing costs—preparation, interviews, follow-up		$994
(Assumption: Hours spent on interviewing activity)	30	
Offer and hiring costs		$500
Total cost of recruiting a new person		**$6,994**

Savings on Recruiting Costs

Normal cost of recruiting each new hire		$6,994
x Number of new hires per year		12,000
(Assumption: Percent of company workforce hired)	10%	
x Percent reduction in recruiting costs for those attracted by company's sustainability image		5%
x Percent that will be attracted by sustainability image		20%
Annual savings on RECRUITING costs		$839,318

Retaining the Best Talent

Assumptions Used To Estimate the Cost of Losing a Good Person		
The person's years of service with the company		5 years
"Decide Time" while the person, privately, decides to leave		1 month
"Save Attempt Time" while management tries to save the good person		0.5 months
"Vacant Time" when the position is vacant		2 months
"New Hire Training Time" for the new hire, by the company		0.5 months
"Department Training Time" for the new person		6 months
Monthly cost of an employee		$5,000
Monthly cost of a manager		$5,833

Cost of Losing of a Good Person		
Person's lost productivity during Decide Time		$2,500
(Assumption: Person's percent lost productivity during Decide Time)	50%	
Managerial lost productivity during Save Attempt Time		$729
(Assumption: Manager's percent lost productivity during Decide Time)	25%	
Person's lost productivity during Save Attempt Time		$1,250
(Assumption: Person's percent lost productivity during Save Attempt Time)	50%	
Payroll and benefits administration		$455
(Assumption: Equivalent days of an employee's time)	2	
Separation allowance		$13,750
(Assumption: Number of weeks' pay)	11	
Lost knowledge, experience, and contacts		$54,000
(Assumption: Percent of salary for 1st year employed	50%	
plus additional percent for each subsequent year)	10%	
Lost training invested in the employee		$12,250
(Assumption: Number of days for 1st year employed	15	
plus additional days for each subsequent year)	5	
Lost customer revenue during Vacant Time		$30,556
(Assumption: Person's share of monthly company revenue	$30,556	
times Vacant Time	2	
divided by credibility factor)	2	
Lost department productivity during Save Attempt and Vacant Times		$6,250
(Assumption: Percent of productivity lost by others	10%	
times number of others affected)	5	
Lost productivity in back-filling person's own work during Vacant Time		$2,500
(Assumption: Percent of productivity lost by back-filling person)	25%	
Lost productivity of manager during Vacant Time		$1,167
(Assumption: Percent of productivity lost by manager)	10%	
Lost productivity in person's job during Vacant Time		$5,000
(Assumption: Percent of productivity lost, despite help from others)	50%	
Savings of person's salary while job is vacant		-$10,000
Total cost of loss of a good person		**$120,406**
Total cost of recruiting a new person		**$6,994**
		See Hiring sheet

Cost of On-Boarding and Training a New Hire

Setting up personnel records, system ids, etc. $227
(Assumption: Equivalent days of an employee's time) 1
New hire training—Cost to company to deliver it $4,900
(Assumption: Cost per day of training $350
times number of days of company training) 14
New hire's own lost productivity during new hire training $2,500
(Assumption: Percent of productivity lost) 100%
Lost productivity of back-filling person's work during new hire training $625
(Assumption: Percent of productivity lost) 25%
Lost productivity of manager during new hire training $292
(Assumption: Percent of productivity lost) 10%
Lost productivity in person's job during new hire training $1,250
(Assumption: Percent of productivity lost) 50%
Cost to deliver formal department training $1,750
(Assumption: Cost per day of training $350
times number of days of department training) 5
New hire's own lost productivity during formal department training $1,136
(Assumption: Percent of productivity lost) 100%
Lost productivity of back-filling person during formal department training $284
(Assumption: Percent of productivity lost) 25%
Lost productivity of manager during formal department training $114
(Assumption: Percent of productivity lost) 10%
Lost productivity in person's job during formal department training $568
(Assumption: Percent of productivity lost) 50%
Buddy's lost productivity in own work during informal training $3,000
(Assumption: Percent of productivity lost 10%
times number of months of informal training) .6
Employee's lost productivity during informal training $15,000
(Assumption: Percent of productivity lost 50%
times number of months of informal training) .6

Total cost of on-boarding and training a new hire . . . . **.$31,646**

Cost of Losing and Replacing One Good Employee
Total cost of loss of a good person . . . . **.$120,406**
Total cost of recruiting a new person . . . . **.$6,994**
Total cost of on-boarding and training a new hire . . . . **.$31,646**

Cost of losing & replacing one good employee . . . . **.$159,046**

x Number of good employees lost each year 1,200
(Assumption: Percent of employee population who leave and 1%
whom we wanted to retain)

Annual cost of losing and replacing good employees $190,855,758

x Percent of these who would not leave if they were attracted to
the company's sustainability initiatives 20%

Annual savings from higher RETENTION rate . . . . **.$38,171,152**

Increased Productivity

Increased Productivity of Individual Employees

Total number of employees	120,000
x Percent who will be energized by the company's sustainability initiatives	20%
x Percent increased productivity from their increased commitment	25%
x Average employee's annual salary	$60,000
Benefit of increased productivity from INDIVIDUALS	**$360,000,000**
Number of full-time equivalent (FTE) employees	**6,000**

Increased Productivity from Improved Teamwork Among Departments

Total number of employees	120,000
x Percent increased productivity from interdepartmental teamwork	2%
x Average employee's annual salary	$60,000
Benefit of increased productivity from improved TEAMWORK	**$144,000,000**
Number of full-time equivalent (FTE) employees	**2,400**

Increased Productivity from Improved Working Conditions

Total number of employees	120,000
x Percent of employees whose working conditions are improved	50%
x Percent increased productivity from improved working conditions	7%
x Average employee's annual salary	$60,000
Benefit of increased productivity from improved WORKING CONDITIONS	**$252,000,000**
Number of full-time equivalent (FTE) employees	**4,200**

Total Benefit of Increased PRODUCTIVITY

Benefit of increased productivity from INDIVIDUALS	**$360,000,000**
Benefit of increased productivity from improved TEAMWORK	**$144,000,000**
Benefit of increased productivity from improved WORKING CONDITIONS	**$252,000,000**
Annual benefit of increased PRODUCTIVITY	**$756,000,000**
Number of full-time equivalent (FTE) employees	**12,600**

Reduced Manufacturing Expenses

Simple, Macro-level Calculation

Hardware revenue $22,000,000,000

(Assumption: Hardware percent of total revenue) 50%

Hardware costs $6,600,000,000

(Assumption: Costs as a percent of hardware revenue) 30%

Sustainability savings in manufacturing costs $330,000,000

(Assumption: Percent of hardware costs saved) 5%

— Savings reinvested in other environmental projects $165,000,000

(Assumption: Percent of savings reinvested) 50%

Annual benefit in MANUFACTURING costs $165,000,000

Checklist For a More Detailed Calculation

Savings from eco-friendly MATERIAL SUBSTITUTIONS

Materials with smaller ecological rucksacks; recycled materials; non-hazardous materials; process redesign

+ Savings from eco-friendly ENERGY SUBSTITUTIONS

Renewable wind and solar energy; in-house generation; fuel cells; mini-generators powered by heat from manufacturing processes; process redesign

+ Savings from MATERIAL REDUCTIONS

Handling savings; zero-waste process redesign

+ Savings from ENERGY REDUCTIONS

Insulation; energy-efficient light fixtures; energy-efficient pumps; thicker, straighter, energy-efficient pipe systems; whole systems thinking when purchasing plumbing and electrical contracts and bids; thicker electrical wires; energy-efficient transformers; increasing off-peak electrical usage; off-the-grid process redesign; plus other energy reduction measures listed in the Reduced Expenses at Commercial Sites worksheet

+ Savings from WATER REDUCTIONS

Recycling and treating wastewater; closed loop, zero-waste process redesign

+ Savings from REDUCING, REUSING, RECYCLING SCRAP MATERIAL

Hazardous waste reduction and elimination; non-hazardous waste reduction, sorting, and elimination; industrial ecology with other companies; zero-waste process redesign

+ Savings from REUSING/RECYCLING RETURNED PRODUCTS

Reuse of products, components, and raw materials; design for disassembly; leasing; selling services instead of products; cradle-to-cradle redesign

+ Savings from LESS PACKAGING

+ Savings from more EFFICIENT TRANSPORTATION of products

More eco-friendly mode of transportation; lighter packaging; batching loads; more efficient routing

+ Savings from FASTER APPROVAL CYCLES

R&D savings; development savings; health and safety savings

Total savings from reduced manufacturing expenses

Reduced Expenses at Commercial Sites

Simple, Macro-level Calculation

Selling, general, and administrative (SG&A) expenses $6,600,000,000
(Assumption: SG&A percent of total revenue) 15%
Energy, water, and consumables costs $132,000,000
(Assumption: Costs as a percent of SG&A expenses) 2%
Savings in COMMERCIAL SITE operating costs $26,400,000
(Assumption: Percent of SG&A expenses saved) 20%

Checklist For a More Detailed Calculation

Savings on EMPLOYEE DISCRETIONARY CONSUMABLES
Paper savings from duplexed printing and copying; office supply savings; other employee suggestions

+ Savings from improved WASTE HANDLING
More sorting at source; composting; cafeteria waste to pig farmers

+ Savings from ENERGY EFFICIENCIES through retrofits
Super-windows; on-site power generation; sunlight; occupancy sensors; eco-efficient right-sized fan and HVAC systems; insulation; task lighting; energy-efficient appliances, office equipment, and lighting fixtures; passive solar heating; plus other measures listed in the Reduced Manufacturing Expenses worksheet

+ Savings from ENERGY EFFICIENCIES in the design of new buildings
All the above; revenue from selling excess energy back to the grid; plus eco-design ideas from multiple stakeholder consultations

+ Savings from EMPLOYEE STEWARDSHIP
Reductions through increased awareness of consumption; using stairs instead of elevators; turning off lights and equipment when not in use

+ Savings from WATER CONSERVATION
Low-flow toilets and plumbing fixtures; closed-loop water treatment using Living Machine approaches

+ Savings from LOWER LANDSCAPING COSTS
Naturalized landscapes; less/no watering or fertilizing; planting trees to offset greenhouse gases from business travel

+ Savings from REDUCED OFFICE SPACE
Telecommuting; e-mail; fewer people because of higher productivity

+ Savings from less BUSINESS TRAVEL
Videoconferencing; teleconferencing

Total savings from reduced expenses at commercial sites

Increased Revenue and Market Share

Simple, Macro-level Calculation

Total revenue today $44,000,000,000

Potential revenue increase because of sustainability initiatives 5%

Increased REVENUE from sustainability initiatives $2,200,000,000

Increased PROFIT from sustainability initiatives **$150,000,000**

(Assumption: Percent of today's revenue that flows to profit) 7%

Checklist For a More Detailed Calculation

Percent of increased mind share of green consumers
x Percent of historic markets share increase per percent of mind share
x Percent of historic revenue per percent of market share

Increased revenue from new green customers

\+ **Increased revenue from more loyal customers**
\+ **Increased revenue from new markets**
\+ **Increased revenue from services through dematerialization and leasing**
\+ **Increased revenue from environmental services**

Total increased new revenue

Reduced Risk

Simple, Macro-level Calculation

Total revenue today $44,000,000,000
Selling, general, and administrative (SG&A) expenses $6,600,000,000
(Assumption: SG&A percent of total revenue) 15%
Part of SG&A expenses associated with risk $330,000,000
(Assumption: Percent of risk-related SG&A expenses) 5%
Expense reductions from REDUCED RISKS $16,500,000
(Assumption: Percent of risk-related SG&A expenses saved) 5%

Methodology For a More Detailed, Scenario-based Calculation

Based on a scenario methodology described in *Pure Profit: The Financial Implications of Environmental Performance* by Robert Repetto and Duncan Austin in a report for the World Resources Institute, 2000.

Step 1: Identify salient future issues

- Identify future environmental, social, and economic forces that are likely to have significant financial impact on the company within the time frame of the assessment (e.g., the next 10 years).
- Consult experts from government agencies, industry, environmental and social activist groups, consultants, and scientists.
- Research published literature.
- Use a matrix of the forces for change (e.g., market prices and availability, regulations, changes to taxes and subsidies, liabilities, and other risks outlined earlier) and the stages of the product cycle (e.g., supply of raw material, manufacturing process, product output, post-consumer take-back) to identify the key value drivers over the range of the product cycle.

Step 2: Build scenarios around each

- Define the range of plausible outcomes associated with each issue.
- Develop two to three scenarios for each issue.

Step 3: Assign probabilities to each scenario

- Especially do this for the best- and worst-case scenarios.

Step 4: Assess company exposure to these issues

- Have industry or company experts rank each issue based on the magnitude of its potential impact on earnings, its timing (the sooner it happens, the greater its impact), and its probability.

Step 5: Estimate financial impacts contingent on the scenarios

- For the forecast period, first build baseline financial forecasts using industry and company trends. Use a valuation technique (e.g., McKinsey's entity discounted cash flow model or Stern Stewart's Economic Value Added model) to equate the value of the company to the sum of the discounted present values of all its separate cost, revenue, investment, and financing streams.
- Then, for each scenario, quantify the outcomes in terms that can be used in a financial analysis (e.g., impact on prices, production costs, revenues, expenditures, investments required, and balance sheet liabilities) for each year in the forecast period. If appropriate, do this for individual company locations.

- Reduce these year-by-year amounts to discounted present values using an estimate of the weighted average cost of capital.
- Add these present values to obtain the net financial impact for the combined scenarios, and express this as a percentage of the company's current market valuation.

Total Bottom-Line Benefit

Totals from Seven Benefit Areas	Annual Savings and Increased Revenue	Annual Profit Increase
Annual savings on RECRUITING costs	$839,318	$839,318
Annual savings from higher RETENTION rate	$38,171,152	$38,171,152
Annual benefit of increased PRODUCTIVITY	$756,000,000	$756,000,000
Annual benefit in MANUFACTURING costs	$330,000,000	$165,000,000
Savings in COMMERCIAL SITE operating costs	$26,400,000	$26,400,000
Increased REVENUE, and resulting PROFIT	$2,200,000,000	$150,000,000
Expense reductions from REDUCED RISKS	$16,500,000	$16,500,000
Total	**$3,367,910,470**	**$1,152,910,470**
Percent of previous year's profits		**38%**
(Assumption: SD Inc. profit in previous year)		$3,000,000,000

Benefits Obtained Over Five Years	Gross Benefit	– Education Investment	Net Benefit	IRR on Education Investment
Year 1: 30% of potential benefit is obtained	$1,010,373,141	$124,109,589	$886,263,552	714%
Year 2: 50% of potential benefit is obtained	$1,683,955,235	$62,054,795	$1,621,900,440	2614%
Year 3: 70% of potential benefit is obtained	$2,357,537,329	$62,054,795	$2,295,482,534	3699%
Year 4: 90% of potential benefit is obtained	$3,031,119,423	$62,054,795	$2,969,064,628	4785%
Year 5: 100% of potential benefit is obtained	$3,367,910,470	$62,054,795	$3,305,855,675	5327%
Total net benefit over 5 years			**$11,078,566,830**	
NPV of 5-year investment in education			**$9,029,019,657**	
(Assumption: Internal cost of money)	6%			

Endnotes

Introduction

1 Forest L. Reinhardt, "Bringing The Environment Down To Earth," *Harvard Business Review* (July-August 1999): p. 150. Reprinted by permission of *Harvard Business Review*. Copyright ©1999 by Harvard Business School Publishing Corporation; all rights reserved.

2 Reuters News Service, "More global firms seeing profits from environment — KPMG," Reuters Daily World Environmental News, The Hague (September 23, 1999).

3 Robert Paehkle, "Green Politics and the Rise of the Environmental Movement," in *The Environment and Canadian Society*, Thomas Fleming, ed. (Scarborough, ON: ITP Nelson, 1997): pp. 251–274.

4 Sonia Labatt, "Corporate Response Toward Environmental Issues: A Case Study of Packaging," (Ph.D. dissertation, Department of Geography, University of Toronto, January, 1995). Also Glen Toner and Tom Conroy, "Environmental Policy," in *Border Crossings: The Internationalization of Canadian Public Policy*, Dorn, Pal, and Tomlin, eds. (Toronto: Oxford University Press, 1996): pp. 108–144.

5 Rodney White and Davis Etkin, "Climate Change, Extreme Events and the Canadian Insurance Industry," *Natural Hazards* 16 (1997): pp. 135–163.

6 Hilary J. Thompson, "The Role of Financial Institutions in Encouraging Improved Environmental Performance," in *Business and the Environment*, Michael D. Rogers, ed. (New York: St. Martin's Press, 1995): pp. 271–281.

7 Stephen Brooks and Andrew Stritch, "Business Organization and Lobbying" in *Business and Government in Canada* (Scarborough, ON: Prentice-Hall, 1991): pp. 208–243.

8 Paehkle, "Green Politics."

9 Sonia Labatt and Virginia Maclaren, "Looking Beyond the Fence: Industry, Its Public and the Environment," *The Journal of Corporate Citizenship* 3 (2001): pp. 69–84.

10 World Business Council for Sustainable Development, *Eco-efficient Leadership for Improved Economic and Environmental Performance* (Geneva, Switzerland: WBCSD, 1995): pp. 5 and 7.

11 Judy Simon, "CIPSI Stalled in Ontario," *Hazardous Waste Materials Management Magazine* (January-February 1996). Available on the web at <http://www.indeco.com/pub_cips.htm>.

12 World Commission on Environment and Development, *Our Common Future* (Oxford: Oxford University Press, 1987).

13 Richard Lamming, Adam Faruk, and Paul Cousins, "Environmental Soundness: A Pragmatic Alternative to Expectations of Sustainable Development in Business," *Business Strategy and the Environment* 8 (1999): pp. 177–188.

14 Stephan Schmidheiny, with the Business Council for Sustainable Development, *Changing Course: A Global Business Perspective on Development and the Economy* (Cambridge, MA: The MIT Press, 1992): p. xii.

15 Livio DeSimone and Frank Popoff, with the Business Council for Sustainable Development, *Eco-efficiency: The Business Link to Sustainable Development* (Cambridge, MA: The MIT Press, 2000): p. 21.

16 Lamming, Faruk, and Cousins, "Environmental Soundness," pp. 182–183.

17 Lorinda R. Rowledge, Russell S. Barton, and Kevin S. Brady, *Mapping The Journey: Case Studies in Strategy and Action Toward Sustainable Development* (Sheffield, UK: Greenleaf Publishing, 1999): p. 36.

18 Brian Nattrass and Mary Altomare, *The Natural Step For Business: Wealth, Ecology and the Evolutionary Corporation* (Gabriola Island, BC: New Society Publishers, 1999): p. 23.

19 Rowledge, Barton, and Brady, *Mapping the Journey*, pp. 26–27.

20 The differentiation between balancing and integrating the three sustainable development dimensions was made by the Honourable Charles Caccia, Canadian member of Parliament and chair of the House of Commons Standing Committee on Environment and Sustainable Development, at York University, Ontario, on March 2, 2001. This was the first of a five-lecture Sustainable Development Lecture Series on the topic of "The Theory and the Practice, the Old and the New Economy." The terminology distinction is taken from personal notes on his remarks.

21 Rosalyn McKeown, *Education for Sustainable Development Tool Kit*. The tool kit can be downloaded free of charge from <http://www.esdtoolkit.org>.

22 Carl Frankel, "Storming The Digital Divide," *Tomorrow* 11, no. 1 (January-February 2001): p. 45.

23 Mary Choquette and George Khoury, "Detailed Findings" in "Social Auditing: Breaking New Ground in Corporate Social Responsibility," Report 288-00 from The Conference Board of Canada: p. 1.

24 Ibid.

25 Social Venture Network website, <http://www.svn.org/home.html>.

26 Gilbert Hedstrom, Stephen Poltorzycki, and Peter Strob, "Sustainable Development: The Next Generation of Business Opportunity," *Prism* (fourth quarter, 1998). Published by Arthur D. Little, Acorn Park, Cambridge, MA 01240-2390.

27 Sustainable Systems Associates. *Applying Sustainable Development to Business: Realizing the Benefit*, Publication 3649E, prepared for the Ontario Ministry of the Environment (Toronto: Queen's Printer of Ontario, 1998): p. i.

28 Matthew Arnold and Robert Day, *The Next Bottom Line: Making Sustainable Development Tangible* (Washington, DC: The World Resources Institute, 1998): p. 3.

29 The Alliance For Environmental Innovation website, *Catalyzing Environmental Results: Lessons in Advocacy Organization-Business Partnerships* (a report sponsored by the J.M. Kaplan Fund) at <http://www.edfpewalliance.org /kapquotes.html> and <http://www.edfpewalliance.org/kapintro.html>.

30 The Alliance For Environmental Innovation website, <http://www.edfpew alliance.org/kapbusiness.html>.

31 "A Green Account: A Management Focus," *The Economist* (September 4, 1993): p. 69.

32 Authors of books about the distressing erosion of carrying capacity of the planet include:

- Lester Brown, Michael Renner, and Brian Halweil, *Vital Signs* 1999: *The Environmental Trends That Are Shaping Our Future* (New York: W.W. Norton & Company, 1999).
- Gail Christianson, *Greenhouse: The 200-Year Story of Global Warming* (Vancouver: Greystone Books, 1999).
- Theo Colborn, Dianne Dumanoski, and John Peterson Myers, *Our Stolen Future: Are We Threatening our Fertility, Intelligence, and Survival?—A Scientific Detective Story* (New York: Plume Books, 1996).
- Anita Gordon and David Suzuki, *It's A Matter of Survival* (Toronto: Stoddart Publishing, 1990).
- Thomas Homer-Dickson, *The Ingenuity Gap: How Can We Solve the Problems of the Future?* (New York: Alfred A. Knopf, 2000).
- Fred Mackenzie, *Our Changing Planet: An Introduction to Earth System Science and Global Environmental Change* (Upper Saddle River, NJ: Prentice Hall, 1998).
- Donella Meadows, Dennis Meadows, and Jorgen Randers, *Beyond the Limits: Confronting Global Collapse, Envisioning a Sustainable Future* (White River Junction, VT: Chelsea Green Publishing, 1992).
- Daniel Quinn, *Ishmael* (New York: Bantam Books, 1993).
- Marq de Villiers, *Water* (Toronto: Stoddart Publishing, 1999).
- Mathis Wackernagel and William Rees, *Our Ecological Footprint: Reducing Human Impact on the Earth* (Gabriola Island, BC: New Society Publishers, 1996).

33 Authors of books about the negative impacts of corporatization and globalization include:

- Maude Barlow and Tony Clarke, *Global Showdown: How the New Activists Are Fighting Global Corporate Rule* (Toronto: Stoddart Publishing, 2001).
- Allan Bloom, *The Closing of the American Mind* (New York: Touchstone Books, 1987).
- John Deverall and Greg Vezina, *Democracy, Eh? A Guide To Voter Action* (Outremont, PQ: Robert Davies Publishing, 1993).
- Murray Dobbin, *The Myth of the Good Corporate Citizen: Democracy Under the Rule of Big Business* (Toronto: Stoddart Publishing, 1998).
- Joe Dominguez and Vicki Robin, *Your Money or Your Life: Transforming Your Relationship with Money and Achieving Financial Independence* (New York: Penguin Books, 1992).
- Riane Eisler, *The Chalice and the Blade: Our History, Our Future* (San Francisco: HarperCollins Publishers, 1988).
- Edward Herman and Noam Chomsky, *Manufacturing Consent: The Political Economy of the Mass Media* (New York: Pantheon Books, 1988).
- Naomi Klein, *No Logo: Taking Aim at the Brand Bullies* (Toronto: Vintage Canada, 2000).
- David Korten, *When Corporations Rule the World* (West Hartford, CT, and San Francisco: Kumarian Press and Berrett-Keohler Publishers, 1995).
- Linda McQuaig, *The Cult of Impotence: Selling the Myth of Powerlessness in the Global Economy* (New York: Viking, 1998).
- Brian Milani, *Designing the Green Economy: The Postindustrial Alternative to Corporate Globalization* (Lanham, MD: Rowan & Littlefield Publishers, 2000).
- John Ralston Saul, *The Unconscious Civilization* (New York: The Free Press, 1995).

34 Authors of books about how business has benefited from a sustainable development agenda include:

- Ray Anderson, *Mid-Course Correction—Toward a Sustainable Enterprise: The Interface Model* (Atlanta, GA: Peregrinzilla Press, 1998).
- Matthew Arnold and Russell Day, *The Next Bottom Line: Making Sustainable Development Tangible* (Washington, DC: World Resources Institute, 1998).
- Thomas Casten, *Turning Off the Heat: Why America Must Double Energy Efficiency To Save Money and Reduce Global Warming* (New York: Prometheus Books, 1998).
- Livio DeSimone and Frank Popoff, with the Business Council for Sustainable Development, *Eco-efficiency: The Business Link to Sustainable Development* (Cambridge, MA: The MIT Press, 2000).

- John Elkington, *Cannibals With Forks: The Triple Bottom Line of 21st Century Business* (Gabriola Island, BC: New Society Publishers, 1998).
- Carl Frankel, *In Earth's Company: Business, Environment and the Challenge of Sustainability* (Gabriola Island, BC: New Society Publishers, 1998).
- Paul Hawken, Amory B. Lovins, and L. Hunter Lovins, *Natural Capitalism: Creating the Next Industrial Revolution* (Boston: Little, Brown and Company, 1999).
- Doug McKenzie-Mohr and William Smith, *Fostering Sustainable Behavior: An Introduction to Community-Based Social Marketing* (Gabriola Island, BC: New Society Publishers, 1999).
- Brian Nattrass and Mary Altomare, *The Natural Step For Business: Wealth, Ecology and the Evolutionary Corporation* (Gabriola Island, BC: New Society Publishers, 1999).
- Forest Reinhardt, *Down To Earth: Applying Business Principles To Environmental Management* (Boston: Harvard Business Review Press, 2000).
- Duncan Austin and Robert Repetto, *Pure Profit: The Financial Implications of Environmental Performance* (Washington, DC: World Resources Institute, 2000).
- Joseph Romm, *Cool Companies: How the Best Businesses Boost Profits and Productivity by Cutting Greenhouse Gas Emissions* (Washington, DC: Island Press, 1999).
- Lorinda R. Rowledge, Russell S. Barton, and Kevin S. Brady, *Mapping The Journey: Case Studies in Strategy and Action Toward Sustainable Development* (Sheffield, UK: Greenleaf Publishing, 1999).
- Stephan Schmidheiny with the Business Council for Sustainable Development, *Changing Course: A Global Business Perspective on Development and the Environment* (Cambridge, MA: The MIT Press, 1992).
- Ernst von Weizsacher, Amory B. Lovins, and L. Hunter Lovins, *Factor Four: Doubling Wealth, Halving Resource Use—The New Report to the Club of Rome* (London: Earthscan, 1997).

The Proposal

1 Stephan Schmidheiny, with the Business Council for Sustainable Development. *Changing Course: A Global Business Perspective on Development and the Economy* (Cambridge, MA: The MIT Press, 1992): p. 86.

2 *Fortune* website, "Fortune Five Hundred 2000, Industry Snapshot: Computers, Office Equipment" at <http://www.fortune.com/fortune/fortune500/ind8.html>.

3 "Dell, IBM Top List of Environmentally Friendly Computer Makers," *Bloomberg News* (September 13, 1999).

4 Environmental data on these computer companies can be found at their corporate environmental websites, as follows:
   - Apple <http://www.apple.com/about/environment/>
   - Compaq <http://www.compaq.com/corporate/ehss/index.html>
   - Dell <http://www.dell.com/us/en/gen/corporate/vision_008_initiatives .htm>
   - Hewlett-Packard <http://www.hp.com/abouthp/environment/>
   - IBM <http://ww.ibm.com/ibm/environment>
   - Pitney Bowes <http://www.pitneybowes.com/company/index.html>
   - Sun <http://www.sun.com/corporateoverview/corpaffairs/enviro.html>

5 Apple Computer website, "Design for Environment at Apple Computer: A Case Study of the Power Macintosh 7200" at <http://www.apple.com/about/ environment/design/case_study/powermac7200.html>.

6 The Alliance For Environmental Innovation website, <http://www.edfpew alliance.org/kapbusiness.html>.

Benefit 1: Easier Hiring of the Best Talent

1 Charles Fishman, "The War For Talent," *FastCompany* (August 1998), <http://www.fastcompany.com/online/16/mckinsey.html>. Reprinted with permission. All rights reserved. To subscribe, please call (800) 542•6029 or visit <www.fastcompany.com>.

2 William M. Mercer, *Beyond the Bottom Line: What CEOs are Thinking* (Toronto: William M. Mercer Company, 1999).

3 Solomon Smith Barney, "IBM's Services Business Is Well Positioned," *Industry Report* (New York: Solomon Smith Barney, September 8, 1999).

4 Roger Herman and Joyce Gioia, Strategic Business Futurists, "Trend Alert: Where Have All the Students Gone?" *Trend Alerts* (August 21, 1999), <http://www. herman.net/archive_8-24-99.html>. Available by calling (800) 227•3566 or from the Herman Group website <www.herman.net>.

5 Elizabeth Axelrod, Helen Handfield-Jones, and Timothy Walsh, "The War For Talent, Part Two," *The McKinsey Quarterly* 2 (2001).

6 Fishman, "The War For Talent."

7 IBM Canada, *Change the World* (a brochure printed by International Business Machines Corporation Canada, 08/97).

8 IBM website, <http://www.ibm.com/employment/>.

9 IBM website, "Is the company's mission important?" at <http://www.ibm.com/ employment/mission.phtml>.

10 Environics, *The Millennium Poll on Corporate Social Responsibility*, conducted by Environics International Ltd., in cooperation with The Prince of Wales Business Leaders Forum and The Conference Board. The survey was done in May 1999,

polling about 1,000 citizens in each of 23 countries on six continents—a total of 25,000 surveys worldwide. The results are accurate to within 3%, 19 times out of 20. Available on the web at <http://www.environics.net/eil/millennium/Environics>.

11 Sustainable Enterprise Academy, *Report on the First Business Leader Seminar, Fall 2000* (Toronto: Sustainable Enterprise Academy, Schulich School of Business, York University, 4700 Keele Street, 2000): p. 11

Benefit 2: Higher Retention of Top Talent

1 Linda Duxbury, Lorraine Dyke, and Natalie Lam, *Building a World-Class Workforce, Executive Summary* (Ottawa: Treasury Board of Canada Secretariat, January 1999): p. 7.

2 Trend Update, "Worker Retention: A Serious Problem Getting Worse," *Trend Letter* (June 10, 1999): p. 2. Published by The Global Network, 1101 30th St. NW, Suite 130, Washington, DC, 20007.

3 KPMG website, "KPMG alliance to offer talent retention tool to high-tech employers," press release, May 5, 1999. Available at <http://www.kpmg.ca/>.

4 "Why Your Workers Might Jump Ship," *Business Week* magazine (March 1, 1999): Up Front section.

5 Bliss & Associates website, "Cost of Turnover" at <http://www.blissassociates.com/articles.html#5>.

6 This is a rule of thumb often quoted in human resources articles and by recruiting specialists.

7 Colin Leduc, excerpts from an Arthur D. Little Inc. presentation on the business case for sustainable development, attached to Colin Leduc's private correspondence to Bob Willard, December 13, 1999.

8 Marcus Buckingham and Curt Coffman, *First Break All The Rules: What The World's Greatest Managers Do Differently* (New York: Simon & Schuster, 1999): pp. 27–29.

9 Tom Terez, Meaning At Work website at <http://www.meaningatwork.com/>.

10 Ibid., "Key Findings" at <http://www.meaningatwork.com/akeyfind.html>.

11 David Dorsey, "The New Spirit of Work," *FastCompany* 16 (August 1998). Also available on the web at <http://www.fastcompany.com/online/16/barrett.html>. Reprinted with permission. All rights reserved. To subscribe, please call (800) 542•6029 or visit <www.fastcompany.com>.

12 Tom Patey, "Graduates focus on green issues and multinationals," *European* (May 16, 1996). The European Graduate Survey 1996 is available from Universum, Box 7053, 103 86 Stockholm, Sweden.

13 Environics, *The Millennium Poll on Corporate Social Responsibility*, conducted by Environics International Ltd., in cooperation with The Prince of Wales Business

Leaders Forum and The Conference Board. The survey was done in May 1999, polling about 1,000 citizens in each of 23 countries on six continents—a total of 25,000 surveys worldwide. The results are accurate to within 3%, 19 times out of 20. Available on the web at <http://www.environics.net/eil/millennium/Environics>.

14 Ibid.

15 John Elkington, *Cannibals With Forks: The Triple Bottom Line of 21st Century Business* (Gabriola Island, BC: New Society Publishers, 1998): p. 27.

16 Dorsey, "The New Spirit of Work."

17 Reuters News Service, "Canadians willing to pay more for 'green' cars," Reuters Daily World Environment News, Toronto (October 13, 1999).

18 B. McNee, C. Smith Ardito, D. Tunick Morello, and E. Zidar, "IT Staff Retention and Recruitment: Addressing a Critical Problem for the IS Organization" (a report from The Gartner Group, September 28, 1998). Available on the web at <http://www.gartner.com>.

Benefit 3: Increasing Employee Productivity

1 David McNally, *Even Eagles Need A Push* (Eden Prairie, MN: Transform Press, 1990): p. 81.

2 James Collins and Jerry Porras, *Built To Last: Successful Habits of Visionary Companies* (New York: HarperCollins, 1994): pp. 8 and 55.

3 Nicholas Imparato and Oren Harari, *Jumping the Curve: Innovation and Strategic Choice In An Age Of Transition* (San Francisco: Jossey-Bass Publishers, 1994): pp. 57 and 58.

4 Robert Reich, "The Company of the Future," *FastCompany* (November 1998). Reprinted with permission. All rights reserved. To subscribe, please call (800) 542•6029 or visit <www.fastcompany.com>.

5 Collins and Porras, *Built to Last*, p. 55.

6 Ibid., pp. 74–76.

7 Ibid., p. 94.

8 Ibid., p. 114.

9 John Miner, *Organizational Behavior: Performance and Productivity* (New York: Random House, 1988): pp. 224–256.

10 Peter Senge, *The Fifth Discipline: The Art and Practice of the Learning Organization* (New York: Doubleday Currency, 1990). The whole book is about the five disciplines.

11 Price Pritchett, *Firing Up Commitment During Organizational Change* (Dallas, TX: Pritchett & Associates, 1994): p. 6.

12 Jim Kouzes and Barry Posner, *The Leadership Challenge* (San Francisco: Jossey-Bass, 1995): pp. 11 and 94.

13 Frances Hesselbein, "The 'How To Be' Leader," in Frances Hesselbein, Marshall Goldsmith, and Richard Beckhard (eds.), *The Leader of the Future*, sponsored by the Peter F. Drucker Foundation (San Francisco: Jossey-Bass, 1996): pp. 122–123.

14 Senge, *The Fifth Discipline*, pp. 205–225.

15 Ken Blanchard and Sheldon Bowles, *Gung Ho! Turn On the People in Any Organization* (New York: William Morrow and Company, 1998): pp. 169–171.

16 Richard Leider, *The Power of Purpose* (Toronto: Fawcett Gold Medal Books, 1985): p. 166.

17 McNally, *Even Eagles Need A Push*, p. 76.

18 Ibid., p. 81.

19 Charles Garfield in McNally, ibid., p. 34.

20 Gail Sheehy in McNally, ibid.

21 Peter Jensen, *The Inside Edge: High Performance Through Mental Fitness* (Toronto: Macmillan Canada, 1992): p. 7.

22 Jim Clemmer, *Growing the Distance: Timeless Principles For Personal, Career, and Family Success* (Canada: TCG Press, an imprint of the Clemmer Group Inc., 1999): pp. 152–153.

23 Warren Bennis and Bert Namus, *Leaders: The Strategies For Taking Charge* (New York: Perennial Library, 1985): p. 17.

24 IKEA website, "IKEA's Vision" at <http://www.ikea.com/content/main.asp?docID=375&tab=4>.

25 Brian Nattrass and Mary Altomare, *The Natural Step For Business: Wealth, Ecology and the Evolutionary Corporation* (Gabriola Island, BC: New Society Publishers, 1999): p. 59.

26 Tom Chappell, *The Soul of a Business: Managing For Profit and the Common Good* (New York: Bantam Books, 1993): pp. 33 and 195.

27 Nattrass and Altomare, *Natural Step for Business*, p. 76.

28 CMP Publications, "Future of computing lies in the power of networks," *Computer Reseller News* (Manhasset: December 4, 1995), Duns: 00-136-8083.

29 This model is from Belgard-Fisher-Rayner, a consulting company that did team training for IBM Canada in the early 1990s.

30 Stephen Rayner, principal of Rayner & Associates, Inc., <http://www.rayner assoc.com>, from e-mail correspondence with Bob Willard, December 10, 1999.

31 Stephen R. Covey, *The 7 Habits of Highly Effective People* (New York: Fireside Books, 1989): p. 76.

32 Tom Peters, *The Tom Peters Seminars: Crazy Times Call For Crazy Organizations* (New York: Vintage Books, 1994): p. 245.

33 Rayner, e-mail.

34 Hay/McBer, "A Framework for Organizational Effectiveness and Change" (in 9612-2599-IBM Framework. brochure used in IBM training): p. 1.
35 Ibid., p. 3.
36 Collins and Porras, *Built To Last*, p. 4.
37 John Elkington, *Cannibals With Forks: The Triple Bottom Line of 21st Century Business* (Gabriola Island, BC: New Society Publishers, 1998): p. 60.
38 Michael Porter and Claas van der Linde, "Green and Competitive: Ending the Stalemate," *Harvard Business Review on Business and the Environment*, Reprint 95507 (originally published in *Harvard Business Review*, September-October 1995): p. 153.
39 Forest L. Reinhardt, *Down To Earth: Applying Business Principles to Environmental Management* (Boston: Harvard Business Review Press, 2000): p. 91.
40 Martin Bennett and Peter James, *The Green Bottom Line: Environmental Accounting For Management* (Sheffield, UK: Greanleaf Publishing, 1998): p. 106.
41 Max DePree, *Leadership Is An Art* (New York: Dell, 1989): p. 23.
42 Nattrass and Altomare, *Natural Step for Business*, pp. 87–88, 99.
43 Reuters News Service, "Silicon Valley not as threatened by energy crisis as some think," Reuters Daily World Environment News, San Francisco (January 14, 2001).
44 Paul Hawken, Amory B. Lovins, and L. Hunter Lovins, "A Road Map for Natural Capitalism," *Harvard Business Review* (May-June 1999): p. 149. Reprinted by permission of *Harvard Business Review*. Copyright ©1999 by Harvard Business School Publishing Corporation; all rights reserved.
45 Joseph Romm, *Cool Companies: How the Best Businesses Boost Profits and Productivity by Cutting Greenhouse Gas Emissions* (Washington, DC: Island Press, 1999): pp. 77–78, 91.
46 Ibid., pp. 219–244.
47 Ibid., pp. 84–98.
48 Rocky Mountain Institute (Alex Wilson, Jennifer L. Uncapher, Lisa McManigal, L. Hunter Lovins, Maureen Cureton, William D. Browning), *Green Development: Integrating Ecology and Real Estate* (New York: John Wiley & Sons, 1998): p. 173. Reprinted by permission of John Wiley & Sons, Inc.
49 Paul Hawken, Amory B. Lovins, and L. Hunter Lovins, *Natural Capitalism: Creating the Next Industrial Revolution* (Boston: Little, Brown and Company, 1999): p. 88.
50 Romm, *Cool Companies*, p. 98.

Benefit 4: Reduced Expenses in Manufacturing

1 Paul Hawken, Amory B. Lovins, and L. Hunter Lovins, "A Road for Natural Capitalism," *Harvard Business Review* (May-June 1999): p. 146. Reprinted by

permission of *Harvard Business Review*. Copyright ©1999 by Harvard Business School Publishing Corporation; all rights reserved.

2 Ernst Von Weizsacher, Amory B. Lovins, and L. Hunter Lovins, *Factor Four: Doubling Wealth, Halving Resource Use—The New Report to the Club of Rome* (London: Earthscan, 1997): p. xx.

3 Based on diagrams and data used by Susan Burns and Gil Friend, environmental consultants, in their breakout sessions at The Natural Step Five-Day Advanced Training conference in Chicago, May 6-10, 1998.

4 Von Weizsacher, Lovins, and Lovins, *Factor Four*, pp. 242–244. The Schmidt-Bleek MIPS measure of material efficiency is from Friederich Schmidt-Bleek, director of the Wuppertal Institute's Division for Material Flows and Eco-Restructuring, *Carnoules Declaration of the Factor Ten Club*, 1994.

5 Ray Anderson, *Mid-Course Correction* (Atlanta GA: The Peregrinzilla Press, 1998): p. 9.

6 World Business Council for Sustainable Development website, "Eco-Efficiency Case Study Collection: Chaparral Steel Case," at <http://www.wbcsd.ch/eedata/chaparra.htm>.

7 Reuters News Service, "Ford, GM set green standards for suppliers," Reuters Daily World Environmental News, Detroit (September 22, 1999).

8 The Delphi Group, *Environmental Performance and Competitive Advantage: a Business Guide*, Publication 3648E, prepared for the Ontario Ministry of the Environment (Toronto: Queen's Printer of Ontario, 1998): p. 9. Copyright ©Queen's Printer for Ontario, 1999. Reproduced with permission.

9 Von Weizsacher, Lovins, and Lovins, *Factor Four*, p. 242.

10 Thomas Casten, *Turning Off The Heat: Why America Must Double Energy Efficiency To Save Money And Reduce Global Warming* (New York: Prometheus Books, 1998): pp. 141 and 198.

11 Robin Pomeroy, "Developing countries are giving polluting fuels ...." Reuters Daily World Environmental News, Trieste, Italy (March 6, 2001).

12 Reuters News Service, "Dupont sets environmental, biotech goals," Reuters Daily World Environmental News, Boston (September 23, 1999).

13 Reuters News Service, "Sainsbury to use wind power at Scots depot," Reuters Daily World Environmental News, London, UK (March 14, 2001).

14 Carl Frankel, *In Earth's Company: Business, Environment and the Challenge of Sustainability* (Gabriola Island, BC: New Society Publishers, 1998): pp. 185–186.

15 "Power to the people," *Tampa Tribune* (July 7, 1999). Available on the web at <http://www.tampatrib.com/>.

16 Hawken, Lovins, and Lovins, "Road Map for Natural Capitalism," p. 157.

17 Ibid., p. 149.

18 The Delphi Group, *Environmental Performance*, p. 3. Copyright ©Queen's

Printer for Ontario, 1999. Reproduced with permission.

19 Hawken, Lovins, and Lovins, "Road Map for Natural Capitalism," p. 157.

20 Tayce Wakefield, "A Systems Approach to Energy Efficiency" (remarks made to Canada's Energy Efficiency Conference, Ottawa, May 1999). Tayce Wakefield is the Vice-President, Corporate and Environmental Affairs, of General Motors of Canada Ltd.

21 The Delphi Group, *Environmental Performance*, p. 29. Copyright ©Queen's Printer for Ontario, 1999. Reproduced with permission.

22 Hawken, Lovins, and Lovins, "Road Map for Natural Capitalism," p. 149.

23 Ibid., p. 149.

24 Ibid., p. 150.

25 Ibid., p.156.

26 Ibid.

27 Wakefield, "Systems Approach to Energy Efficiency."

28 Paul Hawken, Amory B. Lovins, and L. Hunter Lovins, *Natural Capitalism: Creating the Next Industrial Revolution* (Boston: Little, Brown and Company, 1999): p. 53.

29 Scott Johnson, "Application of the Balanced Scorecard Approach," *Corporate Environmental Strategy* 5, no. 4 (summer 1998): p. 40.

30 The Delphi Group, *Environmental Performance*, p. 30. Copyright ©Queen's Printer for Ontario, 1999. Reproduced with permission.

31 "Chocolate Factory Installs 'Living Machine' to Treat Wastewater," *Business and the Environment* (October 1996): p. 10. Available from Cutter Information Corp. in Arlington, MA.

32 The Delphi Group, *Environmental Performance*, p. 5. Copyright ©Queen's Printer for Ontario, 1999. Reproduced with permission.

33 Frankel, *In Earth's Company*, p. 40.

34 Hawken, Lovins, and Lovins, "Road Map for Natural Capitalism," p. 148.

35 Ibid.

36 Frankel, *In Earth's Company*, p. 172.

37 Ibid., p. 173.

38 Madhavi Acharya, "Green is good for business," *The Toronto Star* (September 16, 1999).

39 Frankel, *In Earth's Company*, p. 103.

40 IBM, *Environment and Well-being Progress Report* (International Business Machines Corporation, 1999): p. 24.

41 The Delphi Group, *Environmental Performance*, p. 31. Copyright ©Queen's Printer for Ontario, 1999. Reproduced with permission.

42 Ibid., p. 3. Copyright ©Queen's Printer for Ontario, 1999. Reproduced with permission.

43 Hawken, Lovins, and Lovins, “Road Map for Natural Capitalism,” p. 153.

44 Reuters News Service, “Toyota French Plant to be Eco-Friendly,” Reuters Daily World Environment News, Tokyo (August 4, 1999).

45 Frankel, *In Earth’s Company*, p. 83.

46 The Canadian Eco-Industrial Network, *An Introduction to Eco-Industrial Networking and the Canadian Eco-Industrial Network* (brochure published by the network in 2001): p. 2. Further information is available from <http://www.cein.org>.

47 World Business Council for Sustainable Development website, “Eco-Efficiency Case Study Collection: Chaparral Steel Case” at <http://www.wbcsd.ch/eedata/chaparra.htm>.

48 Canadian Eco-Industrial Network, brochure, pp. 1 and 6–7.

49 Sonia Labatt, “Corporate Response Toward Environmental Issues: A Case Study of Packaging” (Ph.D. dissertation, Department of Geography, University of Toronto, January, 1995): pp. 42–46.

50 Rocky Mountain Institute (Alex Wilson, Jennifer L. Uncapher, Lisa McManigal, L. Hunter Lovins, Maureen Cureton, William D. Browning), *Green Development: Integrating Ecology and Real Estate* (New York: John Wiley & Sons, 1998): pp. 406–407. Reprinted by permission of John Wiley & Sons, Inc.

51 Anderson, *Mid-Course Correction*, p. 14.

52 Sustainable Enterprise Academy, *Report on the First Business Leader Seminar, Fall 2000* (Toronto: Sustainable Enterprise Academy, Schulich School of Business, York University, 4700 Keele Street, 2000): p. 8.

53 Bette K. Fishbein, “EPR: What Does It Mean? Where Is It Headed?” *P2: Pollution Prevention Review*, 8 (1998): p. 16. References are to a copy printed from the web at <http://www.informinc.org/eprarticle.htm>.

54 Hawken, Lovins, and Lovins, “Road Map for Natural Capitalism,” p. 150.

55 The Delphi Group, *Environmental Performance*, pp. 6–7. Copyright ©Queen’s Printer for Ontario, 1999. Reproduced with permission.

56 Martin Bennett and Peter James, *The Green Bottom Line: Environmental Accounting For Management* (Sheffield, UK: Greanleaf Publishing, 1998): based on diagrams on pp. 71 and 313.

57 Ibid., p. 23.

58 Ibid., p. 71.

59 Fishbein, “EPR,” p. 16.

60 John Elkington, *Cannibals With Forks: The Triple Bottom Line of 21st Century Business* (Gabriola Island, BC: New Society Publishers, 1998): p. xii.

61 Bennett and James, *Green Bottom Line*, p. 109.

Benefit 5: Reduced Expenses at Commercial Sites

1 Paul Hawken, Amory B. Lovins, and L. Hunter Lovins, "A Road Map for Natural Capitalism," *Harvard Business Review* (May-June, 1999): p. 149. Reprinted by permission of *Harvard Business Review*. Copyright ©1999 by Harvard Business School Publishing Corporation; all rights reserved.

2 Brian Nattrass and Mary Altomare, *The Natural Step For Business: Wealth, Ecology and the Evolutionary Corporation* (Gabriola Island, BC: New Society Publishers, 1999): pp. 91 and 92.

3 The Delphi Group, *Environmental Performance and Competitive Advantage: a Business Guide*, Publication 3648E, prepared for the Ontario Ministry of the Environment (Toronto: Queen's Printer of Ontario, 1998): p. 4. Copyright ©Queen's Printer for Ontario, 1999. Reproduced with permission.

4 Ibid., p. 19. The quote within the quotation is from the New Bottom Line website. Copyright ©Queen's Printer for Ontario, 1999. Reproduced with permission.

5 Carol Smith, "Voluntary Simplicity Lets Employees Give Themselves a Raise," *Seattle Post-Intelligencer* (May 22, 1998).

6 Environmental Defense Fund website, "Paper Task Force: Synopsis" at <http://www.edf.org/pubs/Reports/ptf/text/synopsis.html>.

7 Nattrass and Altomare, *Natural Step for Business*, p. 26.

8 Hawken, Lovins, and Lovins, "Road Map for Natural Capitalism," p. 150.

9 Ibid.

10 Ibid.

11 World Business Council for Sustainable Development website, "Eco-Efficiency Case Study Collection: Xerox Case" at <http://www.wbcsd.ch/eedata/xerox .htm>.

12 Nattrass and Altomare, *Natural Step for Business*, p. 92.

13 Thomas Casten, *Turning Off The Heat: Why America Must Double Energy Efficiency To Save Money And Reduce Global Warming* (New York: Prometheus Books, 1998): p. 92.

14 U.S. Environmental Protection Agency (EPA) website, "Integrated Approach" at <http://inotes.icfkaiser.com/epa/estar/esbhome/sideepa.html>.

15 EPA Energy Star website for business at <http://yosemite1.epa.gov/estar/business.nsf/webmenus/bins?OpenDocument&pca=Business&type=tools>.

16 Hawken, Lovins, and Lovins, "Road Map for Natural Capitalism," p. 157.

17 Rocky Mountain Institute (Alex Wilson, Jennifer L. Uncapher, Lisa McManigal, L. Hunter Lovins, Maureen Cureton, William D. Browning), *Green Development: Integrating Ecology and Real Estate* (New York: John Wiley & Sons, 1998): p. 329. Reprinted by permission of John Wiley & Sons, Inc.

18 Madhavi Acharya, "Green is good for business," *The Toronto Star* (September 16, 1999).

19 Nattrass and Altomare, *Natural Step for Business*, p. 71.

20 This is a Sound Bite fact from the internal IBM e-speech site, May 1998.

21 Sabu Pathan, "Ryerson Saves As It Expands," *Property Management Report* (February-March 1997): pp. 21–23.

22 Intergovernmental Panel on Climate Change (IPCC), *Climate Change 1995: Impacts, Adaptations and Mitigation of Climate Change: Scientific-Technical Analyses* (contribution of Working Group II to the Second Assessment Report of the Intergovernmental Panel on Climate Change; Summary for Policymakers, 1995): p. 14.

23 Ernst Von Weizsacher, Amory B. Lovins, and L. Hunter Lovins, *Factor Four: Doubling Wealth, Halving Resource Use—The New Report to the Club of Rome* (London: Earthscan, 1997): p. xvi.

24 Ibid., p. 244.

25 Paul Hawken, "Natural Capitalism," *Mother Jones* (March-April 1997): p. 50.

26 Ibid.

27 Von Weizsacher, Lovins, and Lovins, *Factor Four*, pp. 20–29.

28 Natural Resources Canada (NRC) Office of Energy Efficiency (OEE) website, "About Us" at <http://oee.nrcan.gc.ca/fbi/aboutus.cfm>.

29 Ibid.

30 NRC OEE website, "The National Research Council of Canada: Energy Efficiency Pioneer" at <http://oee.nrcan.gc.ca/fbi/casestudies/cs_nrc2.cfm>.

31 Cameron Smith, "A Potent Way To Heat Portables," *The Toronto Star* (February 20, 1999): B6.

32 The Delphi Group, *Environmental Performance and Competitive Advantage: a Business Guide*, Publication 3648E, prepared for the Ontario Ministry of the Environment (Toronto: Queen's Printer of Ontario, 1998): p. iii. Copyright ©Queen's Printer for Ontario, 1999. Reproduced with permission.

33 Von Weizsacher, Lovins, and Lovins, *Factor Four*, pp. 10–12.

34 Paul Hawken, Amory B. Lovins, and L. Hunter Lovins, *Natural Capitalism: Creating the Next Industrial Revolution* (Boston: Little, Brown and Company, 1999): pp. 82–83.

35 Rocky Mountain Institute, *Green Development*, p. 25.

36 Hawken, Lovins, and Lovins, *Natural Capitalism*, p. 87.

37 Ibid., p. 97.

38 CMHC's Healthy House in Toronto website, "Facts & Figures" at <http://www.cmhc-schl.gc.ca/popup/hhtoronto/facts.htm>.

39 Ibid.

40 Hawken, Lovins, and Lovins, *Natural Capitalism*, p. 111.

41 Rocky Mountain Institute, *Green Development*, pp. 25–65.

42 Joel Makower, "How to Make Your PC Earth Friendly," *Co-Op America Quarterly* (spring 1999): p. 9.

43 Acharya, "Green is good for business."

44 Carl Frankel, *In Earth's Company: Business, Environment, and the Challenge of Sustainability* (Gabriola Island, BC: New Society Publishers, 1998): p. 123.

45 Nattrass and Altomare, *Natural Step for Business*, p. 92.

46 Hawken, Lovins, and Lovins, "Road Map for Natural Capitalism," p. 156. Reprinted by permission of *Harvard Business Review*. Copyright ©1999 by Harvard Business School Publishing Corporation; all rights reserved.

47 Hawken, Lovins, and Lovins, *Natural Capitalism*, pp. 219–220.

48 Ian Wylie, "We Recycle Your Air," *FastCompany* (November 2000), <http://www.fastcompany.com/online/40/wf_morrell.html>. Reprinted with permission. All rights reserved. To subscribe, please call (800) 542•6029 or visit <www.fastcompany.com>.

49 Ray Anderson, *Mid-Course Correction* (Atlanta, GA: The Peregrinzilla Press, 1998): pp. 202–203.

50 "Proposal Aims to Encourage Telecommuting," *Washington Post* (July 20, 1999).

51 "Telecommuting Could Change Labor Laws," *Investor's Business Daily* (December 17, 1999). Available on the web at <http://www.investors.com/>.

52 "Proposal Aims to Encourage Telecommuting."

52 Ibid.

54 "Telecommuting Could Change Labor Laws."

55 John B. Horrigan, Frances H. Irwin, and Elizabeth Cook, *Taking a Byte Out of Carbon: Electronic Industries Alliance, and International Cooperative for Environmental Leadership* (Washington, DC: World Resources Institute, 1998): pp. 5–12.

56 Hawken, Lovins, and Lovins, "Road Map for Natural Capitalism," p. 157.

Benefit 6: Increased Revenue/Market Share

1 Forest L. Reinhardt, "Bringing The Environment Down To Earth," *Harvard Business Review* (July-August 1999): p. 150. Reprinted by permission of *Harvard Business Review*. Copyright ©1999 by Harvard Business School Publishing Corporation; all rights reserved.

2 Matthew Arnold and Robert Day, *The Next Bottom Line: Making Sustainable Development Tangible* (Washington, DC: The World Resources Institute, 1998): p. 7.

3 Reinhardt, "Bringing the Environment Down to Earth," pp. 151 and 152.

4 Ibid., pp. 150 and 151.

5 The Alliance For Environmental Innovation website, *Catalyzing Environmental Results: Lessons in Advocacy Organization-Business Partnerships* (a report

sponsored by the J.M. Kaplan Fund) at <http://www.edfpewalliance.org/kapintro.html>.

6 Forest L. Reinhardt, *Down To Earth: Applying Business Principles to Environmental Management* (Boston: Harvard Business Review Press, 2000): p. 40.

7 Reuters News Service, "EPA says will advertise energy star product label," Reuters Daily World Environmental News, Washington (August 13, 1999).

8 Reuters News Service, "U.S., industry energy efficiency program saves 75 bln KW of power," Reuters Daily World Environment News, Washington (March 22, 2001).

9 Yuzo Saeki, "Big Japanese firms embrace 'green accounting'," Reuters Daily World Environmental News, Tokyo (August 7, 1999).

10 Rocky Mountain Institute website, "Home Energy Brief #7: Computers and Peripherals" at <http://www.rmi.org/hebs/heb7/heb7.html>.

11 George Blum, Jerald Blumberg, and Age Korsvold, for the World Business Council for Sustainable Development, *Environmental Performance and Shareholder Value* (WBCSD, 1997): p. 14.

12 Carl Frankel, *In Earth's Company: Business, Environment, and the Challenge of Sustainability* (Gabriola Island, BC: New Society Publishers, 1998): pp. 35–94. Frankel describes four eras in the history of corporate environmentalism, which are loosely related to the five stages in this continuum.

13 The Delphi Group, *Environmental Performance and Competitive Advantage: a Business Guide*, Publication 3648E, prepared for the Ontario Ministry of the Environment (Toronto: Queen's Printer of Ontario, 1998): pp. 29–36. Copyright ©Queen's Printer for Ontario, 1999. Reproduced with permission.

14 Ibid., p. 9. Copyright ©Queen's Printer for Ontario, 1999. Reproduced with permission.

15 Martin Bennett and Peter James, *The Green Bottom Line: Environmental Accounting For Management* (Sheffield, UK: Greanleaf Publishing, 1998): based on diagrams on pp. 238–245.

16 Arnold and Day, *Next Bottom Line*, pp. 44–45.

17 The Delphi Group, *Environmental Performance*, p. 39. Copyright ©Queen's Printer for Ontario, 1999. Reproduced with permission.

18 Ibid. Copyright ©Queen's Printer for Ontario, 1999. Reproduced with permission.

19 Ibid., p. 40. Copyright ©Queen's Printer for Ontario, 1999. Reproduced with permission.

20 The Global Reporting Initiative website, "GRI Overview" at <http://www.globalreporting.org/AboutGRI/Overview.htm>.

21 The Genuine Progress Indicator website, "Questions" at <http://www. cyberus.ca/choose.sustain/Question/GPI.html>.

22 Frankel, *In Earth's Company*, p. 128.

23 Karl-Henrik Robert, founder of The Natural Step in Sweden, "Foreword," in Brian Nattrass and Mary Altomare, *The Natural Step For Business: Wealth, Ecology and the Evolutionary Corporation* (Gabriola Island, BC: New Society Publishers, 1999): p. xiv.

24 Interface, Inc., *Sustainability Report* (Atlanta, GA: Interface, Inc., 1997): p. 11.

25 Bennett and James, *The Green Bottom Line*, p. 103.

26 Stephan Schmidheiny, with the Business Council for Sustainable Development, *Changing Course: A Global Business Perspective on Development and the Economy* (Cambridge, MA: The MIT Press, 1992): p. 86.

27 Karl-Henrik Robert, Herman Daly, Paul Hawken, and John Holmberg, *A Compass For Sustainable Development* (a handout of in-depth articles and related readings given to participants at The Natural Step Five-Day Advanced Training conference in Chicago, May 6–10, 1998.

28 John Elkington, *Cannibals With Forks: The Triple Bottom Line of 21st Century Business* (Gabriola Island, BC: New Society Publishers, 1998): p. 5.

29 Ibid.

30 The Delphi Group, *Environmental Performance*, p. 3. Copyright ©Queen's Printer for Ontario, 1999. Reproduced with permission.

31 Donella Meadows, "Two Mindsets, Two Visions of Sustainable Agriculture," *The Global Citizen* (July 29, 1999).

32 Ibid.

33 Reuters News Service, "J. Sainsbury eyes gin as organic food sales double," Reuters Daily World Environment News, London (September 8, 1999).

34 Reinhardt, *Down to Earth*, p. 39.

35 Ibid., p. 37.

36 Frankel, *In Earth's Company*, p. 140.

37 Ibid., p. 141.

38 Elkington, *Cannibals With Forks*, pp. 6 and 124.

39 Frankel, *In Earth's Company*, p. 140.

40 Reuters News Service, "Renewable supplier sees significant UK demand," Reuters Daily World Environment News, London (October 1, 1999).

41 Reuters News Service, "Canadians willing to pay more for 'green' cars," Reuters Daily World Environment News, Toronto (October 13, 1999).

42 Sustainable Enterprise Academy, *Report on the First Business Leader Seminar*, Fall 2000 (Toronto: Sustainable Enterprise Academy, Schulich School of Business, York University, 4700 Keele Street, 2000).

43 Ibid., p. 11.

44 David Dorsey, "The New Spirit of Work," *FastCompany* 16 (August 1998). Also available on the web at <http://www.fastcompany.com/online/16/

barrett.html>. Reprinted with permission. All rights reserved. To subscribe, please call (800) 542•6029 or visit <www.fastcompany.com>.

45 Rocky Mountain Institute (Alex Wilson, Jennifer L. Uncapher, Lisa McManigal, L. Hunter Lovins, Maureen Cureton, William D. Browning), *Green Development: Integrating Ecology and Real Estate* (New York: John Wiley & Sons, 1998): p. 332. Reprinted by permission of John Wiley & Sons, Inc.

46 Scott Johnson, "Application of the Balanced Scorecard Approach," *Corporate Environmental Strategy* 5, no. 4 (summer 1998): p. 40.

47 World Business Council for Sustainable Development website, "Eco-Efficiency Case Study Collection: Electrolux Case" at <http://www.wbcsd.ch/eedata/electrolux.htm>.

48 The Delphi Group, *Environmental Performance*, p. 3. Copyright ©Queen's Printer for Ontario, 1999. Reproduced with permission.

49 Brian Nattrass and Mary Altomare, *The Natural Step For Business: Wealth, Ecology and the Evolutionary Corporation* (Gabriola Island, BC: New Society Publishers, 1999): pp. 99 and 100.

50 Reinhardt, "Bringing the Environment Down to Earth," p. 152.

51 "How Green Is Your Market?" *The Economist* (January 8, 2000). Also available on the Environics website at <http://www.environics.net/eil/articles/green/>.

52 Stuart Hart, "The Bottom of the Pyramid," *Tomorrow* magazine 11, no. 1 (January-February 2001): pp. 9–11.

53 Carl Frankel, "Let There Be Light Bulbs." *Tomorrow* magazine 11, no. 1 (January-February 2001): pp. 12–13.

54 Carl Frankel, "Storming the Digital Divide," *Tomorrow* magazine 11, no. 1 (January-February 2001): pp. 42–45.

55 Malcolm Gladwell, *The Tipping Point: How Little Things Can Make a Big Difference* (New York: Little Brown and Company, 2000).

56 Paul Hawken, Amory B. Lovins, and L. Hunter Lovins, "A Road Map for Natural Capitalism," *Harvard Business Review* (May-June, 1999): p. 146. Reprinted by permission of *Harvard Business Review*. Copyright ©1999 by Harvard Business School Publishing Corporation; all rights reserved.

57 Ibid., p. 154.

58 Ibid.

59 Bennett and James, *The Green Bottom Line*, p. 261.

60 Ibid., p. 270.

61 *Green Business Letter*, 1997, p. 7.

62 Bennett and James, *The Green Bottom Line*, p. 266.

63 "Centerbeam tells Businesses: Don't Buy Computers, Buy Services," *New York Times* (August 9, 1999).

64 Paul Hawken, Amory B. Lovins, and L. Hunter Lovins, *Natural Capitalism:*

Creating the Next Industrial Revolution (Boston: Little, Brown and Company, 1999): p. 19.

65 Stuart Hart, "Beyond Greening: Strategies For a Sustainable World," *Harvard Business Review on Business and the Environment*, Reprint 97105 (originally published in *Harvard Business Review*, January-February 1997): pp. 108 and 116.

66 KPMG website, "KPMG in unique link with Body Shop," international press release, December. 14, 1998. Available at <http://www.kpmg.com/>.

67 Reuters News Service, "Fujitsu launches software for 'Green' management," Reuters Daily World Environment News, Tokyo (August 24, 1999).

Benefit 7: Reduced Risk, Easier Financing

1 Forest L. Reinhardt, "Bringing The Environment Down To Earth," *Harvard Business Review* (July-August 1999): p. 155. Reprinted by permission of *Harvard Business Review*. Copyright ©1999 by Harvard Business School Publishing Corporation; all rights reserved.

2 KPMG website, "1999 Risk Survey Report" at <http://www.kpmg.ca/risk/surmain.htm>.

3 Innovest Strategic Value Advisors website, "EcoValue'21: An In-depth Description" at <http://www.innovestgroup.com/ecovalue_indepth.html>.

4 International Council of Chemical Associations website, <http://www.cefic.be/activities/hse/rc/rc.htm>.

5 Reinhardt, "Bringing the Environment Down to Earth," p. 155.

6 Brian Nattrass and Mary Altomare, *The Natural Step For Business: Wealth, Ecology and the Evolutionary Corporation* (Gabriola Island, BC: New Society Publishers, 1999): pp. 50–51.

7 Ibid., pp. 51–52.

8 Ibid., p. 52.

9 Paul Hawken, Amory B. Lovins, and L. Hunter Lovins, "A Road Map for Natural Capitalism," *Harvard Business Review* (May-June 1999): p. 155.

10 David Wright, "New Rules: Name Game," *Risky Business* 2 (2001): p. 6. Available from PricewaterhouseCoopers in Toronto.

11 Martin Bennett and Peter James, *The Green Bottom Line: Environmental Accounting For Management* (Sheffield, UK: Greanleaf Publishing, 1998): based on diagrams on p. 125.

12 Forest L. Reinhardt, *Down To Earth: Applying Business Principles to Environmental Management* (Boston: Harvard Business Review Press, 2000): p. 137.

13 Hawken, Lovins, and Lovins, "Road for Natural Capitalism," p. 155.

14 Reuters News Service, "Major disasters killed 17,000 people and caused about $38 billion," Reuters Daily World Environmental News, Zurich (January 11, 2001).

15 Hawken, Lovins, and Lovins, "Road for Natural Capitalism," p. 155.

16 Sustainable Systems Associates, *Applying Sustainable Development to Business: Realizing the Benefits*, Publication 3649E, prepared for the Ontario Ministry of the Environment (Toronto: Queen's Printer of Ontario, 1998): p. 5.

17 Ibid., p. 6.

18 Reinhardt, "Bringing the Environment Down to Earth," p. 155.

19 Nattrass and Altomare, *Natural Step for Business*, p. 27.

20 Innovest,"EcoValue'21," <http://www.innovestgroup.com/ecovalue_indepth .html>.

21 Frank Dixon, managing director, Research & Development, Innovest Strategic Value Advisors, personal correspondence, July 30, 1999.

22 Michael Jantzi Research Associates Inc. website, "Socially Responsible Stock Index Launched," press release, February 15, 2000. Available at <http://www. mjra-jsi.com>.

23 Sustainable Enterprise Academy, *Report on the First Business Leader Seminar, Fall 2000* (Toronto: Sustainable Enterprise Academy, Schulich School of Business, York University, 4700 Keele Street, 2000): p. 9.

24 Reuters News Service, "More global firms seeing profits from environment – KPMG," Reuters Daily World Environmental News, The Hague (September, 23, 1999).

25 The Delphi Group, *Environmental Performance and Competitive Advantage: a Business Guide*, Publication 3648E, prepared for the Ontario Ministry of the Environment (Toronto: Queen's Printer of Ontario, 1998): p. 8. Copyright ©Queen's Printer for Ontario, 1999. Reproduced with permission.

26 Ibid. Copyright ©Queen's Printer for Ontario, 1999. Reproduced with permission.

27 Sustainable Systems Associates, *Applying Sustainable Development to Business*, pp. 26–27.

28 Carl Frankel, "Happy Old Year," *Tomorrow* magazine 11, no. 1 (January-February 2001): p. 61.

29 Roger Adams, "Linking Financial and Environmental Performance," *Environmental Accounting and Auditing Reporter* 2, no. 10 (May 1997).

30 Ibid.

31 Duncan Austin and Robert Repetto, *Pure Profit: The Financial Implications of Environmental Performance* (Washington, DC: World Resources Institute, 2000): p. 3.

32 Sustainable Systems Associates, *Applying Sustainable Development to Business*, p. 6.

33 The Delphi Group, *Environmental Performance*, p. 7. Copyright ©Queen's Printer for Ontario, 1999. Reproduced with permission.

34 Stephan Schmidheiny, with the Business Council for Sustainable Development,

Changing Course: A Global Business Perspective on Development and the Economy (Cambridge, MA: The MIT Press, 1992): p. 64.

35 The Delphi Group, *Environmental Performance*, p. 8. ©Queen's Printer for Ontario, 1999. Reproduced with permission.

36 George Blum, Jerald Blumberg, and Age Korsvold, for the World Business Council for Sustainable Development, *Environmental Performance and Shareholder Value* (WBCSD, 1997): p. 15.

37 Austin and Repetto, Pure Profit, p. 47.

38 IBM, IBM *Annual Report 1999* (New York: IBM Stockholder Relations, IBM Corporation, 1999): p. 79.

39 Austin and Repetto, *Pure Profit*, pp. 1–38.

Conclusion

1 Forest L. Reinhardt, "Bringing The Environment Down To Earth," *Harvard Business Review* (July-August 1999): p. 157. Reprinted by permission of *Harvard Business Review.* Copyright ©1999 by Harvard Business School Publishing Corporation; all rights reserved.

2 William M. Mercer, *Beyond the Bottom Line: What CEOs are Thinking* (Toronto: William M. Mercer Company, 1999).

3 Paul Hawken, Amory B. Lovins, and L. Hunter Lovins, "A Road Map for Natural Capitalism," *Harvard Business Review* (May-June, 1999): p. 155. Reprinted by permission of *Harvard Business Review.* Copyright ©1999 by Harvard Business School Publishing Corporation; all rights reserved.

4 Scott Johnson, "Application of the Balanced Scorecard Approach," *Corporate Environmental Strategy* 5, no. 4 (summer 1998): p. 35; and Robert Kaplan and David Norton, *The Balanced Scorecard: Translating Strategy Into Action* (Boston: Harvard Business School Press, 1996).

5 Reinhardt, "Bringing the Environment Down to Earth," p. 150.

6 Michael Porter and Claas van der Linde, "Green and Competitive: Ending the Stalemate," *Harvard Business Review on Business and the Environment*, Reprint 95507 (originally published in *Harvard Business Review*, September-October 1995): p. 145.

7 Carl Frankel, *In Earth's Company: Business, Environment, and the Challenge of Sustainability* (Gabriola Island, BC: New Society Publishers, 1998): pp. 104–109.

8 Christopher Plant and Judith Plant (eds.), editorial introduction to Debra Lynn Dadd and Andre Carothers' "A Bill Of Goods? Green Consuming In Perspective" in *Green Business: Hope or Hoax?* (Gabriola Island, BC: New Society Publishers, 1991): p. 11.

9 Brian Nattrass and Mary Altomare, *The Natural Step For Business: Wealth, Ecology*

and the Evolutionary Corporation (Gabriola Island, BC: New Society Publishers, 1999): p. 64.

10 Thea Singer, "Can Business Still Save The World?" *Inc. Magazine* (April 1, 2001).

11 Debra Lynn Dadd and Andre Carothers, "A Bill Of Goods? Green Consuming In Perspective" in Christopher Plant and Judith Plant (eds.), *Green Business: Hope or Hoax?* (Gabriola Island, BC: New Society Publishers, 1991): p. 14.

12 "Surveys Find Consumers Distrustful of Corporate Environmental Practices," *Green Market Alert* (March 1991): p. 4.

13 Christopher Plant and David Albert, "Green Business in a Gray World—Can It Be Done?" in Christopher Plant and Judith Plant (eds.), *Green Business: Hope or Hoax?* (Gabriola Island, BC: New Society Publishers, 1991): p. 4.

14 Forest L. Reinhardt, *Down To Earth: Applying Business Principles to Environmental Management* (Boston: Harvard Business Review Press, 2000): p. 5.

15 Paul Hawken, Amory B. Lovins, and L. Hunter Lovins, *Natural Capitalism: Creating the Next Industrial Revolution* (Boston: Little, Brown and Company, 1999): p. xi.

16 Peter Sandman, "It's the outrage, stupid," *Tomorrow magazine*, 2 (March/April 1996).

17 Johnson, "Application of the Balanced Scorecard," p. 35.

18 Matthew Arnold and Robert Day, *The Next Bottom Line: Making Sustainable Development Tangible* (Washington, DC: The World Resources Institute, 1998): pp. 42–43.

19 Thomas Casten, *Turning Off The Heat: Why America Must Double Energy Efficiency To Save Money And Reduce Global Warming* (New York: Prometheus Books, 1998): p. 92.

20 Ibid., pp. 92 and 93.

21 Hawken, Lovins, and Lovins, "Road for Natural Capitalism," p. 148.

22 Ibid., p. 156.

23 The Alliance For Environmental Innovation website, *Catalyzing Environmental Results: Lessons in Advocacy Organization-Business Partnership* (a report sponsored by the J.M. Kaplan Fund) at <http://www.edfpewalliance.org/kapcompany.html>.

24 Frankel, *In Earth's Company*, p. 124.

25 Ibid., p. 123.

26 Ibid., p. 125.

27 George Blum, Jerald Blumberg, and Age Korsvold, for the World Business Council for Sustainable Development, *Environmental Performance and Shareholder Value* (WBCSD, 1997).

28 Noah Walley and Bradley Whitehead, "It's Not Easy Being Green," *Harvard*

Business Review on Business and the Environment, Reprint 94310 (originally published in *Harvard Business Review*, May-June 1994): pp. 99 and 101.

29 John Elkington, *Cannibals With Forks: The Triple Bottom Line of 21st Century Business* (Gabriola Island, BC: New Society Publishers, 1998): p. 38.

30 Arnold and Day, *Next Bottom Line*, p. 5.

30 Reinhardt, "Bringing the Environment Down to Earth," p. 153.

Bibliography

THE FOLLOWING BOOKS AND ARTICLES were used as source material for this book. They may be of interest to leaders interested in further exploring the business case for sustainable development and the power of engaging employees in meaningful work. See the Endnotes for additional excellent web resources.

Adams, Roger. "Linking Financial and Environmental Performance." *Environmental Accounting and Auditing Reporter* 2, no. 10 (May 1997).

Anderson, Ray. *Mid-Course Correction—Toward a Sustainable Enterprise: The Interface Model.* Atlanta GA: The Peregrinzilla Press, 1998.

Arnold, Matthew and Robert Day. *The Next Bottom Line: Making Sustainable Development Tangible.* Washington, DC: The World Resources Institute, 1998.

Austin, Duncan and Robert Repetto. *Pure Profit: The Financial Implications of Environmental Claims.* Washington, DC: World Resources Institute, 2000.

Bennett, Martin and Peter James. *The Green Bottom Line: Environmental Accounting For Management.* Sheffield, UK: Greanleaf Publishing, 1998.

Bennis, Warren and Bert Namus. *Leaders: The Strategies For Taking Charge.* New York: Perennial Library, 1985.

Blanchard, Ken and Sheldon Bowles. *Gung Ho! Turn On the People in Any Organization.* New York: William Morrow and Company, 1998.

Blum, George, Jerald Blumberg, and Age Korsvold. *Environmental Performance and Shareholder Value.* World Business Council for Sustainable Development, 1997.

Buckingham, Marcus and Curt Coffman. *First Break All The Rules: What The World's Greatest Managers Do Differently.* New York: Simon & Schuster, 1999.

Casten, Thomas. *Turning Off The Heat: Why America Must Double Energy Efficiency To Save Money And Reduce Global Warming.* New York: Prometheus Books, 1998.

Chappell, Tom. *The Soul of a Business: Managing For Profit and the Common Good.* New York: Bantam Books, 1993.

Clemmer, Jim. *Growing the Distance: Timeless Principles For Personal, Career, and Family Success.* Canada: TCG Press, an imprint of the Clemmer Group Inc., 1999.

Collins, James and Jerry Porras. *Built To Last: Successful Habits of Visionary Companies.* New York: HarperCollins, 1994.

Covey, Stephen R. *The 7 Habits of Highly Effective People.* New York: Fireside Books, 1989.

The Delphi Group. *Environmental Performance and Competitive Advantage: a Business Guide.* Publication 3648E. Prepared for the Ontario Ministry of the Environment. Toronto: Queen's Printer of Ontario, 1998.

DePree, Max. *Leadership Is An Art.* New York: Dell, 1989.

DeSimone, Livio and Frank Popoff, with the Business Council for Sustainable Development. *Eco-efficiency: The Business Link to Sustainable Development.* Cambridge, MA: The MIT Press, 2000.

Dorsey, David. "The New Spirit of Work." *FastCompany* 16 (August 1998). Available at <http://www.fastcompany.com/online/16/barrett.html>.

Duxbury, Linda, Lorraine Dyke, and Natalie Lam. "Executive Summary" of *Building a World-Class Workforce.* Treasury Board of Canada Secretariat. January 1999.

Elkington, John. *Cannibals With Forks: The Triple Bottom Line of 21st Century Business.* Gabriola Island, BC: New Society Publishers, 1998.

Environics. *The Millennium Poll on Corporate Social Responsibility*, conducted by Environics International Ltd., in cooperation with The Prince of Wales Business Leaders Forum and The Conference Board.

Fishbein, Bette K. "EPR: What Does It Mean? Where Is It Headed?" *P2: Pollution Prevention Review* 8 (1998). Available at <http://www.informinc.org/eprarticle.htm>.

Fishman, Charles. "The War For Talent." *FastCompany* (August 1998). Available at <http://www.fastcompany.com/online/16/mckinsey.html>.

Frankel, Carl. *In Earth's Company: Business, Environment and the Challenge of Sustainability.* Gabriola Island, BC: New Society Publishers, 1998.

———. "Let There Be Light Bulbs." *Tomorrow* magazine 11, no. 1 (January-February 2001).

———. "Storming the Digital Divide." *Tomorrow* magazine 11, no. 1 (January-February 2001).

Hart, Stuart. "Beyond Greening: Strategies For a Sustainable World." *Harvard Business Review on Business and the Environment.* Reprint 95507. Originally published in *Harvard Business Review* (January-February 1997).

———. "The Bottom of the Pyramid." *Tomorrow* magazine 11, no. 1 (January-February 2001).

Hawken, Paul, Amory B. Lovins, and L. Hunter Lovins. "A Road Map for Natural Capitalism." *Harvard Business Review* (May-June 1999).

———. Natural Capitalism: Creating the Next Industrial Revolution. Boston: Little, Brown and Company, 1999.

Hedstrom, Gilbert, Stephen Poltorzycki, and Peter Strob. "Sustainable Development: The Next Generation of Business Opportunity." *Prism* (fourth quarter, 1998). Published by Arthur D. Little, Acorn Park, Cambridge, MA 01240-2390.

Hesselbein, Francis, Marshall Goldsmith, and Richard Beckhard (Editors). *The Leader of the Future.* Sponsored by the Peter F. Drucker Foundation. San Francisco: Jossey-Bass, 1996.

Imparato, Nicholas, and Oren Harari. *Jumping the Curve: Innovation and Strategic Choice In An Age Of Transition.* San Francisco: Jossey-Bass Publishers, 1994.

Interface, Inc. *Sustainability Report.* Atlanta, GA: Interface, Inc., 1997.

Intergovernmental Panel on Climate Change. *Climate Change 1995: Impacts, Adaptations and Mitigation of Climate Change: Scientific-Technical Analyses.* Contribution of Working Group II to the Second Assessment Report of the Intergovernmental Panel on Climate Change. Summary for Policymakers, 1995.

Jensen, Peter. *The Inside Edge: High Performance Through Mental Fitness.* Toronto: Macmillan Canada, 1992.

Johnson, Scott. "Application of the Balanced Scorecard Approach." *Corporate Environmental Strategy* 5, no. 4 (summer 1998).

Kaplan, Robert and David Norton. *The Balanced Scorecard: Translating Strategy Into Action.* Boston: Harvard Business School Press, 1996.

Kouzes, Jim and Barry Posner. *The Leadership Challenge.* San Francisco: Jossey-Bass, 1995.

Leider, Richard. *The Power of Purpose.* Toronto: Fawcett Gold Medal Books, 1985.

McNally, David. *Even Eagles Need A Push.* Eden Prairie, MN: Transform Press, 1990.

McNee, B., C. Smith Ardito, D. Tunick Morello, and E. Zidar. *IT Staff Retention and Recruitment: Addressing a Critical Problem for the IS Organization.* The Gartner Group Industry Trends & Directions (ITD), September 28, 1998.

Miner, John. *Organizational Behavior: Performance and Productivity.* New York: Random House, 1988.

Nattrass, Brian and Mary Altomare. *The Natural Step For Business: Wealth, Ecology and the Evolutionary Corporation.* Gabriola Island, BC: New Society Publishers, 1999.

Patey, Tom. "Graduates focus on green issues and multinationals." *European* (May 16, 1996). The European Graduate Survey 1996 is available from Universum, Box 7053, 103 86 Stockholm, Sweden.

Peters, Tom. *The Tom Peters Seminars: Crazy Times Call For Crazy Organizations.* New York: Vintage Books, 1994.

Porter, Michael and Claas van der Linde. "Green and Competitive: Ending the Stalemate." *Harvard Business Review on Business and the Environment.* Reprint 95507. Originally published in *Harvard Business Review* (September-October 1995).

Pritchett, Price. *Firing Up Commitment During Organizational Change.* Dallas, TX: Pritchett & Associates, 1994.

Reich, Robert. "The Company of the Future." *FastCompany* (November 1998).

Reinhardt, Forest L. "Bringing The Environment Down To Earth." *Harvard Business Review* (July-August 1999).

———. *Down To Earth: Applying Business Principles to Environmental Management.* Boston: Harvard Business Review Press, 2000.

Rocky Mountain Institute (Alex Wilson, Jennifer L. Uncapher, Lisa McManigal, L. Hunter Lovins, Maureen Cureton, William D. Browning). *Green Development: Integrating Ecology and Real Estate.* New York: John Wiley & Sons, 1998.

Romm, Joseph. *Cool Companies: How the Best Businesses Boost Profits and Productivity by Cutting Greenhouse Gas Emissions.* Washington, DC: Island Press, 1999.

Rowledge, Lorinda R, Russell S. Barton, and Kevin S. Brady. *Mapping The Journey: Case Studies in Strategy and Action Toward Sustainable Development.* Sheffield, UK: Greenleaf Publishing, 1999.

Schmidheiny, Stephan, with the Business Council for Sustainable Development (BCSD). *Changing Course: A Global Business Perspective on Development and the Economy.* Cambridge, MA: The MIT Press, 1992.

Senge, Peter. *The Fifth Discipline: The Art and Practice of the Learning Organization.* New York: Doubleday Currency, 1990.

Sustainable Systems Associates. *Applying Sustainable Development to Business: Realizing the Benefits.* Publication 3649E. Prepared for the Ontario Ministry of the Environment. Toronto: Queen's Printer of Ontario, 1998.

Sustainable Enterprise Academy. *Report on the First Business Leader Seminar, Fall 2000.* Toronto: Sustainable Enterprise Academy, Schulich School of Business, York University, 4700 Keele Street, M3J 1P3, 2000.

Von Weizsacher, Ernst, Amory B. Lovins, and L. Hunter Lovins. *Factor Four: Doubling Wealth, Halving Resource Use—The New Report to the Club of Rome.* London: Earthscan, 1997.

Walley, Noah and Bradley Whitehead. "It's Not Easy Being Green." *Harvard Business Review on Business and the Environment.* Reprint 94310. Originally published in *Harvard Business Review* (May-June 1994).

William M. Mercer. *Beyond the Bottom Line: What CEOs are Thinking.* Toronto: William M. Mercer Company, 1999.

World Business Council for Sustainable Development. *Eco-efficient Leadership for Improved Economic and Environmental Performance.* WBCSD, 1995.

World Commission on Environment and Development (WCED). *Our Common Future.* Oxford: Oxford University Press, 1987.

Wright, David. "New Rules: Name Game." *Risky Business* 2 (2001). Available from PriceWaterhouseCoopers in Toronto.

Index

About the Author

BOB IS A LEADING EXPERT on the business value of corporate sustainability strategies and in the last three years has given over 120 keynote presentations to corporations, consultants, academics, and nongovernmental organizations.

During his 34-year IBM career, Bob held leadership positions in marketing, technical support, education, and human resources, including 20 years in management. Between 1990 and 2000, Bob led leadership development for IBM's 2,000 managers and executives in Canada. Since taking early retirement in 2000, he has worked full time on applying his business and leadership development experience to engage the business community in proactively avoiding risks and capturing opportunities associated with sustainability.

Bob recently served on the boards of Eco-Energy Durham and the Ontario Sustainable Energy Association (OSEA). He currently serves on the advisory boards of The Natural Step, Canada, and the Certificate in Adult Training and Development at OISE/University of Toronto.

A resident of Ontario, he is a delighted owner of one of the first Honda Civic hybrid-electric cars sold in Canada. More information about Bob and his books can be found at www.sustainabilityadvantage.com. He can be reached at bobwillard@sympatico.ca.

DANCING WITH THE TIGER

Learning Sustainability Step by Natural Step

Brian Nattrass & Mary Altomare

Foreword by Nicholas C. Sonntag

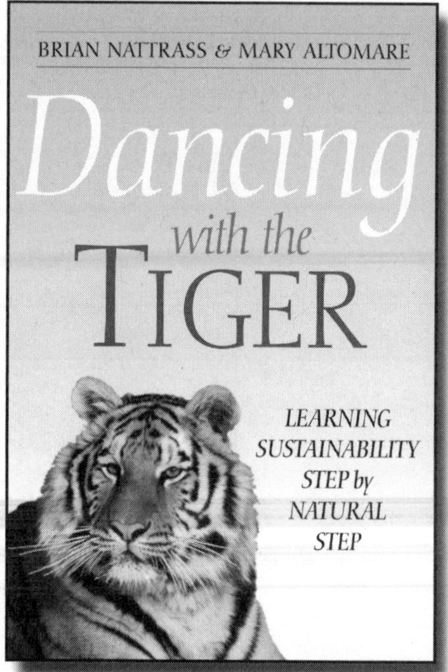

Making social and ecological change happen is not easy. At both the planetary and organizational levels, it is a dance that is fraught with danger for both the change agents themselves and their organizations. It is like dancing with a tiger.

For corporations, communities and other organizations, the choreography of the dance toward sustainability has been systematized by The Natural Step: a framework that provides the science, analysis, methodologies and tools to use in the quest for sustainability. *Dancing with the Tiger* presents the stories of individuals, teams and organizations learning about change and sustainability, and then acting on that learning. Case studies include some of the most successful companies and communities in North America:

- **Nike:** its struggles, victories and setbacks on the road to sustainability
- **Starbucks:** the tension of modeling corporate responsibility with alarming growth
- **CH2MHill:** its gradual evolution from environmental to sustainability engineering
- **Whistler:** grappling with the paradox of sustainability in a high profile resort town

— as well as Home Depot, Norm Thomson Outfitters, the municipalities of Seattle and Santa Monica, and others.

Following on the success of *The Natural Step for Business*, this book takes a deeper look at the real business impacts of sustainability. It will be of special interest to business people, government officials, and students of business, organizational development and the environment.

Brian Nattrass: lawyer, CEO, Chairman of Earth Day International, and author of a book on corporate finance.

Mary Altomare: academic administrator at Yale and Duke universities, and consultant with the World Bank and US AID. Both are now practice leaders for The Natural Step in North America.

320 pages 6" x 9" Hardcover

Business & Economics

ISBN 0-86571-455-X

US$29.95 / Can$42.95 – available June 2002

THE NATURAL STEP STORY

Seeding a Quiet Revolution

Karl Henrik-Robèrt

Foreword by Ray Anderson

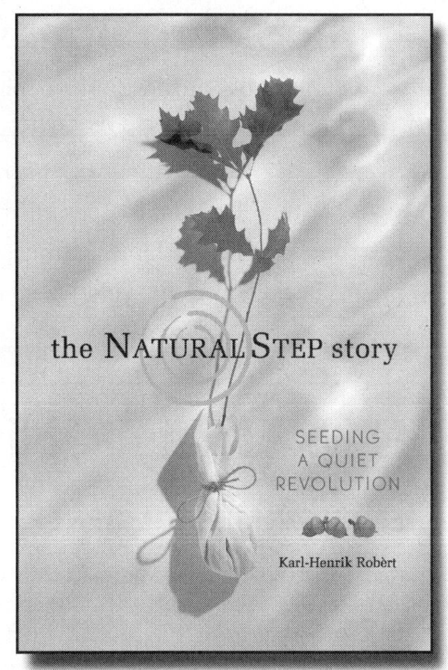

It may be unlikely that a Swedish karate champion, family man, and cancer scientist could be at the center of developing a systems approach to life on Earth that could revolutionize the way humans operate in the world, but this is the story of just that: the idea, and the man behind it.

As a cancer specialist, Karl-Henrik Robèrt faced a stream of parents who would sacrifice anything to save their children. Yet that same selflessness did not seem to extend to saving the environment. For debate on how to achieve sustainability was divided, with no agreement on universal principles. But Robèrt's experience convinced him that consensus on how to meet the most basic requirements of life should be possible.

Thus began a long process of consultation among scientists and others that eventually led to the definition of four system conditions essential for the maintenance of life on Earth: conditions that have now been agreed upon world-wide and encapsulated as The Natural Step framework. Supported by the King of Sweden, Robèrt's original ideas were mailed to every household in Sweden. Exported around the world, they were elaborated, refined and eventually adopted by companies like IKEA and McDonald's, and business leaders such as Ray Anderson, CEO of US carpet company Interface, and Paul Hawken, successful entrepreneur and author who later headed the US Natural Step organization.

Dramatic, visionary and inspiring, *The Natural Step Story* will appeal to all with a passion for sustainability including business leaders, academics, journalists, activists, and students.

Karl-Henrik Robèrt is a cancer scientist and Professor of Resource Theory at the University of Gothenburg in Sweden. Having initiated The Natural Step movement in 1989, he was awarded the Green Cross Award for International Leadership in 1999, and the Blue Planet Prize (the 'environment Nobel') in 2000.

288 pages 6" x 9" Hardcover

Business & Economics / Biography / Cultural Studies

ISBN 0-86571-453-3

US$29.95 / Can$42.95 – available April 2002

New Society Publishers

ENVIRONMENTAL BENEFITS STATEMENT

New Society Publishers has chosen to produce this book on New Leaf EcoBook 100, recycled paper made with 100% post consumer waste, processed chlorine free, and old growth free.

For every 5,000 books printed, New Society saves the following resources:[1]

29	Trees
2,609	Pounds of Solid Waste
2,870	Gallons of Water
3,744	Kilowatt Hours of Electricity
4,742	Pounds of Greenhouse Gases
20	Pounds of HAPs, VOCs, and AOX Combined
7	Cubic Yards of Landfill Space

[1]Environmental benefits are calculated based on research done by the Environmental Defense Fund and other members of the Paper Task Force who study the environmental impacts of the paper industry.

For more information on this environmental benefits statement, or to inquire about environmentally friendly papers, please contact New Leaf Paper – info@newleafpaper.com Tel: 888 • 989 • 5323.

NEW SOCIETY PUBLISHERS